USING DATA TO
Assess Your
Reading
Program

Emily Calhoun

Association for Supervision and Curriculum Development
Alexandria, VA USA

Association for Supervision and Curriculum Development
1703 N. Beauregard St. • Alexandria, VA 22311-1714 USA
Phone: 800-933-2723 or 703-578-9600 • Fax: 703-575-5400
Web site: http://www.ascd.org • E-mail: member@ascd.org
Author guidelines: www.ascd.org/write

Gene R. Carter, *Executive Director;* Nancy Modrak, *Director of Publishing;* Julie Houtz, *Director of Book Editing & Production;* Tim Sniffin, *Project Manager;* Judi Connelly, *Senior Graphic Designer;* Barton Matheson Willse & Worthington, *Typesetter;* Dina Seamon, *Production Specialist.*

Paperback ISBN: 0-87120-968-3 • ASCD product #102268 • List Price: $34.95
($27.95 ASCD member price, direct from ASCD only)   s10/04

Library of Congress Cataloging-in-Publication Data

Calhoun, Emily.
    Using data to assess your reading program / Emily Calhoun.
        p. cm.
    Includes bibliographical references and index.
    ISBN 0-87120-968-3 (alk. paper)
    1. Reading—Evaluation.   2. Action research.   I. Title.

    LB1050.42.C35 2004
    372.48—dc22   2004013242

10 09 08 07 06 05 04   12 11 10 9 8 7 6 5 4 3 2 1

Critical Definitions

Reading program: All that is being done by the school or district organization to support students' reading development. A reading program comprises four elements: curriculum (what is taught), instruction (how curriculum content and processes are taught), assessment (how curriculum content and processes are evaluated), and the organization of the learning environment (how students and staff are deployed and how time is allocated).

Commercial reading materials: Physical stuff that can be purchased to provide teachers and students with a standard written curriculum and to support teachers in using specific instructional approaches, for example, basal reading series. These materials are sometimes confused with the reading program (see above).

Teaching: To cause to know a subject or to know how something works; to instruct by precept, example, or experience. Good teaching by thoughtful teachers orchestrates the four elements of the reading program with live students to make sure reading proficiency develops for almost all students, no matter what commercial reading materials are used.

Using Data to Assess Your Reading Program

Preface

Change is ever with us. One of our continuous challenges is to make sure the changes we make in our classrooms and schools have positive benefits for our students. Working together to assess and improve the reading program is one way school staff can address challenges and accelerate the reading development of students.

This book is about assessing student progress in reading and assessing the elements of the elementary school reading program, but it is also about using a proactive, problem-solving approach to accomplish these tasks. The diversity of experience found in school staff and in students who attend our schools requires an approach that increases curriculum coherence, builds professional community, and pulls the whole organization toward excellence.

The framework I suggest for reading program improvement, schoolwide action research, is one that I've often used to help school teams inquire into the quality of their literacy programs. Schoolwide action research is a form of disciplined inquiry conducted by school staff to gather information, analyze educational practices, and improve student achievement. It can be used to strengthen curriculum standards and assessment procedures and to build a professional community. My primary goal is that readers will be able to use this framework, along with the contents of this book, to increase the reading proficiency of their students.

Because I feel as if we are working together studying reading programs and their effects on students, I often use the pronouns *I, we,* and *you.* I use the terms *staff* and *faculty* to indicate the need for collective, schoolwide knowledge and work. I also write as if you—as individuals or teams—will be using the data discussed and helping others use it to make changes, if needed, in the reading programs students are experiencing.

My work has convinced me that these fundamentals—clarifying the learning of the student population and analyzing it as a function of the program of study—need attention in many classrooms, schools, and districts. If you need to assess your reading program or strengthen your use of data on the performance of groups of students, you'll find tools here to support your work—as well as lots of camaraderie.

PART ONE

Introduction

When we assess a reading program, what matters most is how well it works for students. To clarify how well a program is working, we examine student performance in major dimensions of reading development and determine whether students are making good progress. If the results show us anything less than almost all students reading on or above grade level, reading extensively, and acquiring information and experience through reading, then there is work to be done on that reading program.

The study process outlined in this book is called action research, and it entails collective, disciplined inquiry with the intent of improving a school's reading program and its effects on students. This disciplined inquiry requires faculty to gather data about students and their levels of achievement; to gather information about the reading program students are experiencing; and to cull information from the external knowledge base as we explore what scholars and scholar-practitioners recommend for improving student performance and strengthening instruction. Three big ideas shape this approach to reading program assessment:

1. Student performance and reading program elements should be studied simultaneously,
2. Current performance and changes in performance should be measured, and
3. Collective inquiry should be used to inform and guide changes in practice.

These ideas provide a conceptual and operational framework for examining reading programs and their effects on students. We can use them to guide our investigation into the reading program in our schools and districts.

To determine how effective our program is and where we need to make improvements, we need to study both student performance and the elements of the reading program (curriculum, instruction, assessment, and organization of the learning environment). Student performance is a "reading program effect"; since levels of student performance are direct results of our program, we cannot determine reading program effectiveness except in relation to student progress.

One of my favorite William Glasser quotes is particularly apropos in regard to the necessity of a tight linkage between studying student performance data and reading program components. He says, "If we are not going to try to improve what we do, there is little sense in assessing it." The operative word is *improve*. Assessment as we use it here is not a search for data that label a reading program as "Excellent" or "Poor." All programs can be improved, and with careful study and good measurement tools, we can determine how effective our reading program is in terms of how well our students are achieving, and then make changes where they are needed.

The purpose of school and district reading programs is to support growth in reading. So when we assess the quality of a program, we need to look at current student performance *and* at the amount of gain students make as they participate in the program. Optimally, the reading assessment system at the elementary school level provides data on students' progress several times during the school year, as well as data on students' year-to-year growth. For individual students and groups of students, the results of regular assessments of student performance allow us to design instruction that will accelerate their literacy

development. If we study performance data and student gain over time, these data will allow us to predict what our reading program promises students who enter our school or district, as well as what it promises for subgroups within our student population.

We also need to assess changes in our own practices and changes in the learning environment provided in our school. As individuals and faculties, we identify the reading knowledge, processes, and strategies in which students need to become more skilled. We study the information from the external knowledge base on literacy and learning. We inquire into how this knowledge and these processes are represented in our written curriculum and our actual classroom curriculum, how they are taught, and how they are assessed. If we find gaps in our reading program, we must take actions and study the changes we make and their effects on students. We will most likely find that positive changes in student achievement are highly correlated with changes in instructional practices.

As we sift, sort, and reflect on the information we gather, we will find student effects that are pleasing and instructional practices that are very effective—and we will celebrate these! We will also find student effects we do not like, critical curriculum content that is missing, or limited repertoires for teaching certain reading strategies—and we will make plans to change these and study what happens. New information will generate new questions and problems, but we know we can make education work better for our students and ourselves. And our inquiries continue.

Since these ideas describe interactive, nonlinear processes, structuring a book to help readers understand how they work together and how they can be applied has been problematic. However, as you can tell from the Table of Contents, I've organized the book into four sections:

1. Schoolwide or organization-wide action research;
2. School and student data;
3. The content of the reading curriculum and assessing student performance up close; and
4. Planning and organizing collective work.

Depending on your immediate needs and interests, some readers may find it more useful to read Part Three prior to Part Two.

Now, let's take a closer look at how faculties can use action research to improve student performance and the quality of the reading program.

1

Using Action Research for Reading Program Assessment

Action research can be conducted on almost any process, but for school improvement purposes, it should be directed primarily toward improving student learning. This is broad territory, involving not only student learning in all the academic domains but also the study of curriculum, instructional practices, assessment procedures, and the organization of the learning environment by teachers, administrators, and others engaged in supporting student learning. In this book, we will focus on reading, applying the action research process to improving student proficiency in reading and to examining the quality of our reading program.

Along with the No Child Left Behind Act (http://www.ed.gov/nclb), passed in 2001, the flood of new books on teaching reading, and the proliferation of new assessment packages, there are numerous articles and books reminding us that we need to improve student performance, increase teachers' knowledge of content and pedagogy, improve leadership skills, and increase the learning occurring at all levels of the organization (e.g., Bransford, Brown, & Cocking, 1999; Bryk, Sebring, Kerbow, Rollow, & Easton, 1998; Darling-Hammond & Ball, 1998; and Elmore, 2000). Those of us who work in and with schools can respond to the federal regulations, the reminders from our colleagues, and the goal of the No Child Left Behind Act by using our collective experiences and our knowledge base in reading to develop more effective curriculum and instruction for students and more successful professional development for ourselves.

Action research is one of the tools we can use to help us respond in an integrative and informed manner, instead of a reactive or merely compliant manner. The action research process provides a structure for continuously assessing the effects of actions and seeking more effective ones if needed. When used organization-wide by school and district staff, the process can increase individual professional expertise and build strong professional communities. Aimed directly at student learning and accompanied by training to expand instructional and curricular practices, this technique can also yield improved student achievement (Joyce et al., 1996; Joyce, Calhoun, & Hopkins, 1999; Joyce, Hrycauk, Calhoun, & Northern Lights Kindergarten Teachers, 2003).

The nice thing about using an action research approach is that a school team or faculty can use it to study students' progress in reading and the breadth, depth, and multidimensionality of their program, whatever materials are being used—be they commercially published (such as High/Scope, Scholastic, Open Court, Guided Reading) or a locally developed curriculum. For action research is simply a structured process for addressing a problem or answering questions with the intention of using the resulting information to make improvements. Additionally, the research process can be conducted individually by a single teacher in a classroom or collaboratively among several persons with similar interests. I am going to write as if you and I were engaging in schoolwide or organization-wide action research. This allows us to look at what is happening to all students in our setting and to consider more fully the curriculum and instructional experiences they encounter.

The Action Research Framework

Because the process for examining reading programs described in this book uses a schoolwide or districtwide action research framework, it's important to understand what that framework is, how it works, and when it's useful. We need to ask ourselves the following questions:

Who are our students, and what programs are currently available in the school to support their development as readers? How are they responding to the learning environment of the school? How well are our students performing in literacy, especially in reading? Do we want to improve the current levels of performance? Are we satisfied with their rate of progress (gain)? And are there changes we can make in curriculum, instruction, assessment, or the organization of the learning environment that are likely to improve literacy learning in our setting?

To help us pursue the information we need to answer these questions, we have the Action Research Matrix (Figure 1.1), a graphic organizer that focuses simultaneously on student learning and the learning environment provided for students. Faculties can use the six cells, which represent lines of inquiry, as a framework for structuring collective inquiry into student learning. Some of you may be familiar with using this matrix to design plans for schoolwide action research (Calhoun, 1994, 2002).

The matrix includes a place to identify the student learning goal that a faculty selects for its collective focus as well as six domains, or cells, of inquiry and action. The structure of the matrix is designed to help groups study and use on-site and external information about student learning and the learning environment. Cells 1, 2, and 3 focus on learners' current performance and what is possible in terms of student achievement. Cells 4, 5, and 6 focus on the formal learning environment, which in this

--- FIGURE 1.1 ---

Action Research Matrix
What Do We Know? What Do We Do?

Date: _____

Schoolwide Focus: _____

(Academic student learning goal in a curriculum area)

	Learner (Students)		Learning Environment (School)	
On-Site Information (Information at the school level)	1. Current student information	3. Student performance and responses we would like to see	4. Information about the current learning environment in our school	6. Learning environment we would like to see
External Information (Study of literature, standards, & best practices)	2. External information about learners/students		5. External information about the learning environment	

Source: Adapted from Calhoun, E. F. (1998). Action research matrix. St. Simons, GA: The Phoenix Alliance.

case comprises the reading program elements: curriculum, instruction, assessment, and the organization of students and staff.

School and district staff are asked to use both on-site and external information as they set their benchmarks and desired levels of performance for students (Cell 3) and as they select actions to study and implement in their classrooms and schools (Cell 6). The sequence of the matrix is designed to help staff explore the research base and move beyond what is currently known or done in their school or setting. However, it is only a guide to domains of inquiry and action, not a rigid set of steps.

Let's visit Elwood Elementary, where the staff are learning to use action research to study the development of reading vocabulary. The actions of the Elwood staff help illustrate the six domains of inquiry in the Action Research Matrix (Figure 1.1).

The Research Matrix in Action

Elwood Elementary is a prekindergarten through grade 5 school in a small town near a large metropolitan area. Sixty percent of its 622 students participate in the free and reduced-price lunch program. The race/ethnicity composition of the student population is 43 percent white, 38 percent black, 16 percent Hispanic, and 3 percent other ethnicity (mostly from Asia and some of the former Russian republics).

Two years ago, a new principal, Helen, came to Elwood. She has put a lot of energy into studying student results from the past five years, meeting with parents and community members, inviting board members for regular visits to the school, and reading books or team teaching in classrooms almost every day. Helen is determined to improve student achievement, and she and the staff have decided to tackle reading first and use action research to structure their collective work. Susie, the curriculum director for the district, is a skilled action research facilitator, and Helen has asked Susie to work closely with them as they get started.

The year after she arrived, Helen formed a School Leadership Team (made up of seven teachers, the counselor, and the principal) that facilitates across classroom study and action, and she has asked teachers to form study groups. Each leadership team member serves as team leader of a study group, which is composed of four staff members who work and plan as peer partners for some tasks and as a group at other times. Helen believes these group structures provide social support, facilitate communication, distribute leadership, and make whole-school improvement possible.

The School Leadership Team has worked with the district office, the community, and the staff as they have developed and implemented steps toward improving literacy. They began using the *High/Scope Active Learning Practices* materials (Hohmann et al., 2002) in their prekindergarten program the previous year because of its promised effects and its use of reading and writing in building students' literacy and communication skills, and they also added the *Preschool Child Observation Record* (High/Scope, 2003) to help them monitor student progress. This year all the kindergarten and 1st grade teachers have been participating in a yearlong staff development course offered by their intermediate service agency. The course focuses on instructional techniques that help accelerate the development of oral and written language, including a lot of work with phonological awareness activities. First and 2nd grade teachers are seeing some improvements in students' use of language, and their impressions are confirmed by the data from informal reading inventories. Third through 5th grade teachers have been working with reciprocal teaching to improve reading comprehension; however, most of their students still struggle with any but the simplest text. The staff know they must do more. They still have far too many students reading far below grade level.

Their students' needs are so great that the staff could begin with any priority student learning goal or major curriculum standard and make progress. However, as they began their action research process, they decided that their school focus would be on "expanding reading vocabulary and word analysis skills" because they think bringing that about would make the most difference in accelerating literacy for the most students. Observe how the Elwood staff, with some support from Susie, uses the structure of the Action Research Matrix to guide their collective work.

Cell 1—Current Student Information

One of the first things Elwood's leadership team did was organize the existing and easily available student achievement data from the previous year's reading results on the norm-referenced tests administered statewide at the 3rd and 5th grades. Figure 1.2 shows these results.

As you can see, at 3rd grade, 37 percent of Elwood students were in the bottom quartile in reading overall, with

---

FIGURE 1.2

Elwood Elementary Students' Achievement Test Scores: Reading

Percentile Range	3rd Grade (87 Students Enrolled)		5th Grade (82 Students Enrolled)	
	Number of Students	Percent	Number of Students	Percent
75th–99th	5	6%	10	12%
50th–74th	20	23%	17	21%
25th–49th	27	31%	23	28%
1st–24th	32	37%	24	29%
Not tested	3	3%	8	10%

68 percent of the students scoring below the 50th percentile. The results for Elwood's 5th grade students were a little better, with 29 percent in the bottom quartile and 57 percent scoring below the 50th percentile. However, when these data were shared with the staff, one of the teachers noted that 10 percent of the 5th grade students did not take the tests, and if that number were eliminated in calculating percentages, then 64 percent of their students were below the 50th percentile. Another teacher said, "Well, our scores below the 50th percentile pretty much match our demographics. We do have 60 percent of our students on free and reduced lunch." Both of these comments generated some heated discussions among staff members.

The leadership team also organized the data on the vocabulary and comprehension sections of the local curriculum assessments from the previous three years, and the staff could see how similar the results were from grade to grade, with approximately 60–65 percent of the students struggling below the "Proficiency" level. (These tests are administered in grades 2 through 5.) In reviewing these results, staff also noticed that after the first year, scores were somewhat higher on vocabulary than on reading comprehension. Questions were raised about whether this was related to the content of the tests, to the fact that the same tests had been used for three years, or to the possibility that students' understanding of vocabulary had exceeded their reading comprehension skills. There were many opinions voiced,

but no answers to these questions. Susie and Lisa, the 3rd grade team leader, decided to evaluate the content of the tests, and Susie told them that she would look up the districtwide scores to see if there were similar patterns in the other elementary schools. Helen was pleased that the questions were raised in the consciousness of the staff, but she felt students were performing so poorly in both dimensions that small increases in vocabulary over two years didn't seem of great moment and thus were not worthy of much of their precious staff development time.

Several teachers brought up the issue of high student turnover at Elwood, so the principal and two leadership team members decided to use student ID numbers and organize results from the previous year's 5th graders who had been in the school for at least three years. When these data were shared with all staff members at their next meeting, they found that about two-thirds of the students tested on both state and local assessments had been with them for three or more years. Some of the 3rd and 4th grade teachers wanted to look at the same kind of data for the previous year's 3rd graders, but the leadership team wanted staff to start looking at some results other than their own. They had several reasons. They could feel the defensiveness of some colleagues, and they wanted to counter the frequent comments of, "Well, look at our children. What else can we expect from so many one-parent families and poor neighborhoods?"

Cell 2—External Information About Learners/Students

In an attempt to learn more about how vocabulary develops and to provide a base for high expectations, the leadership team sought resources on how vocabulary is acquired and on student achievement in other settings. They located and studied the research synthesis "Conditions of Vocabulary Acquisition" by Beck and McKeown (1991), "The Vocabulary Conundrum" by Anderson and Nagy (1992), and several pieces by Linnea Ehri on how students learn to read words (they especially liked the directness and clarity of the 1999 AERA paper). The curriculum director used the Web and state report card information to organize and share data from five elementary schools with similar demographics that had made significant improvements in vocabulary and comprehension for three years in a row.

The leadership team and their study groups also reviewed local curriculum documents. Although they found vocabulary mentioned frequently, there was not much guidance on what was most worth teaching and when. At the next leadership team meeting, members reported by grade level and special needs. As Susie listened to their comments about what was missing, she realized that she might be able to use some of their work to improve the district curriculum standards. She also realized that the district's curriculum documents needed to provide teachers with a better conceptual map of how reading, vocabulary, and word analysis skills develop.

Cell 3—Student Performance and Responses We Would Like To See

The leadership team led the staff through an exercise to help everyone reflect on the student results they had looked at earlier, on information about how students develop vocabulary, and on student achievement data from comparable schools. Then they led the staff in setting some targets for the next year.

The principal opened the session by encouraging the staff to set high expectations for students. She was concerned that they—including her—had fallen into a pattern of setting low targets so they would be more likely to attain them. By the time the discussions were over, the staff had decided that for the state's norm-referenced tests, they would aim for increasing the school mean by 10 percentile points and having at least 40 percent of their students at the 50th percentile or higher. They would also attempt to move at least 20 percent of their students out of the bottom quartile of the vocabulary and comprehension portions of the local curriculum assessments by the time the tests were administered the next spring.

There was some discussion about how to involve students in assessing their own reading and vocabulary growth, but neither the leadership team nor the staff wanted to set any performance benchmarks yet. Teachers who were especially interested in pursuing student self-assessment were asked to put together some ideas and try them out. As this effort evolved, three pairs of teachers for grades 1, 3, and 4 were going to try different assessment techniques: (1) have students keep vocabulary boxes of new words and words they were learning; (2) have students keep vocabulary journals about new words and words they were learning; and (3) interview students about the strategies they used when they encountered an unfamiliar word. These teachers would report the results and work with colleagues to resolve issues before any recommendations were made.

Cell 4—Information About the Current Learning Environment in Our School

Staff members reported on the instructional techniques they used in teaching vocabulary and provided specific examples of assessments. The members of the leadership team also decided to ask their study groups for especially good resources they had used in teaching vocabulary and word analysis skills. However, when the team evaluated the collection, some of which were their own favorites, they discovered, with Helen's help, that most of the resources were good activities but not very good conceptually. For example, there were a number of games and worksheets (both manual and computerized) that called for students to blend sounds and form words, match words and meanings, and find words in rows and columns of letters, as well as some simple crossword puzzles for older students. Some of the more promising techniques shared were using phonetic spelling and writing activities; using books on CD-ROM, such as those by Broderbund that allow students to listen to a story on the computer and also click on words they want

repeated; and keeping the *American Heritage Talking Dictionary* CD-ROM available in the classroom writing center.

Cell 5—External Information About the Learning Environment

The team had to go beyond their current school resources to find out more about what elements would make up an optimal vocabulary development curriculum, which instructional techniques and models of teaching were most effective, and which ways were most effective for teachers to assess growth. Lisa had just finished her master's thesis, titled "Strategies for Building Vocabulary for Kindergarten Through Third Grade." The team asked her to present a summary of her research review, the best references and teaching resources she had found, and her student results. The following points made by Lisa generated quite a bit of discussion among team members:

- A variety of approaches to teaching phonics for decoding unfamiliar words are effective as long as they are systematic.
- Asking students to locate and write definitions is not an effective approach to building vocabulary or word meaning.
- Requiring struggling and average readers to use print dictionaries is not effective in building vocabulary.
- Beginning around grade 3, the amount a student reads is the major determinant of his vocabulary growth.
- Most textbooks do not include enough information about key concept words to help students under-

stand the concepts or add the words to their sight vocabulary.

Lisa shared some of the resources on vocabulary instruction she had used to design interventions in her individual teacher research. She had found several strategies that were effective with her students in Stahl's (1999) *Vocabulary Development,* and she had found Beck, McKeown, and Kucan's (2002) descriptions of how to develop "student friendly explanations" of words in *Bringing Words to Life* especially helpful. Other resources that were brought to the team as part of this initial screening included two that the 1st grade teachers had used during their yearlong staff development: an article by the Cunninghams (1992) titled "Making Words: Enhancing the Invented Spelling-Decoding Connection," and a short book by Calhoun (1999) titled *Teaching Beginning Reading and Writing with the Picture Word Inductive Model.* The curriculum director also found two resources she particularly liked: a chapter by Graves (1992) titled "The Elementary Vocabulary Curriculum: What Should It Be?" and a research synthesis by Ehri, Nunes, Stahl, and Willows (2001) titled "Systematic Phonics Instruction Helps Students Learn to Read: Evidence from the National Reading Panel's Meta-Analysis."

Elwood's staff had four weeks left before their February 15 faculty development retreat. The principal and curriculum director arranged for multiple copies of each resource so that each would be read by at least four team members. Team members signed up to evaluate the resources and complete a structured response sheet prior to the retreat. On the response sheets, they are to identify the curriculum emphases and instructional techniques that, according to the authors, hold the most promise for accelerating literacy, especially for building reading vocabulary.

Cell 6—Learning Environment We Would Like to See

At the culmination of the February retreat, after a strenuous day of sifting through many apparently effective techniques and identifying recommendations and resources to share with the staff, the team felt comfortable with the student learning focus and the plan to work on expanding sight vocabulary and teaching students word recognition strategies they could use to add words to their reading and writing storehouses. After some debates and compromises, the team finally agreed to five curriculum, instruction, and assessment initiatives to recommend for schoolwide support and study in their focus area of expanding reading vocabulary and word analysis skills: (1) ask every teacher to teach students at least two strategies for building reading vocabulary and to help students assess their use of these strategies; (2) increase read-alouds to students from prekindergarten through grade 5; (3) increase the amount of reading by all students, K–5, from picture books to chapter books; (4) use the picture-word inductive model with beginning readers K–2 and as part of social studies units in grades 3 through 5; and (5) select or begin to build a common set of up-close assessments of students' sight vocabulary and word analysis skills in both reading and writing.

The principal and team leader agreed to draft these five initiatives into an action and staff development plan along with timelines, resources, and a budget, and to get it back to the team within two weeks. (The principal was concerned about the March 22 district deadline for the next year's school plans and budgets.) The curriculum director and Lisa planned to contact the regional intermediate service agency consultant to see if she could provide staff development on strategies for building reading vocabulary and on assessing vocabulary growth. Other staff members would be asked to lead staff development and planning sessions on their other three initiatives (read-alouds, wide reading, and the picture-word inductive model).

Once the team reviewed the action plan and made necessary modifications, it went to all staff members for review, along with several resources and excerpts that forecast what the staff would be studying and implementing under these initiatives.

As the school action plan was submitted to the staff and commitments were made, a number of social and school culture issues began to swirl around Elwood's next steps. Leadership team members worried about getting their study group members to read articles and research. The six teachers who would be providing staff development on read-alouds, wide reading, and the picture word inductive model worried about how to get their colleagues to study

implementation and plan lessons and instructional moves the way they did. In as many ways as she could, Helen thanked those concerned for their willingness to lead and reassured them that she would be participating in everything—the reading and study group discussions, the staff development, and learning and implementing the strategies—and that time would be protected at least twice a month for staff to work together, not counting their regular study group sessions.

* * * * *

Of course, this was just the beginning of Elwood's journey toward accelerating literacy for all students. Action research provides them with a structure for cycles of continuous inquiry into student and staff learning, and the will of the leaders—the principal, the teachers, and the curriculum director—provides the energy that will make it possible. Let's juxtapose a few of the actions of the Elwood faculty to attributes of successful school improvement efforts: focus on student learning, focus on staff learning, use of data, whole-school participation, use of the research base, use of external technical assistance, cross-role learning by all members of the organization, and leadership that elevates the organization.

Elwood focused its collective study on student learning, specifically student development in reading. While faculty members examined existing student data on both vocabulary and reading comprehension, they decided to work first on improving reading vocabulary. The other dimensions of reading development were not ignored; they were just not in the foreground for systematic formal study by the faculty as a unit.

Faculty members used their existing school and district data and sought out assessment tools that would give them more information about students' vocabulary development and use of word analysis skills. They are familiar with the demographic data that describe their student population, and they used these data as they analyzed their test results and thought about the implications. They looked for ways to involve students in assessing their own vocabulary acquisition processes.

Elwood's leadership team is made up of teachers, the principal, and the counselor. The district curriculum director works with the team as a technical assistant to model the action research process and help the team learn to use it. However, it is not just team members involved in studying the data, analyzing instructional and assessment practices, and studying the knowledge base in reading; all faculty members participate in the collective study. Leadership team

members are simply willing to try things first and provide support to colleagues as the faculty struggles to become a more powerful learning community. The principal and many teachers—but not all of them—believe that student achievement in reading can improve. They have arguments—most of which are resolved civilly—but this does not stop the school improvement momentum. The strength and skills of the organizationally designated leaders, the principal and the curriculum director, work in tandem to make this kind of professional study and discourse possible.

And finally, Elwood uses its school action plan to organize collective study and serve as a binding agreement for actions. Tasks are scheduled; materials and human resources are secured. Obstacles to the development of a healthy learning community have not disappeared; they are almost always present in human organizations. But—at least while these leaders and teachers are supported—collective, disciplined inquiry into student learning and educational practices will be a part of the fabric of school life at Elwood.

2

Building Reading
Curriculum Coherence

One of the reasons for using action research to examine the quality of the reading program is that it provides faculty members with a process for making informed decisions and reaching agreements about what they will teach and systematically assess. These agreements represent curriculum and assessment coherence; their presence can help us improve students' reading performance.

For an individual teacher, curriculum and assessment coherence includes knowledge of the components that make up a discipline or subject area, how these components are connected, and what needs to be taught to help students develop expertise. As the teacher works with students and assesses what they can and cannot do, the teacher's knowledge of the continuum of development within the discipline guides instruction. For a group of teachers, such as a school or district faculty, it means the same thing, but its implementation is far more complex.

Over the years, educators have tried various mechanisms to standardize curriculum content because they know that teachers and administrators differ in their knowledge of and orientation toward subject areas. In reading, the most common techniques have been the adoption of a single basal reading series and the development of districtwide curriculum guides that include standards and benchmarks.

The creation of such documents generally has limited success. A document produced by committees or experts does not necessarily reflect the expertise of the teachers responsible for "delivering" this curriculum, nor does it mean that those teachers have reached agreements about what and how to teach or in what order to teach it. Making collective agreements about curriculum content is not an easy task, even in an area as basic as reading. For example, in the United States, the reading wars continue. Educators seeking agreements about the optimal content of reading curriculum have developed documents as diverse as *Preventing Reading Difficulties in Young Children* (Snow, Burns, & Griffin, 1998) and *Teaching Children to Read* (National Reading Panel, 2000).

16

Besides, if curriculum guides and teaching manuals could do the job, the United States would have the highest-achieving students in the world; the academic curriculum reforms of the 1960s would have been successful; "new math" would have been easily implemented; and science as inquiry would be a part of the elementary school experience for all students. The problem is not a lack of good curriculum documents; it is a problem of implementation. The sad truth is that teachers are not always provided with the opportunities for effective professional development to help them implement the best curriculums. Along with the lack of follow-up and support when they return from workshops, they have little opportunity within the school day for discussions that would help them understand, for example, why the new mathematics curriculum is more conceptually coherent than basic arithmetic or why teaching students the scientific process—how to think and behave like scientists—would be more effective in helping students learn the content and process of science than their current lessons.

Our country probably leads the world in producing and providing reading curriculum materials for use in our elementary school classrooms. I've visited schools in 14 countries. Whether in Thailand, New Zealand, Finland, or the United Kingdom, I never encountered as many teachers' guides and manuals for teaching reading as can be found in most elementary schools in this country.

Considering the quantity and weight of the documents that currently exist,

it's almost as if someone believes that teachers cannot think or that teacher expertise cannot be developed. Perhaps this is just a side effect of trying to help schools and control the curriculum. As educational decision makers and policymakers sought materials to help school faculties standardize curriculum content and provide a broad spectrum of activities to support student learning, publishers and marketers responded. The level of detail and quantity of recommended activities in the teachers' guides that accompany basal reading series frequently surpass the ability of teachers to put them into practice.

So what do we need to do? We need to support our own professional development and curriculum implementation. We need to design our work schedules (weekly, monthly, yearly) so that faculties can discuss research on reading; compare what they read to their current practices; reach agreements about teaching and assessing a set of commonly valued, research-based curriculum standards; and be supported in implementing necessary changes.

Let's think about what was happening at Elwood. The district has adopted a basal reading series. Elwood teachers all have copies of their district curriculum standards and of *Put Reading First: The Research Building Blocks for Teaching Children to Read* (Armbruster, Lehr, & Osborn, 2001), but these were not much practical help in developing a comprehensive program for building reading vocabulary. However, by the time faculty members complete their own examination of building reading vocabulary—studying and discussing information about vocabulary and word recognition skills from the external knowledge base, expanding their instructional practices, and examining student performance—they will have a conceptual framework of the components that help children learn to read words and expand their vocabularies. They will have strengthened their understanding of the connections among these components and be able to help students use them all—sight words, phonics and decoding, meaningful word parts, and context—to build reading vocabulary. The reading curriculum will be more effective across classrooms, not just on paper.

The kind of study this book is designed to support can help faculties move beyond lists of reading curriculum standards, benchmarks, and syntheses of research into discussions about the rationale for standards and for reading program components and into collective agreements about curriculum and assessment content. In the following section are some ideas for identifying reading curriculum emphases and for tightening the connection between curriculum and assessment.

Sources of Curriculum Emphases

To determine if the content we are teaching and assessing is likely to develop high levels of reading proficiency, we must develop responses to two questions:

1. What do proficient (expert) readers do?
2. What do students need to know and do to indicate they are making

good progress on the reading development continuum?

Our responses address basic curriculum issues: What is the purpose of the reading program? What are the program's long-term goals? What is included in the program? How is the program organized? Even if we are fortunate enough to have the "best" research-proven reading program materials that ever existed, we still need to articulate our own personal responses to these questions. They provide the rationale for our curriculum and instructional decisions and guide our daily actions and use of resources.

Our responses identify the knowledge, skills, and processes we want students to develop. They help us focus on key reading curriculum content for classroom instruction and schoolwide emphases. And they help us identify what needs to be systematically assessed. Working with colleagues to develop responses may lead to debates about what to include in the reading curriculum, which should eventually give way to agreements about schoolwide curriculum emphases and the identification of a few common assessments.

As you think about what defines reading proficiency, try to see through and beyond your current curriculum. Do your current student-learning goals and outcomes, along with the instructional activities you introduce each day, lead to the development of highly proficient readers who enjoy reading and read extensively? Put your ideas into a compact K–8 developmental perspective so that you can "see" what the school reading program is trying to bring into reality.

Of course, I don't know what your school's reading curriculum and standards of proficiency look like. Nor do I know how reading is taught in your setting. What I do know is that if you want to improve students' reading performance schoolwide, discussions about how reading proficiency develops are crucial. And discussions about the components or strands of those dimensions that will be emphasized and assessed across classrooms are critical for building a sturdy curriculum scaffold for students.

Using the External Knowledge Base to Identify Curriculum Emphases

Let's think about where reading curriculum comes from and how it relates to local curriculum emphases and standards. The reading curriculum has come a long way since the McGuffey readers—just consider the weight and size of the stacks of teachers' editions in most elementary school classrooms!

Reading curriculum is derived from an understanding of how language works, how literacy develops, how people learn to read and use printed language, and what good readers do. I'll take these four areas and give an example from each one that demonstrates the changing nature of knowledge and how these changes influence our reading program.

From "how language works" emerged the idea that reading comprehension involves constructing meaning from and interacting with text. This definition of reading comprehension connotes active communication between the author and the reader. It evokes the purposes for reading and the prior knowledge that readers bring to their encounters with text and that affect what they take away from these encounters. It goes beyond earlier conceptions of reading comprehension as a passive gathering of the author's ideas. Many of the changes in literacy curriculum over the last 30 years owe much to the studies of social and cognitive psychologists and linguistic scholars on "how language works." It's not just about how print works and rules that govern word formation and expression; the purpose of language is communication.

From "how literacy develops" comes our emphasis on how students develop concepts about print and our understanding of how social settings and cultural practices influence their development. We understand that children's experiences and interactions with print and its use and functions in their home and community affect their ease of entry into conventional reading and writing. These concepts about print (for example, that what is said can be written down, that what is written down can be said, that print carries a message, that print is made up of words and words are made up of letters) are present in all kindergarten curricula. We know that some students will come to us already using these concepts, and others will need intensive instruction and immersion in reading and writing experiences before they acquire these concepts. This is different from earlier conceptions of reading readiness as the mental age at which students were mature enough to profit from reading skills instruction in kindergarten or 1st grade.

From "how people learn to read" comes our understanding of how students build a reading vocabulary. While you and I may place vocabulary under different curriculum headings and emphasize different components, we know that students build a reading vocabulary by learning to read words automatically, by decoding, by using word parts such as suffixes, and by using context. And we know that the purpose of these word-level curriculum emphases is to promote reading comprehension development, not just the accurate decoding of words.

From "what good readers do" comes our emphasis on self-monitoring. Good readers are aware of when they understand the text and when they are having problems with some aspect. When they have a problem, they have strategies for fixing it. They may begin by rereading, they may diagram the connections made thus far, or they may seek additional information. They are conscious of words, continually monitoring for meaning and expanding their vocabulary and their knowledge of the world. Most reading curricula now address the development of metacognitive and self-regulatory processes.

Engaging in a School- or District-Based Study of the Reading Curriculum

Information from these four areas of knowledge shapes the reading curriculum. Thousands of books and articles have been written about these areas. Scholars and scholar practitioners synthesize and distill this information, and it shows up in documents that are designed to influence our school curriculum. Documents such as *Preventing Reading Difficulties in Young Children* (Snow et al., 1998) and *Reading and Writing Grade by Grade: Primary Literacy Standards for Kindergarten Through Third Grade* (New Standards Primary Literacy Committee, 1999) find their way into our schools.

We use some of these documents and our own experiences as we decide what the reading development continuum looks like and what it takes to support student progress from emergent literacy to highly proficient reading. Then we take this content knowledge and group it into curriculum components that make sense to us. Figure 2.1 is an example.

Figure 2.1 lists four dimensions of reading development that I believe need to be represented in any reading curriculum. Each dimension has two or more components that "go together" because of the role they play in reading development or how they relate to each other. For example, "Emergent Literacy Skills" includes three components necessary for the development of conventional literacy: concepts about print, letter recognition, and phonological and phonemic awareness. "Comprehension of Connected Text" includes three components: two that address how students come to understand and use expository nonfiction prose and narrative fiction prose, and one component that addresses basic processes supporting comprehension of connected text. Other genres could be

—————— FIGURE 2.1 ——————

Dimensions of Reading Development Recommended for Study

Emergent Literacy Skills
Concepts About Print
Letter Recognition
Phonological and Phonemic
Awareness

Building Reading Vocabulary
Sight Words
Phonics and Decoding Skills
Structural/Morphological Analysis
Contextual Analysis

Comprehension of Connected Text
Understanding and Learning from
Expository Nonfiction Text
Understanding and Relating to
Narrative Text (Primarily Fiction)
Basic Processes That Support
Comprehension: Fluency and
Self-Monitoring

Reading Habits and Attitudes
Extensive Reading
Positive Attitude Toward Reading

added to this dimension, but the skills and strategies students need to understand and relate to text would be similar, as would their need for fluency and self-monitoring.

I recommend that you systematically examine your reading program and students' levels of knowledge and performance in the four dimensions of reading development listed in Figure 2.1. I will treat the study of each dimension and its components in detail in Chapters 9 through 12. I do not pretend that these 12 components represent an all-inclusive reading curriculum; there could be many additions. They do, however, represent knowledge and behaviors that need to be included in any elementary school reading program. And they can serve as a content guide for examining your reading curriculum.

While maturation and experiences outside the school setting do affect the pace of reading development, we are going to concentrate on what curriculum and instruction can do to support progress.

Focusing Your Action Research Lens

What students need to know and do to become good readers guides our curriculum emphases and our assessment content. In a very simplistic fashion, Figure 2.2 illustrates these matches and the special role that assessment plays in showing us the progress students are making and in directing our next curriculum and instructional moves.

Student performance in each component can be represented on a continuum from little or no knowledge or expertise to extensive knowledge and expertise. The up-close measures described in Chapters 9 through 12 help us assess student progress in the knowledge and skills they need to become good readers

--- FIGURE 2.2 ---

Using Dimensions of Reading Development as Curriculum and Assessment Emphases

Dimensions of Development		Curriculum Emphases
Emergent Literacy Skills		**Emergent Literacy Skills**
Concepts About Print		Concepts About Print
Letter Recognition	< A >	Letter Recognition
Phonological and Phonemic Awareness	< S >	Phonological and Phonemic Awareness
Building Reading Vocabulary	< S >	**Building Reading Vocabulary**
Sight Words	< E >	Sight Words
Phonics and Decoding Skills		Phonics and Decoding Skills
Structural/Morphological Analysis	< S >	Structural/Morphological Analysis
Contextual Analysis	< S >	Contextual Analysis
Comprehension of Connected Text	< M >	**Comprehension of Connected Text**
Understanding and Learning from Expository, Nonfiction Text	< E > < N >	Understanding and Relating to Expository, Nonfiction Text
Understanding and Relating to Narrative Text (Primarily Fiction)	< T >	Understanding and Relating to Narrative Text (Primarily Fiction)
Basic Processes: Fluency and Self-Monitoring		Basic Processes: Fluency and Self-Monitoring
Reading Habits and Attitudes		**Reading Habits and Attitudes**
Extensive Reading		Extensive Reading
Positive Attitude Toward Reading		Positive Attitude Toward Reading

and make decisions about what to teach next.

If you can do a careful study of students' progress in these four dimensions, you will know how well the reading program is serving students and where to focus additional instructional resources and staff development. If you and your colleagues inquire into them with depth—studying what behaviors and knowledge the students put into action, how these behaviors and knowledge are related, how they develop over time, how they are supported instructionally,

and how they can be assessed accurately and productively—you can provide a reading program that not only "leaves no child behind" but accelerates the literacy development of all children, whatever their level of performance.

The good news is that you do not need to study all dimensions of development at once. Selecting one dimension or component that needs improvement and beginning your action research can benefit your students and help increase the population of highly proficient readers in your school.

3

Clarifying a Few Key Terms

My experience is that many of the most common and important words we use when talking about student achievement and school improvement in reading have different meaning for different group members, even among staff who have been teaching in the same grade or same school for many years. To facilitate our communication, I want to define some of the key terms used throughout this book: *reading, literacy, reading program, assess,* and *gain.*

As we consider the meanings of these terms, think about how you would define them and describe their development or use. Thinking about what each term means to you will serve as a useful conceptual set for this inquiry into reading program assessment. In addition, discussing the definitions of the terms as a group is a good starting point for a team about to embark on such an assessment, as these differences in interpretations and variations in beliefs about what is most worth teaching, when it should be taught, how it should be taught, and how it should be measured are part of the normal complexity of reading program improvement.

Reading

What is reading? What would you say if asked to define the act of reading? What does being an excellent reader require? What combination of cognition, skills, and strategies are needed?

In this book, reading is defined as processing written symbols and text, as well as graphic information, to derive meaning. The complex process we call *reading* requires knowledge and skill in various linguistic, literary, and cultural domains. For example, highly proficient readers have procedural knowledge about

- The conventions and structures of written English text (concepts about print, names of letters);

- The letter and sound relationships that make up spoken and written language (the alphabetic principle and phonemic awareness; phonics and the graphophonic system);
- The patterns and relationships of words in phrases, sentences, and extended text (syntax);
- The meanings of words (semantics) and the analysis of words;
- Reading comprehension processes and strategies; and
- Text elements and characteristics of a variety of genres.

In addition, cultural background, both that of the reader and that represented in the text, and the social context in which reading occurs can influence a reader's interaction with text and the ease with which she can derive author-based meaning and intent, appreciate the nuances of meaning, and use the information fully.

Think about the skills and processes that are involved in reading and the literal and cultural knowledge you bring to the act as you read this excerpt from *The New York Times Book Review* by Emily Eakin:

> Once an obscure ape dwelling in remotest Zaire, the bonobo surged to celebrity in the mid-1990s on a groundswell of liberal sentiment. Here was a primate tailor-made for the age of political correctness: vegetarian, peace-loving, female-dominant . . . . (Sunday, July 14, 2002, p. 26)

Only you know exactly which and how many skills and sources of knowledge you drew on as you read those two sentences. Mine ranged from using phonics

to fluent phrasing to using prior knowledge about changes in the feminist movement in the last decade and many more. As adult good readers, we often equate *reading* with *reading comprehension,* because that's what we do when we read something. A complication we have in studying reading curriculum is that reading comprehension is both a primary goal of the reading program and a component of it. As a component, I define it as constructing meaning from and interacting with text, generally using prior knowledge as well as the information in the text.

The meaning of *proficient* also appears to be changing. When I use it, as in "We want our students to be proficient readers," I intend the traditional dictionary meaning of "advanced in a branch of knowledge," with synonyms such as "adept, skilled, skillful, expert" (Merriam-Webster, 1994, p. 931).

Literacy

What is literacy? What does it mean to be a literate person? What helps build literacy? What is the relationship between reading and literacy?

Here, literacy means using printed and written information to develop knowledge, to achieve goals, and to function in society. Literacy includes reading and writing, but is more than that: it is one of the ways people make sense of their world—both by acquiring information and ideas from others and through the process of expressing themselves. Therefore, literacy involves *doing* something, not just *knowing* something. Literate persons can understand and make sense of what others have written and can communicate effectively through writing.

Think about this definition of literacy in terms of the following scenario. You're reading a book. You think, "This is great. I can use it with my students and Jeanie will just love it!" Jeanie is the language arts coordinator in the next district, and she has been struggling with helping staff members use more up-close assessments of students' reading behaviors. She hasn't been particularly satisfied with what she's been doing. Next time you're responding to e-mails, you send Jeanie one identifying the book and telling her what you liked about it and how you think it might be helpful in guiding staff use of assessments.

Some of the aspects of literate behavior represented in this scenario include the ability to read the book, to identify uses for the content, to write about the content, and to share that information with someone without the effort taking much cognitive energy. You can assimilate large amounts of print information and respond efficiently in print because you are a literate person.

Very early, children desire to be part of and control some aspects of their environment. They seek meaning and rapidly learn to understand and speak whatever language or languages are used in the home. As children begin to read and write, they learn more about and participate more fully in their culture. Language facility and skill in reading and writing support their sense of belonging, provide some control in social interactions, expand their choices, and facilitate interactions with other members of the culture. In many countries, the greater the level of literacy, the broader the range of choices about the life one lives and how to shape that life. Today, in the 21st century, students need to leave school with high levels of literacy, able to participate fully in their culture, able to exercise their rights as U.S. citizens, and well on their way to becoming literate world citizens.

Growth in literacy is facilitated by the application of all the language arts—reading, writing, speaking, and listening—and consideration of the connections among them. Students need many opportunities at every grade level to gather meaning from and interact with text as readers, and to make meaning and interact with others as writers. They need social settings in which they can discuss these meanings with other readers and writers and encounter different perspectives from those who read the same material or wrote about the same content.

While we will focus our examination of student performance primarily on reading, we will look closely at the use of the reading-writing connection in curriculum and instruction. While not identical processes, reading and writing are naturally connected forms of communication; they can be learned simultaneously, and they can be used together to rapidly and effectively advance growth in language use.

Reading Program

What is a "reading program"? How would you describe the reading program in your classroom, school, or district?

In this book, the term "reading program" describes what is being provided by teachers and by the school as an organization to develop literacy among all students, and especially what is done in the teaching of reading. Elements of the reading program include the curriculum content and materials chosen to facilitate reading skill and literacy development, the nature of instruction that is provided, the nature and use of assessment, and the organization of persons and resources for supporting literacy development. These program elements shape the formal learning environment of our students.

Sometimes when I ask folks to describe their reading program, they respond by saying, "We use Scholastic" or "We use *Road to the Code*" or "We use whole language" or "We use guided reading." These responses identify curriculum materials or instructional approaches that are parts of a school reading program, but they do not represent the entirety of the reading program.

Assess

What does it mean to assess something? You do not have to describe the differences between or relationships among assess, measure, evaluate, diagnose, and test, but "assess" is a very common term in our profession. What does it mean when you use it?

I use "assess" to mean "gather information about and determine the presence of some variable or combination of variables." In education, variables are often judged on continua, ranging from "no presence or evidence of" to "strongly present and appropriately used"; from "no knowledge or understanding of" to "full and comprehensive understanding"; or for skills and processes, from "novice" to "expert." We assess the knowledge and processes that make up our curriculum standards and objectives in order to determine the progress students are making on the reading development continuum. The results of our assessments allow us to make curriculum decisions and design instruction to move students forward at a good pace. When we can, we involve students in self-assessment and the use of the results so they can celebrate the progress they are making, participate more fully in monitoring progress and in designing learning experiences, and develop metacognitive control of their own learning processes.

In terms of student performance in reading development, we need to assess both knowledge and the use of skills, processes, and strategies that indicate developmental progress or level of expertise in that dimension. For example, in vocabulary development we might assess students' knowledge of high-frequency words in 1st grade, their knowledge of vocabulary words that we expect them to know in 4th grade, their skill in using selected prefixes and suffixes to determine word meaning or build words, or their strategies for using context to determine word meaning.

Gain

How do we know our instruction is successful?

We look at gain—the amount of growth made or movement forward on a novice–expert continuum when comparing knowledge, skill, or expertise from one assessment event to another—for individual students and for groups of students. Here is a very simple example. When Marvina entered kindergarten, she could recognize 10 of the 26 lowercase letters of the English alphabet. Three months later, she could recognize 24 letters, a gain score of 14. Her gain in letter recognition is greater than Abby's, who entered kindergarten recognizing 21 of the letters, and who three months later recognizes all 26, a gain score of 5.

We could organize the letter recognition status of all students in our kindergarten class so that we could select curriculum materials and design instructional activities most appropriate to their current state of development. To determine the progress students are making and to determine the effects of our curricular and instructional choices, we would record the letters they recognize at one point in time and then again, three months later. We would use these comparisons in performance to study individual gain, gain for groups of students, and if we wish, mean gain for the class as a unit. Mathematically, we are looking at the difference between the level of knowledge, skill, or expertise indicated on an earlier measure subtracted from or considered in relation to current knowledge, skill, or expertise.

It is *gain* in reading proficiency that tells us how effective our program really is, not what students bring with them to the classroom door.

PART TWO

Assessing Student Progress and Reading Program Effects

In this section, we will review the types of data involved in setting up a basic system for assessing the effects of school and district reading programs. Cell 1, "Current Student Information," and Cell 3, "Student Performance and Responses We Would Like to See," in the Action Research Matrix in Figure 1.1 provide a framework and a starting place for our data collection efforts.

In classrooms, schools, and districts, an ongoing system of data collection and use helps responsible parties make informed decisions. Such a system helps individual teachers and faculties become more knowledgeable about the student population, track student progress in reading, and make decisions that help accelerate student learning. By analyzing student performance and rates of progress in reading, faculty members can identify problems in the reading program.

An ongoing system of reading program assessment should include general school data about the student population and students' participation in categorical and optional programs provided to support reading development. Prosaically, the study of students begins by counting them, answering the question "How many students are we working with?" in each class, each grade, and the school as a whole. Then we add demographic data, particularly characteristics that are historically related to progress in reading, such as gender, socioeconomic status, ethnicity, and English language proficiency. We may develop a multiyear profile of our student population by combining the data on population size (how many students) with our data on socioeconomic status or ethnicity and study how stable our population has been, or look for trends or demographic shifts.

We pay attention to demographic characteristics for many reasons. The two most important ones for our discussion are that we will use them as we analyze student progress and we will use them in analyzing the effectiveness of our reading program. Successful reading programs reduce the potentially negative influence of certain demographic characteristics that have commonly placed students at a disadvantage. They do this by increasing the learning strategies of *all* students.

Next, we build into our system those data that inform us about students' presence for instruction and their participation in programs other than the "regular classroom curriculum." We need to know how much instructional time our students experience. We need to know who is being served in special programs and how effective these programs have been in supporting their development in reading. We also need to know how many staff are available and how they are deployed, because as we study what works and does not work in our reading program, we may make changes in how the adults are organized. And finally, we need to know how we are engaging parents and other caregivers in supporting their children's education.

Our system also needs to include data on student achievement and performance in reading and on reading habits and attitudes. As we monitor student progress in reading, we will find that occasional ad hoc data collection is not very useful and that the reliance on once-a-year test batteries does not help individual teachers or faculties learn what they need to do better in order to help their students right now. To develop a relatively accurate picture of individual student performance in reading and the performance of groups of students, we need to include data from multiple sources in our system. Some data we collect and study once a year,

such as the results from high inference measures like standardized, norm-referenced tests. Some data we collect and analyze three times a year, such as the results from up-close measures of comprehension and fluency collected as students read graded passages. Other data, such as the grades teachers assign to indicate student progress in reading, we may only collect and study when we are focusing on reading program improvements. And finally, our system will need to include some information about students' attitudes toward reading and the kind of habits our reading program is helping them establish.

Figure II.1 provides a list of all of the types of data and variables that school staff need to study as they make informed decisions about the reading program. Each chapter in Part 2 will be devoted to discussion of one of these data categories, proceeding from common data sources that exist in most schools to less common but necessary sources. Almost all schools have general school data, grades, or other teacher-assigned indicators of student progress in reading, as well as results from norm-referenced or criterion-referenced tests for some portion of their student population. Far fewer schools have data from up-close, performance-based measures used for monitoring progress and guiding instruction throughout the year. And even fewer schools systematically collect data on student habits and attitudes toward reading.

You will notice that for each category in Figure II.1, I have provided one or more questions as a conceptual set for

---

FIGURE **II.1**

Types of Data and Questions to Explore in Clarifying Collective Knowledge of the School Population and Students' Progress in Reading

Type of Data and Variables	Questions to Explore
General School Data	
Characteristics of the student population	Who are we working with and responsible for?
Presence for instruction	To what degree are students present for instruction? Do they want to be in our school and classrooms?
Special programs	What have we added to the school's organizational structure beyond the regular classroom? Who participates? And how effective are these programs?
Staff characteristics and parent/caregiver participation	Who are we? How are we involving parents and caregivers?
Teacher- or School-Assigned Indicators of Student Performance (e.g., Grades)	
Student progress in reading as designated by teachers and/or school policy	What do we learn about student progress in literacy when we study the results of the evaluations and judgments that we have made about student achievement during the school year and from year to year?
Indicators of Student Performance Derived from Norm-Referenced Tests (NRTs) or Criterion-Referenced Tests (CRTs)	
Student progress in reading as indicated by the results of group-administered NRTs or CRTs	What do we learn about student progress and achievement when we look at the results of group-administered tests designed to compare the test taker's performance to the performance of a representative sample (national, state, or district) or to an established set of criteria?
Indicators of Student Performance Derived from "Up-Close," Performance-Based Measures with Standard Criteria for Administration, Content, and Scoring	
Student progress in reading and literacy development as indicated by the results of up-close measures	What do we learn about student progress when we look across classes and grade levels at the results from standard measures designed to provide both progress and diagnostic information for use in daily instruction and for grouping students within the class?
Indicators of Reading Attitudes and Habits	
Student engagement with and attitudes about reading	How do students feel about reading? About themselves as readers? What choices do they make?

—————————————————— FIGURE II.2 ——————————————————

Variables and Data Sources for Use in Building Collective Knowledge of the School Population and Students' Progress in Reading

Type of Data	Variables and Data Sources
A. General School Data	*Characteristics of the Student Population* Number of students (Table 1, Figure 4.1) Ethnicity (Table 2, Figure 4.1) Gender (Table 3, Figure 4.1) Socioeconomic background (Table 4, Figure 4.1) Native languages and language proficiency (Tables 5 and 6, Figure 4.1) *Presence for Instruction* School attendance and presence for instruction (Figure 4.3) Disciplinary actions *Special Programs* Who is being served (Figure 4.4) Staff deployment and computer availability What are the effects (Figure 4.5) Number and effects of optional programs What are the costs (Figure 4.5)
B. Teacher- or School-Assigned Indicators (e.g., Grades)	*Student Progress in Reading as Designated by Teachers and/or School Policy* Grade distributions (Figure 5.1) Student progress distributions for terms such as "Excellent" or "Needs Improvement" Retentions (Figure 5.3)
C. Indicators of Student Performance Derived from Norm-Referenced Tests (NRTs) or Criterion-Referenced Tests (CRTs)	*Student Progress in Reading as Indicated by the Results of Group-Administered NRTs or CRTs* Results of norm-referenced tests (Figures 6.8–6.10) Results of criterion-referenced tests
D. Indicators of Student Performance Derived from "Up-Close," Performance-Based Measures	*Student Progress in Reading and Literacy Development as Indicated by the Results of Up-Close Measures* Results of emergent literacy measures (Figure 10.1) Results of reading vocabulary measures (Figures 11.6, 11.7, and 11.10) Results of comprehension measures (Figure 12.4)
E. Indicators of Reading Attitudes and Habits	*Student Attitudes and Habits* Self-report data from surveys Self-report data from interviews Observations of student actions Records of student actions (Figures 13.1–13.3)

studying the school's population, its general academic health, its use of special programs, and its student performance. These "big" questions are designed to focus inquiry and discussion during the school year, as well as from year to year. They represent lines of inquiry for a faculty and are not meant to yield one-time, short-answer responses.

In Figure II.2, I've listed variables and data sources for each of the five categories. Think about which sources your staff already use schoolwide or across several grade levels.

Now, you may say, "Whew! That's just too much. We don't have time for that. We have to teach! We have to run the school." Remember the old adage about eating an elephant one bite at a time. The purpose of these figures is to help you think about developing a system and routines for using multiple sources of data about students and to think about the kinds of information teachers, students, parents, and other decision makers need.

Some readers may look at the instruments for measuring up-close performance and think, "She's describing an individual diagnostic assessment that isn't designed to provide information about groups of students." Well, if it is good enough to provide the classroom teacher with student reading levels, fluency and reading rate, and identifications of student strengths in word recognition, then it is good enough for us to look at in terms of community progress. Whenever reasonable, we want to use those assessments that provide us with quality information about students in our classrooms to also provide us with quality information about the student population as a whole.

Other readers reviewing Figures II.1 and II.2 may say, "Our staff already study these data and use them during the year and from year to year to design learning experiences in literacy and monitor student progress. We already triangulate multiple data sources and use the information for assessing individual and group progress in reading proficiency, for monitoring aspects of the reading curriculum, for evaluating student performance, and for generating individual student profiles and group profiles as needed." If you are in this group, your school or district already has a very good assessment system in place, and you may only need to skim Chapters 4 through 8.

4

Studying General School Data: Demographics and Program Participation

With whom are we working and for whom are we responsible? How are the students responding, in general, to the school as an institution? What is our current organizational structure beyond the "regular classroom and curriculum" and how are these additional programs working? Who are we, and how are we involving parents and caregivers?

In this chapter, I review how general school data can be organized and used in assessing the performance of groups of students and in examining the quality of a school's reading program. We begin by looking at student demographics and where and how students are being served. These data give staff a picture of the composition of the student population, of student participation in the school setting, and of organizational programs and structures designed to support students' educational progress.

Characteristics of the Student Population

Organizing our enrollment and demographic data helps us develop an accurate description of the student population. We can determine its *size*—how many students we are responsible for in the school as a unit and in each grade level; its *gender distribution*—what the male/female ratio in the school is; its *ethnic richness*—how many ethnic groups are represented; *the variety of native languages present*—how many native languages are represented and what the current levels of English proficiency are; and its *socioeconomic status*—what the range of socioeconomic comfort and resources represented is.

If you want to ensure that no student is "left behind" in literacy development, you will need to know more than is traditional about the characteristics of the student population and about how to use these data. This "knowing and using" is not the same thing as having the data available in the school files or in tables embedded in comprehensive school improvement plans. It means that teachers, administrators, and other support persons are using these data as they study the external knowledge base on best practices, as they plan daily and yearly learning experiences, and as they monitor individual and group progress in literacy development.

Therefore, the school leadership team will need to select or develop tables depicting the following information (if such tables are not already in use by the staff):

- Total *number of students* attending the school and the number of students at each grade level.
- *Gender* across the total population and within each grade level.
- *Ethnicity* across the total population and within each grade level.
- *Native languages* represented, organized according to gender and number or percent of students speaking these languages across the total population and within each grade level.
- *Levels of English proficiency* of English as a Second Language (ESL) students.
- *Socioeconomic or income background data,* if available (for example, the number and percent of students receiving free school meals).

Tables 1 through 6 in Figure 4.1 are examples of ways to organize basic demographic data for study. Although all of the characteristics of the student population mentioned above could be consolidated into one table, the number of variables in these tables is limited in order to focus attention on particular characteristics of the population.

You will notice that several of these tables allow space for data for up to five years. While data from one year provide useful information, faculty members also need to study multiple-year profiles. When comparing data from one year to the next, set a date and use almost that same date each year or each quarter. For example, look at enrollment the sixth week of school from year to year, or look at attendance the third week in each quarter.

Whether we are examining demographic data or student performance data in reading, we need multiple-year profiles to help us develop an understanding of what students are experiencing, and eventually, to determine if there are patterns or trends that need to be addressed by the faculty. Some patterns or trends simply need to be recognized so that the school can make sure it is ready, such as those that indicate changes in the demographic characteristics of the population (for example, increased numbers of students living in poverty or increased numbers of ESL students). Some changes should be celebrated by the school community, such as those that indicate positive moves in student performance or attitude. Some signal the need for concerted action by the staff, such as those that indicate a pattern of declining student performance. And some patterns provide information for both celebrating and for renewed study and action, such as when student achievement for the previous three years has steadily increased for three subgroups but has remained almost flat for one subgroup of the school population.

—— FIGURE **4.1** ——

Tables for Organizing Demographic Data

On CD-ROM
Tables 1–6

1 Enrollment

School: _____ Data Organized by: _____

Principal's Name: _____ Shared with Staff: _____
(Date)

	Grade __ No. of Students	Grade __ No. of Students	Grade __ No. of Students	Grade __ No. of Students	Grade __ No. of Students	Grade __ No. of Students	
Enrollment by Grade and Total							
Year							Total No.
2003							
2004							
2005							
2006							
2007							

Source of Data: _____ Time of Year Collected: _____

2 Student Characteristics: Race and Ethnicity

School: _____ Data Organized by: _____

Principal's Name: _____ Shared with Staff: _____
(Date)

	White		Black		Hispanic		Asian/Pacific Islander		American Indian/Alaskan		
Students by Race and Ethnicity											
Year	No.	%	No.	%	No.	%	No.	%	No.	%	Total No.
2003											
2004											
2005											
2006											
2007											

Source of Data: _____ Time of Year Collected: _____

3 Student Characteristics: Gender

School: _____ Data Organized by: _____

Principal's Name: _____ Shared with Staff: _____
(Date)

		Total No./% for School		K		1st		2nd		3rd		4th		5th	
Students by Gender															
Year		No.	%	No.	%	No.	%	No.	%	No.	%	No.	%	No.	%
2003	M														
	F														
2004	M														
	F														
2005	M														
	F														
2006	M														
	F														
2007	M														
	F														

Source of Data: _____ Time of Year Collected: _____

(continues)

FIGURE **4.1** CONTINUED

Tables for Organizing Demographic Data

On CD-ROM

Tables 1–6

4   Student Characteristics: Socioeconomic Status

School: _____   Data Organized by: _____

Principal's Name: _____   Shared with Staff: _____
                                               (Date)

Students on Reduced/Free Lunch Program		
Year	**No.**	**%**
2003		
2004		
2005		
2006		
2007		

Source of Data: _____   Time of Year Collected: _____

5   Student Characteristics: Native Languages

School: _____   Data Organized by: _____

Principal's Name: _____   Shared with Staff: _____
                                               (Date)

	Students' Native Languages											
	English											
Year	No.	%	No.	%	No.	%	No.	%	No.	%	No.	%
2003												
2004												
2005												
2006												
2007												

Source of Data: _____   Time of Year Collected: _____

6   Student Characteristics: English Language Proficiency

School: _____   Data Organized by: _____

Principal's Name: _____   Shared with Staff: _____
                                               (Date)

	Students' English Language Proficiency							
Year	**English Only**		**Limited English Proficient**		**Redesignated**		**Fluent English**	
	No.	%	No.	%	No.	%	No.	%
2003								
2004								
2005								
2006								
2007								

Source of Data: _____   Time of Year Collected: _____

— FIGURE 4.2 —

Student Characteristics: Race and Ethnicity

School: _____Elwood_____   Data Organized by: _____Simmons_____

Principal's Name: _____Simmons_____   Shared with Staff: _____10-17-02_____

Year	White		Black		Hispanic		Asian/Pacific Islander		American Indian/ Alaskan		Total
	No.	%	No.	%	No.	%	No.	%	No.	%	No.
1999	330	61%	173	32%	16	3%	22	4%	0	0%	541
2000	330	58%	177	31%	40	7%	23	4%	0	0%	570
2001	302	51%	208	35%	65	11%	18	3%	0	0%	593
2002	267	43%	236	38%	99	16%	19	3%	0	0%	622
2003											

Source of Data: _____Enrollment_____   Time of Year Collected: _____6th Week of School_____

For example, we can go back to Elwood Elementary to see how such data can help us understand what kind of actions need to be taken in our school. Figure 4.2 displays Elwood's student enrollment between 1999 and 2002. Some things that affect space and staff stand out immediately when you review this short enrollment history. Each year since 1999, the school has added about 30 students a year. This means more teachers and more classrooms are needed. Since teacher allocation is based on average daily attendance, funding was not a problem. However, when Helen came in as principal in August 2000, she recognized that there had been an increase in the Hispanic student population, so she wanted to hire some bilingual teachers and paraeducators. Thus far, she has hired four bilingual (Spanish/English) paraeducators and one teacher.

In terms of space, in the first two years the staff was able to manage by giving up a resource room and teacher workroom located off the library; this last year the district added two portable buildings. Helen is trying to convince the district of the need for a new wing. The space is available, but funding doesn't look likely, even though district projections indicate that Elwood's population will continue to grow.

If you looked at the changes in socioeconomic status for Elwood students over this same time period, the kind of data that would be organized in

Table 4, you would see that the percentage of students participating in the free and reduced-price lunch program had increased from 41 percent in 1999 to 60 percent in 2002. When the percentage of children living in poverty is high, the burden on the staff to create a rich, multidimensional literacy program increases.

As part of a general policy of keeping data available for staff use, hard copies of Tables 1–6 or similar ones should be included in the teacher's handbook for easy reference, as well as in the classified or general staff handbook, and updated annually. I highly recommend this practice, even if the information is available on the district Web site, and even in settings that have a high turnover in student population during the school year.

After the demographic data on students have been organized in simple tabular form, the leadership team or school facilitator needs to help staff study these data and their various uses. If this isn't done, teams or individuals often respond with, "So what?" Reviewing these data and discussing their implications help keep faculty members up-to-date about the demographic characteristics of the whole school community and position them as informed citizens for generating possible avenues of action as changes occur or problems are identified.

Making Use of Data About Student Characteristics

Table 1 in Figure 4.1 presents the number of students by grade level. At a glance, it lets us know how many students we are responsible for at each

grade level and in the school community as a whole. These simple enrollment data have many uses if you are trying to determine the effectiveness of your school's reading program.

It is almost impossible to interpret test results and what they mean about student performance in a school unless one knows how many students are enrolled at each grade level in which the test was administered. We must know the number of students at each grade level and how many students took the test in order to calculate the participation rate.

The participation rate indicates the percentage of the total student population who were assessed and are represented in the school or grade level mean and other summary statistics commonly provided to schools and districts. Size of student population may seem a simple and innocuous variable, but without it, test results representing groups of students (such as a class or grade level group) can rarely be interpreted accurately. For example, even in the same school district, I often find participation rates that vary from 98 percent in one school to as low as 78 percent in another school. Think about what a difference it makes to the mean or to the standard deviation (variation from the mean) if 20 to 30 percent of the student population are not represented in the data. This is true whether we are studying results of norm-referenced tests, informal reading inventories, or reports of how many students are reading "on level."

There will be much uproar about the 95 percent participation rate in the annual state assessments in reading/ language arts and mathematics required as part of the No Child Left Behind Act. (Currently, this requirement is scheduled to go into effect in 2005–2006 and will include grades 3–8 and one year in the 10th–12th grade span.) What we need to do is make this requirement work for us instead of against us. While we must avoid testing situations that are harmful to children, many schools and districts should have been including more students in their testing program and in their student averages than they had been. This is an opportunity to standardize test administration procedures so that we can look at school and district performance from year to year. It won't be easy, because there is, and will continue to be, stress attendant to test scores and public reporting until our literacy programs are strong enough to produce better results.

We also need the description of the student population provided by enrollment disaggregations (Tables 2–6) to determine if we are successfully educating *all* students. Historically in many public schools and school systems, the variables that simply describe student characteristics have become factors that predict how well students will perform academically. Here are a few examples:

- Young males in the primary grades have a higher failure rate than females, particularly in reading, which often influences their entire school career. Many young males do not read as well as their female classmates. See, for example, the National

Assessment of Education Progress, 4th Grade Reading, 2000, in which the percentage of "good readers" breaks down to males, 37 percent, and females, 63 percent (Donahue, Finnegan, Lutkus, Allen, & Campbell, 2001; National Center for Educational Statistics [NCES], 2001).

- Black and Hispanic students often have a much higher failure rate based on school grades, and they have lower achievement on standardized test measures than do white and Asian students (Haycock, 2002; NCES, 2001, 2003).
- Across all grade levels, poor students—those from "low socioeconomic status" backgrounds—have greater difficulty making progress in schools, have poorer academic records, and are much less likely to attend college (Cooley, 1993; Haycock, 2002; McGill-Franzen & Allington, 1991).

There are numerous examples of schools where these student characteristics do not predict performance (Haycock, 2002; Joyce & Calhoun, 1996; Slavin, Karweit, & Wasik, 1994; Taylor, Pearson, Clark, & Walpole, 2000). When an educational institution and its learning environment are working optimally for all students, these variables do not predict success or a lack thereof.

Table shells like those in Figure 4.1 help to organize descriptive data about the school population. We use these descriptive data in studying the effects of the reading program, and any categorical and optional literacy programs, on all students. As we inquire into student achievement and reading performance data, we can find out if gender, ethnicity, native language, English language proficiency, and socioeconomic status are factors in predicting a student's success or failure in our school.

Presence for Instruction

Once you know the enrollment and demographic characteristics of your student population, you can look at who is and who is not present for the literacy instruction being provided. To clarify this picture, review data on school attendance and disciplinary actions. Most of these data are accumulated already, either at the request of the local education authority or to complete school improvement reports. However, they are often not available for staff in easy-to-

read charts that communicate how the student population and groups within that population are responding to the school as a place to be. Analyzing these data provide us with diagnostic information about the climate of the school. For teachers and educational leaders concerned with student progress in literacy, degree of presence for instruction is often an influential variable.

In this category, let's use data on attendance as an example. Look at the table "Students' Attendance and Suspension" (Figure 4.3). It is designed to give staff an easy-to-follow picture of the average percentage of students attending school during one year and the general status and severity of absences from instruction. If you have been evaluating your school's climate and working with parents and caregivers on keeping stu-

FIGURE 4.3

Table for Student Attendance and Suspension

School: _____   Data Organized by: _____

Principal's Name: _____   Shared with Staff: _____
(Date)

Year:	No. of Students Enrolled	Average Daily Attendance		Absent More Than ___ Days		In-School Suspension More Than 5 Days		Out-of-School Suspension More Than 5 Days	
		No.	%	No.	%	No.	%	No.	%
1st Quarter	M								
	F								
2nd Quarter	M								
	F								
3rd Quarter	M								
	F								
4th Quarter	M								
	F								

Source of Data: _____   Time of Year Collected: _____

dents in school, the table lets you know how successful the interventions have been thus far. If increasing student attendance is a current emphasis, then a table that displays attendance monthly or quarterly is needed. I also added gender as a variable to consider in relation to school attendance and suspension. There may or may not be a relationship between gender and absences in your school, but if there is, the staff and community need to know. Just as I added gender, you could add any variable that you are concerned about, such as ethnicity, language proficiency, or socioeconomic status.

Data about discipline referrals and other disciplinary actions are accumulated by most schools. Data sources include records of disciplinary actions, such as who is referred to the principal's or counselor's office; reasons for referrals; the number of incidents; and the consequences of these referrals, such as individual counseling with students, conferences with parents, in-school suspension, after-school suspension, suspension from school for a number of days, placement in programs for behavior-disordered children, placement in an alternative school, expulsion from school, or the relinquishment of students into the care of law enforcement officials. While these data are routinely accumulated in many schools, they often move immediately into the school archives with little reflection by faculty members on what they mean for the educational progress of the student population as a whole. Someone needs to organize these data into schoolwide pro-

files and help the faculty inquire into the cumulative effect of the school's discipline code on instruction.

Combining data on school attendance and disciplinary actions with the demographic data on the student population can help determine if there are patterns that are not good for student progress or for the climate of the school. For example, are students from some cultural backgrounds at high risk of failure because of absence from instruction or behavior patterns? Are Hispanic students overrepresented in absences? Are black students overrepresented in disciplinary referrals? If they are, why? What types of infractions are most common? Are there general schoolwide patterns? Are males overrepresented in terms of discipline referrals? If so, how early does this begin—kindergarten, 1st grade? Whether students are missing prime instructional time because they are not present in school or because they are sitting in in-house suspension, their likelihood of feeling successful in school or of learning the curriculum offered by the school is decreased.

The challenge for staff as they look at data on disciplinary actions and what these data mean in terms of absence from instruction and effects on student membership in the school community is to find a reasonable balance when student behavior is disruptive to student progress. The overuse of disciplinary actions that remove students from their heterogeneous social group and lead to a "send them down the hall or across town" solution may be extremely unhealthy for the maturation of students and for the self-esteem of the staff, and it is almost certainly detrimental to student progress in literacy.

Student Participation in and Effects of Special Programs

The third type of general school data we study provides information about special programs available in the school or district, who is participating in these programs, and how effective they have been in supporting student progress. Let's look at two kinds of programs that have been added to supplement or extend regular classroom instruction and curriculum: categorical programs and optional programs.

Categorical programs—special education and compensatory programs such as Title I—are required or made possible through legislation and state or federal guidelines. In most cases, they were added to the school in an attempt to support the education of students most in need or those who might not receive an optimal education with the standard curriculum or in the regular classroom environment. *Optional programs* are activities or routines that staff have added to the school or to certain grade levels for some worthy reason related to literacy. Some of these optional programs are activities with materials (such as Accelerated Reader), and some provide additional personnel (such as Grandparents as Partners). Some are costly in terms of time, money, and personnel; others are relatively inexpensive. In order to study the effects of these categorical and optional programs on the student popu-

lation, we need to organize data about their number, nature, costs, and effects on students.

The Effects of Categorical Programs

Start by examining categorical programs. The intent of these programs is that they go beyond regular classroom instruction and (1) remediate student performance, such as through compensatory programs in reading; (2) add knowledge or skills essential to success within the school, such as through immersion programs to teach the English language; (3) enhance and provide enrichment beyond the regular classroom curriculum, such as through classes for those labeled as gifted; and (4) provide an education, to the extent possible, for students whose mental ability severely limits their participation in regular classroom instruction. Our focus is especially on Title I and special education programs, including those for gifted students as well as those for learning disabled students. Over 70 percent of Title I students are in programs to improve reading, and another 24 percent are in programs to improve language arts (U.S. Department of Education, 1999). And, as McGill-Franzen and Goatley (2001) have reminded us, the largest category of special education students is "specific learning disability"—and the majority of these students have deficits in reading.

As we inquire into special categorical programs, we need data that help clarify both their role in the school as a whole and their effects on student progress in reading. Look first at the breadth and impact of categorical programs on the

FIGURE 4.4

Tables for Student Participation in Special Categorical Programs

On CD-ROM
Tables 8–9

8   By Grade Level and Gender

School: _____   Data Organized by: _____

Principal's Name: _____   Shared with Staff: _____
(Date)

School Year: _____

		Total Enrolled		Special Education		Gifted		Title I		Not Served by Special Programs	
		No.	%	No.	%	No.	%	No.	%	No.	%
Whole School											
Kindergarten	M										
	F										
1st Grade	M										
	F										
2nd Grade	M										
	F										
3rd Grade	M										
	F										
4th Grade	M										
	F										
5th Grade	M										
	F										

Source of Data: _____   Time of Year Collected: _____

9   By Student Need

School: _____   Data Organized by: _____

Principal's Name: _____   Shared with Staff: _____
(Date)

From _____   To _____
(School Year)   (School Year)

Year	Total No. Enrolled	Special Education		Gifted		Title I		Not Served by Special Program	
		No.	%	No.	%	No.	%	No.	%
2003									
2004									
2005									
2006									
2007									

Source of Data: _____   Time of Year Collected: _____

school and how they serve the student population. The school leadership team can select or develop tables that depict the number of programs currently in place in the school—for example, Title I reading, bilingual programs, English immersion programs, or gifted and other special education programs—and the number and percent of students being served. The tables in Figure 4.4 are examples of initial tables for collective study. Table 8 allows the staff to see how many students are served in each grade level for one school year. Table 9 helps staff study changes across several years in the numbers of students who need these programs.

You can develop tables to look at any variable of interest to you and your

---
FIGURE **4.5**

Table for Analyzing Efforts of Special Programs

On CD-ROM
Table 10

School: _____   Data Organized by: _____

Principal's Name: _____   Shared with Staff: _____
(Date)

School Year: _____   Total Number of Students Enrolled: _____

Program	Population Served		Redesignated		3 Years or More		Impact on Students Check One				Documentation Source	Total Funds Allocated
	No.	%	No.	%	No.	%	High	Medium	Low	Don't Know		
Title I Reading												
Bilingual												
Special Ed.												

Source of Data: _____   Time of Year Collected: _____

colleagues as you explore the effectiveness of categorical programs in your setting.

If you find that your categorical programs have not been as effective as you would like in accelerating literacy, you are not alone. Evaluations of Chapter I/Title I in the 1990s indicated that the longer students were in these categorical programs, the more they lagged behind their peers (Puma et al., 1997). The good news is "that students with reading disabilities may need the same kind of effective instruction as students without disabilities" (McGill-Franzen & Goatley, 2001).

Think about how the categorical programs are structured, the nature of the literacy curriculum and reading instruction being provided to participating students, and the cost of these programs (including salaries, materials, staff development and support, and space) in relation to the programs' general impact on student achievement. These inquiries can be hard on the social system of the school and district, especially on the directors and staff in these programs, but organizers such as Figure 4.5 are good places to start the discussion. I suggest you begin with student data from the previous school year. If you find this information of value, you may want to develop a three-year profile as a baseline.

Most of the time, when faculties study how students get into Title I and learning disabilities programs and what happens to those students over time, they find disturbing data that serve as a call to action. It may be that a disproportionate number of young males are entering special needs programs at the beginning of 2nd, 3rd, and 4th grades and never exiting. It may be that 25 percent of the students in English immersion classes exit still lacking enough facility with the language to productively use the curriculum materials available to them. Armed with these data, the leadership team and faculty members can make changes that make the school program work better for their students. For example, they can identify students in mid–1st grade who are struggling as emergent readers and engage them in skilled one-on-one tutoring sessions and at-home mentoring efforts. As Juel reminds us so cogently, few students who are behind in reading at the end of 1st grade ever catch up unless they are in a school with a strong intervention program (Juel, 1988, 1992).

I have encountered several settings in which an administrator did not want the number of students receiving special education services to decrease because of the financial ramifications to the school district, and in some cases to individual schools. In some of these locations, what I consider inordinate amounts of money were paid to outside contractors to evaluate students. It seemed as if the goal was not to serve the students and help them be successful in the regular classroom, but to have a large number of students designated as "in need." I pray that such places are rare and that you will not have to deal with similar unpleasant situations.

The good news is that today, many schools with a high percentage of Title I students have opportunities to engage in strong schoolwide professional develop-

ment efforts. In fact, this has been the case since the Hawkins-Stafford Elementary and Secondary School Improvement Act Amendment of 1988, and even more so with the Elementary and Secondary Education Act (ESEA) reauthorizations of 1994 and 2001. Earlier regulations that divided staff (and students) and limited collective discourse have been changed. Now we just need to exploit these changes and design sustained staff development and collective study of our curricular and instructional interventions.

The Effects of Optional Programs

In addition to evaluating categorical programs, we need to look at the number, nature, cost, and effects of optional programs that have been added to the school or to certain grade levels in an effort to provide more literacy learning opportunities. This includes programs such as Accelerated Reader, after-school tutorials, and DEAR (Drop Everything and Read) time. We need similar information about these optional actions and programs to that we obtained about our special categorical programs. While these data may be messy and hard to analyze, just grappling with the task can help staff think about the choices that have been made about instructional time and resource use.

We have a tendency in education to add activities we like to our classroom routines and our school day. Many of these are worthwhile, yet we don't always study whether they yield the promised effects. Also, some of us hesitate to offend the advocates of current or new programs and so don't challenge the use of time or resources dedicated to carrying them out. We simply opt not to follow the program in our classrooms or to recommend it to parents and other community members. This would be all right if each of us were running our own private little red schoolhouse, but it is not a healthy way to handle disagreements in a professional community responsible for common curriculum standards and accelerating student literacy.

The effects of these optional activities or programs don't always need to yield increased student achievement, but we do need to be clear about what they are providing and about their costs in terms of staff time and resources. For example, let's consider the effects of two relatively low-cost optional programs, a voluntary tutoring program for students having difficulty in reading and a Reading Buddies program, in which high school students take turns reading with their 3rd grade buddies twice a week. The voluntary tutoring program may bring more community members into the school, but it may have very little direct, documented effect on student achievement. This does not mean it should be eliminated, but we might want to look into its impact on instructional time and students' approach to reading. A Reading Buddies program may lead to improved attitudes about reading for some students and the development of good mentoring relationships for some. What we should think about with programs such as these is timing. If I were still teaching first grade, I would much rather have my Reading Buddies come at 2:00 p.m. rather than at 9:00 a.m. because most of

my students would be excited about it whenever they came, and while a worthwhile literacy activity, I would not want it interrupting the structure of the morning's language arts block.

In many schools, categorical and optional programs serve a large portion of the student population. Too often, once a program has been put in place to serve the special needs of students or to fill a curriculum gap or instructional need, we tend to assume we have "taken care of" those needs. You want to build time for staff to inquire into the general effects of these programs on the educational progress of your students, on the health of the organization, and on the integrity of these programs to best instructional practices and to the goals of the school. Eventually, routines for regularly scanning the effects of these programs on students and school climate should be implemented. While in-depth, up-close attention to the effects of current programs often causes social turmoil and even animosity, if leadership team members and staff persist and focus on student effects and data, a more powerful learning environment will evolve.

Staff Characteristics and Parent or Caregiver Participation

In major program improvement efforts, it's often necessary to take a closer look at staff composition and deployment and at how we are involving parents and community members in educating their children. This may include organizing data about staff characteristics such as population size, gender, role designations, cultural background, or fluency in languages other than English. We need to know how many parents and community members are serving in advisory groups, as mentors, as volunteer tutors, as classroom observers, and as leaders of school or district initiatives. And we need to know how representative they are of our student population.

5

Studying Teacher- or School-Assigned Indicators of Student Performance

What do grades in reading mean in your school? What do they tell students, parents, and school staff about students as readers and where they are on the reading development continuum?

Let's think about what grades and school retention policies can tell us about the quality and effects of the reading program. Teachers assign grades or complete performance summaries at regular intervals during the school year; these ratings serve as summative evaluations of student performance in reading. They also provide evidence about whether the learning environment of the school and current instructional practices are working or not.

We study grade distributions in reading and the number of promotions and retentions because the grades students receive, despite variations in grading procedures from teacher to teacher, are the major currency of success in schools. While high-stakes tests are catching up fast, class grades—more than any other indicator of student performance—reflect a student's successful or unsuccessful progress through school. This is true even in the primary grades, where word labels, such as "Independent" or "Developing," may be used instead of letters or numbers, or where lists of skills are used to assign ratings to student performance in reading. Timely progress in literacy development is so critical to students' success in school that individual teachers and the staff as a unit need to have a profile of student grades that have been assigned to evaluate this progress.

My use of the word "assigned" in no way implies that students have not earned a particular grade or performance rating. There are a number of reasons I use the verb "assigned" to describe what we do when we evaluate student performance in the classroom. The major one is to encourage reflection and discussion about the criteria used to determine summative indicators of performance. Many of us are familiar with cases in which students in differ-

FIGURE 5.1

Table for K–5 Student Achievement in Reading

On CD-ROM
Table 11

School: _____ Data Organized by: _____

Principal's Name: _____ Shared with Staff: _____
                                                              (Date)

School Year: _____		Quarter (Circle One):	1st	2nd	3rd	4th					
		A		B		C		D		F		Total
Grade Level		No.	%	No.	%	No.	%	No.	%	No.	%	No.
K	M											
	F											
1st	M											
	F											
2nd	M											
	F											
3rd	M											
	F											
4th	M											
	F											
5th	M											
	F											

Source of Data: _____ Time of Year Collected: _____

ent classrooms are similar in reading performance, yet they have very different grades assigned to this performance on their report card or progress report.

Whether we are thinking of grades assigned by classroom teachers or percentile rankings "assigned" or derived from tables that accompany norm-referenced tests, the criteria and bases used for performance ratings need to be public knowledge. Faculty discussions and the establishment of a few decision rules about the relationships between curriculum standards and how grades are assigned strengthen curriculum alignment. Curriculum standards, however accurate and appropriate they may be for a grade level or school, have not been implemented fully until they are present in instruction and represented in the assessment of the effects of that instruction and the grades assigned to students.

Of course, student grades and program effectiveness are related. Thus, another benefit of organizing student grades is that a composite analysis of grades or teacher-assigned progress indicators serves as a school faculty's rating of the effectiveness of the current reading program.

You may want to organize student grades and progress report data to present information about the school as a unit or about a designated grade level. Let's look at a schoolwide example. Organizers, such as the Table 11 (Figure 5.1), can be used to provide a frequency distribution of the number and percent of the student population receiving each designation on the grading scale. This provides the staff with a profile of

—————————————— FIGURE 5.2 ——————————————

Student Achievement in Reading by Class: Quarterly Grades or Other Progress Indicators by Gender

School: _____Elwood_____   Grade Level: _____2nd_____

Principal's Name: _____Simmons_____   Teacher's Name: __Huett 6/2001__
                                                                                    (Date)

Quarter		A		B		C		D		F		Total No. of Students
		No.	%	No.	%	No.	%	No.	%	No.	%	
1st	M	0	0%	6	60%	2	20%	2	20%	0	0%	10
	F	0	0%	10	77%	2	15%	1	8%	0	0%	13
2nd	M	0	0%	6	60%	3	30%	1	10%	0	0%	10
	F	0	0%	10	77%	3	23%	0	0%	0	0%	13
3rd	M	0	0%	7	70%	2	20%	1	10%	0	0%	10
	F	0	0%	12	86%	2	14%	0	0%	0	0%	14
4th	M	1	10%	7	70%	1	10%	1	10%	0	0%	10
	F	8	53%	6	40%	1	7%	0	0%	0	0%	15

kindergarten through grade 5. I added gender as a variable, but you could add ethnicity, socioeconomic status, or other variables you are concerned about.

If the reading program is working, the grade distribution for our students should show almost all grades skewed to the high end of the grading scale ("Excellent," "Good Progress"; As and Bs; or most students making good progress on most of the skills listed on the report card). The results of instruction in public schools should be criterion-based, not norm-referenced, with curriculum standards serving as the criteria. If the reading program is not working very well, then students' grades may spread across the scale, looking more like a normal dis-

tribution, with few As and Fs, more Bs and Ds, and most of the students making Cs or "Average."

Going back to the Elwood Elementary scenario, Figure 5.2 displays one of the tables from the school's first analysis of grades. At the end of Helen's first year, she asked the leadership team to have study group members record their grades for the year. The data in Figure 5.2 are from one 2nd grade teacher at Elwood. Of course, this class is one of the extreme cases, but there were six such extreme cases in this school, representing 126 students. Many teachers were amazed at the gender differences in their classrooms. The results of these individual analyses by classroom and grade level

FIGURE 5.3

Table for Retention by Number and Ethnicity

On CD-ROM
Table 12

School: _____   Data Organized by: _____

Principal's Name: _____   Shared with Staff: _____

(Date)

School Year: _____

	Total Enrolled No.	White		Black		Hispanic/Latino		Asian/Pacific Islander		American Indian/Alaskan	
		No.	%	No.	%	No.	%	No.	%	No.	%
Whole School											
Kindergarten M											
F											
1st Grade M											
F											
2nd Grade M											
F											
3rd Grade M											
F											
4th Grade M											
F											
5th Grade M											
F											

Source of Data: _____   Time of Year Collected: _____

teams also made the leadership team want to look at grades by ethnicity.

If the school district has a policy for retaining students, the school's leadership team can use table shells like Figure 5.3 to study how many students are being retained at each grade level and the ethnicity of the retainees. In general, grade level retention has not been effective in accelerating literacy development (Karweit, 1999).

When staff study the grade distributions or student progress designations schoolwide, by both grade and curriculum area, and then look at what happens to students whose grades in reading are "Unsatisfactory," or when they follow the academic careers of students who were retained, they almost always find something that needs to be changed by the adults in the system. It may be that

the new "flexible grouping" by class is just a new name for the old practice of tracking, and that once students are placed in the bottom group, they almost always remain in the bottom group or track. Or it may turn out that 75 percent of the students retained in grades 1 to 4 dropped out of school.

These important data—reading grades or the labels we assign to student performance in reading—are ignored in many settings. Yet they serve an evaluation role as value judgments about student progress on the reading development continuum, an assessment role as indicators of student progress on this continuum, and a program quality role as indicators of the effectiveness of the current reading program. If you are in a school or district that has worked on strengthening the reliability and validity of its grading system and its connection to curriculum standards, you know how testy some of us can get when we are pushed by our colleagues to be specific about the criteria we use for grading. If you haven't tackled this yet in your school or district, a good place to begin is by having teachers organize grades or whatever progress labels are used at the classroom level and begin discussing how they were derived and their implications for students.

6

Studying the Results of Norm-Referenced and Criterion-Referenced Tests

Does your school or district use group-administered, norm-referenced achievement tests or criterion-referenced tests? If it does, are tests included for measuring reading and vocabulary? What do their results tell you about student achievement in reading? How are the results of these tests used in your school and district?

Large-scale, group-administered testing is on the rise. Thanks in part to the No Child Left Behind Act, many elementary school staff, students, and parents will soon be coping with far more of these tests than ever before. Using the results wisely will challenge all of us.

Let's define the measures in this category, discuss their appropriate use, clarify what their results mean, and think about how we might make better use of them without spending an inordinate amount of time organizing and analyzing data. I'm going to address the characteristics of norm-referenced tests (NRTs) and criterion-referenced tests (CRTs) briefly, then spend most of this section on interpreting and using the results of NRTs, both because these tests are more commonly administered across classrooms and because the task of interpreting what they mean in terms of student performance is far more complex.

Defining NRTs and CRTs

Norm-referenced tests are used to compare a student's performance to that of a large and representative group of students who took the test at a specific time in their school career. *Criterion-referenced tests* are used to compare a student's performance to a fixed standard of performance or a well-defined domain of behavior. The results of both types of tests also provide information about the knowledge and skills of groups of students.

Norm-referenced tests and state and district criterion-referenced tests are often referred to as "standardized tests." The word *standardized* simply means that these tests are uniform in content and have predetermined, common guidelines for administration and scoring. This standardization, which is by no means perfect in terms of the variability in administration, allows for comparison of results across classrooms, schools, school districts, and states. In this chapter, I will focus on group-administered, norm-referenced achievement tests and criterion-referenced tests that have been standardized for national or statewide administration.

Norm-referenced achievement tests are based on the assumption that levels of student performance on the content being measured will resemble a normal curve, with most students' scores falling in the middle of the distribution, while the rest of the scores are thinly but evenly distributed on either side. (The tests are also designed so that this distribution will occur, usually by adding and subtracting more difficult or less difficult items in the pretesting or developmental phase of the test.) In these tests, standards of performance are relative: whether a student score indicates high achievement, average achievement, or low achievement is determined by how the norming group responded to the items on the test. This is why they are called *norm*-referenced: students' scores are derived through comparison to the scores of the norm group. For example, if Elena scored at the 60th percentile on the "Vocabulary" subtest, she scored in the middle of the distribution, and better than 60 percent of the students who participated in the norming of the test.

Criterion-referenced tests are designed to measure performance in relation to a standard "good" performance. They are often designed to measure specific objectives and skills within a discipline. In contrast to norm-referenced tests, the standards of performance are absolute: whether a student score indicates high, average, or low achievement is not determined in relationship to how other students scored, but is dependent on his mastery of the content, processes, or skills being measured. Criterion-referenced tests are generally more responsive to instruction than are norm-referenced achievement tests, and they can thus be used to measure the effects of instruction on student knowledge.

Here is a simplified example: a criterion-referenced test designed to measure five major reading outcomes—determining main idea, summarizing information from expository prose, using multiple sources of information, evaluating author's purpose, and fluency. The section that measures student skill in summarizing information includes four expository passages, each with varying levels of text complexity and comprehension demands. After a student has provided her summaries, they are scored using rubrics that indicate the major message and key points that need to be included. For mastery at each level of complexity, a student would have to include an accurate explanation of the major message and all key points. To be proficient, a student must summarize three of the four. Let's say that Elena completed three summaries correctly, but missed some of the key details on the fourth item. She is assessed as proficient in summarizing expository prose. How well she scores depends on how well she addressed the task, and had nothing to do with how anyone else scored. If Elena had been unable to summarize any of the passages accurately or could only respond to the simplest one, we may not know exactly why she is having difficulty, but we know she is not proficient and that we need to work with her on summarization.

In the 1970s and 1980s, I helped develop district and statewide criterion-referenced tests in reading and language arts in a variety of settings. I gained an up-close appreciation of how difficult it is to construct appropriate test items and affect classroom instruction positively. For example, it's easy to agree that we want students to be able to summarize what they have read and that we want to assess their proficiency in the process; but it takes much time and expertise to write performance tasks that use text at the appropriate levels, design scoring criteria that indicate levels of proficiency in summarizing, and put together tests that measure knowledge and skill in summarizing and other aspects of reading development, not to mention being group-administered and scored accurately (and inexpensively). Part of the difficulty is in describing the performance tasks and evaluative criteria for scoring,

and part is in making sure these descriptions and the items that comprise the tests do not limit or reduce the classroom curriculum that students experience.

"Curriculum reductionism" (Popham, 2001b, p. 19) is a common problem of high-stakes tests, tests whose results can lead to penalties, loss of status, or no rewards. What happens in many settings is that as pressure to increase test scores rises, teachers are "encouraged" to focus instructional time on teaching what is on the tests, which can restrict both the curriculum content that students experience and reduce the levels of cognitive tasks designed into their daily learning experiences. However, when performance descriptions and test items are developed that match the most important curriculum outcomes, the results of these tests provide useful instructional information for teachers and explicit performance indicators for students and parents. Currently, some of the better examples of criterion-referenced tests are the National Assessment of Education Progress (NAEP) for grades 4, 8, and 12 (National Center for Educational Statistics, 2004) with their clear standards of reading proficiency, items that are part of the New Standards in Writing at the primary grades (New Standards Primary Literacy Committee, 1999), and some of the advanced placement tests at the secondary level.

These nice, clear distinctions between norm-referenced tests and criterion-referenced tests used to work so well. However, today I'm seeing state and district tests that are called "criterion-referenced," but the use of curriculum sampling and the way the results of the tests are interpreted make them more like norm-referenced achievement tests. NRTs are simply not as useful in guiding classroom instruction because they are designed to serve a different purpose. As concerned educators, we need to direct attention to making sure some of the new state tests are criterion-referenced and matched to a few key reading outcomes instead of a thin sampling of achievement across the complex area we call "reading." Norm-referenced, standardized tests dominate state- and district-mandated assessments of reading at the elementary school level. The five most widely used national NRTs providing data on student achievement in reading are the *California Achievement Tests,* the *Comprehensive Tests of Basic Skills,* the *Iowa Tests of Basic Skills,* the *Metropolitan Achievement Tests,* and the *Stanford Achievement Tests.* The companies that construct these five tests also construct most of the state-customized, standards-based tests (Popham, 2001b).

Interpreting and Using the Results of NRTs

To use NRT results productively, I suggest school teams engage in four tasks: (1) clarify the meaning of the individual student and group summary results received by the school; (2) study how different subgroups perform; (3) keep an eye on participation rate by grade level and school; and (4) study the distribution of scores. You'll notice that most of these tasks involve using the test results to understand how *groups* of students perform.

Clarifying the Meaning of the Results

If your school or district uses a national standardized test, you have 20 or more different reports of results available, depending on what was ordered from the company's scoring service. If you have a plain-speaking test coordinator in your district or school, he can help you interpret these reports. Whether you have a test coordinator or not, request and study the *interpretation guides* for the test, both the guide for administrators and the one for teachers, and the description of reports that can be provided. Take examples of the reports you have. Study and ask questions until you understand the data provided. I say this because I have been an audience member for many, many presentations on standardized test results, and I remain amazed both at how much information is provided and at how little most of us understand and take away. Often what we leave these meetings with is, "Oh, our scores are about the same," or "We've made some improvements in reading comprehension," or "It looks like scores are creeping up," or "Well, what can they expect when we have so many poor children?" And sometimes these are the only messages that are delivered.

I'm afraid I have led sessions on interpretation of these results that probably delivered the same messages, with very little active construction of meaning by participants. As I came to be somewhat more comfortable with interpreting these results myself—by working with the data, studying the manuals, calling company representatives, and talking with university and state department colleagues with educational psychology backgrounds—I became better at helping others work with and understand what such results represent in terms of student performance.

Clarifying the Meaning of Individual Student Results

Let's look at the meaning of individual student results—those numbers that are sent back to us as descriptors of the performance of an individual student. We look at these first because teachers have so many to interpret, and because these are the numbers from which school summary results are generated.

We'll start with an individual student's reading scores. Leon is 8 years, 8 months old. He is in 3rd grade and was tested in the fall. Leon took the standardized reading, language, and mathematics tests required at 3rd grade in his state and the science and social studies tests required in his school district. Over a period of five days, he responded to

multiple-choice questions designed to measure knowledge and skills in these five academic areas. The primary item format used on these large-scale achievement tests is multiple choice. Each item generally includes a passage, graphic, or other material; a stem or question; and four or five choices from which students select a response.

Figure 6.1 shows Leon's reading test results. Let's assume they represent his best work and that we can use them to make valid score-based inferences about Leon's current reading knowledge and skills. What do the test scores tell us about Leon's reading skills and those of the rest of the students in his district?

Leon's test results compare his performance to that of other students who took the same test. These results—in fact, all the results received by the school—are derived from comparisons of students' scores with the scores of the norm group for that edition of the test. For example, Leon responded correctly to 27

FIGURE 6.1

Leon's Reading Scores

Score	Vocabulary	Reading Comprehension	Total
Raw Score	19	27	46
National Percentile Rank	76th	87th	83rd
Standard Score	189	204	196
Grade Equivalent	4.0	5.1	4.5
Normal Curve Equivalent	57	63	60
Local Percentile Rank	71st	86th	80th

of the 36 items on the "Reading Comprehension" subtest. All the scores listed in the "Reading Comprehension" column of Figure 6.1 were determined based on where that 27 placed Leon in relation to the raw scores of norm group members. In measurement terms, Leon's raw score was converted to scores that can be compared across time and different levels of the test. Each one of the derived scores we look at gives us a general estimate of Leon's achievement and indicates that Leon is doing well on the reading achievement continuum.

Let's look at "National Percentile Rank." Here Leon's raw score placed him at the 87th percentile in reading comprehension, meaning that his raw score was the same as or better than 87 percent of the students who were tested at the same time of year during the national standardization of this edition of the test. That is good. And that's basically all we know. We can say he scored "high average," but we cannot say he scored "well above average," because "average" could range from the 16th through the 84th percentile (one standard deviation below and above the mean, which is the 50th percentile). It is, however, becoming common to think about percentile scores of 25 and below as indicating "below average," those from 26 to 75 as indicating "average," and those from 76 on up as indicating "above average."

As we burrow a little deeper into Leon's scores, we begin to understand why we don't want to put too much emphasis on individual student results and why we want to help parents and policymakers consider these results as

only one indicator of Leon's performance in reading. The "Reading Comprehension" subtest Leon took has 36 items measuring a range of reading knowledge and skills (for example, determining explicit and implicit main ideas, identifying key relevant details, recognizing and using sequences, using context, drawing conclusions, and applying information). Because these 36 items sample such a broad range of possible reading behaviors, we know very little about what specific reading knowledge and skills Leon has or where he excels or needs help. Also, although Leon's percentile rank score is 87, he responded correctly to only three-fourths (n = 27) of these 36 items.

We could look at the item analysis for this test, which would show us how many items were used to measure student knowledge and skill in each content division. However, these items are designed to spread scores out and have a wide range of difficulty levels. In addition, some areas only have 2 items while others have 10. Without studying the actual items on the test, we still know little about how to support Leon instructionally. But guiding instruction is not the purpose of NRTs; their purpose is differentiating students' levels of performance in reading.

So what do all these scores tell us about Leon's performance and his school district? For a 3rd grader who took the test in the third month of 3rd grade (3.3), Leon's scores look good. On both the vocabulary and reading comprehension subtests, he scored better than three-quarters of the national norm group and ranked at about the same position in comparison to all the 3rd graders in his district. He seems stronger in comprehension than in vocabulary, based on his performance on this test. The similarity between Leon's national ranking and his local ranking appears to indicate that students in this school district have very similar scores to those of the national norm group.

Clarifying the Meaning of Group Summary Results

Schools can receive a number of different reports describing the reading achievement of groups of students, including subgroups such as those identified in the tables of Figure 4.1. For example, you can ask for reports on all 5th graders; all the 5th grade girls; all the 5th grade boys; each ethnic group in the population; and so on. Some of these school-level reports provide mainly summary statistics, such as mean scores; some provide lists of the numbers and percentages of students performing at different levels organized by percentile rank, standard scores, grade equivalents, or normal curve equivalent (NCE) scores; and others provide rosters with a printout of student performance in each academic area measured (and the content and skill divisions within each area).

Some of these summary reports are far more useful than others. While their names vary from company to company, the reports that provide the following information are especially useful: (1) the school or building averages, including student norms; (2) the subgroups' scores; (3) the skills analysis or cluster

scores; and (4) the list of student scores. After individual test results, reports that give us summary statistics, especially *means* or *averages,* are the most commonly used from school to school and district to district as staff describe the performance of groups of students. However, they are also the reports that I see misinterpreted the most. Because of the amount of data summarized and our lack of in-depth understanding of many of the terms used in reporting the results, productive use is often difficult. The good news is that once we become skillful in interpreting these reports, their analysis doesn't take very long.

To interpret these group summaries accurately, we need to know how they are developed. Once the raw scores of Leon and all his 3rd grade classmates who took the test were entered into the testing company's database, they were used to derive the relative scores of individual students and groups within the school. If we take a set of raw scores on the reading comprehension subtests from across all 3rd grade classes in a school, total the scores, and divide by the number of scores, we have the mean, or average, for the set. The mean indicates the most representative score in a normal distribution, or the point around which most other scores are clustered. Subtracting this mean value from each raw score in a set, squaring each resulting number, totaling these numbers, dividing by the number of raw scores, and taking the square root results in the *standard deviation* for that set. If a statistician has the mean (the average value), the standard deviation (the degree of dispersion), and

— FIGURE 6.2 —

The Relationship Between the Normal Curve and the Standard Deviation (SD)

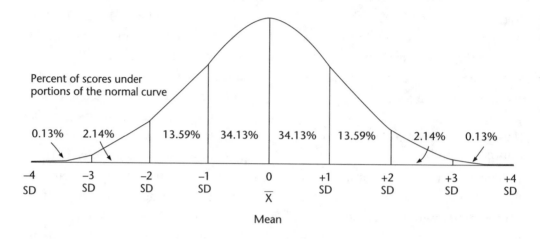

the number of scores in a set, she can plot a graphic frequency distribution such as the normal curve in Figure 6.2.

If we had a large, nationally representative sample of 3rd grade reading achievement test scores, the graphic depiction of the scores would look like Figure 6.2. In normal distributions, the mean also represents the 50th percentile and an NCE of 50.

Because of the special relationship between the standard deviation and the normal curve, in a distribution that is approximately normal, we know that 68 percent of students' raw scores will fall between one standard deviation (SD) above and one standard deviation below the mean, 95 percent of students' scores will fall within two standard deviations above and below the mean, and 99.7 percent will fall within three standard deviations above and below the mean. You'll notice that Figure 6.2 displays the

standard deviations from –4 to +4 and the percentage of raw scores that would be found under each portion of the curve in a large, random sample of normally distributing data such as achievement test scores. For example, only 2 percent of students' raw scores would fall between the +2 SD and +3 SD (98th to 99th+ percentile).

Remember, norm-referenced, standardized achievement tests are designed so that one-half of the students who take the test will score above the 50th percentile and one-half below the 50th percentile. When field-testing new editions, the test company wants the distribution of scores from the norming groups to form a pattern that matches the normal curve depicted in Figure 6.2: a symmetrical, bell-shaped curve with the mean bisecting it.

Let's apply this brief statistics review to a real school report. For this example,

—— FIGURE 6.3 ——

Results from "School Average Report"

Grade 4	Reading Vocabulary	Reading Comprehension
Number of Students (No Exceptional or ESL)	145	145
Average—All Students Mean NCE	46	54
Percentile	43rd	50th
Stanine	4	5

I've selected a school and school district with different demographics and reading achievement history from Leon's and one that uses a different national test. The "School Average Report" provided to this school indicated that mean NCE scores were used to identify the percentile score. Some companies use mean NCE scores for this; some use the mean standard score for identifying the "average" percentile score for a group of students. (Percentile scores are ordinal data, unlike the interval data of standard and NCE scores, and cannot be averaged.) No standard deviations are provided in the report.

In this school district, standardized tests are administered at grades 2 through 5 in the spring. In the school summary report shared here, the tests were administered in April, in contrast to Leon's school district, where the tests were administered in the fall. The testing company simply uses spring norms instead of fall norms for deriving student scores.

Take a look at the results reported to this school in Figure 6.3. For both clarity and emphasis, I'm just going to address the results of the reading comprehension subtest.

The reading comprehension scores look about average, right?

Well, for the sake of understanding the meaning of *means* and what they can mask about student achievement, I have plotted the percentile distribution for this school's 4th grade. I used the school's "Percentile High to Low Report," which lists each student's percentile score on each test and subtest of this achievement battery. Figure 6.4 shows the frequency distribution of the reading comprehension scores for 145 students from nine 4th grade classrooms. Compare it to the normal curve in Figure 6.2. Does it look like what you expected for a school that has its "mean" right at 50? What do you think will happen to the distribution of these reading comprehension scores when we plot them by gender?

Studying Subgroup Performance

You know how important it is to disaggregate school summary data so we can look at how different groups in our

Figure 6.4

Grade Level Distribution of Percentile Scores on Reading Comprehension Subtest: Grade 4

Subtest: Reading Comprehension										
				X						
				X						
				X						
				X						
				X						
				X						
				X						
				X						
				X	X		X			
				X	X		X	X		
	X			X	X	X	X	X		
	X			X	X	X	X	X		
	X	X	X	X	X	X	X	X		
	X	X	X	X	X	X	X	X		
	X	X	X	X	X	X	X	X		
	X	X	X	X	X	X	X	X	X	
	X	X	X	X	X	X	X	X	X	
	X	X	X	X	X	X	X	X	X	
	X	X	X	X	X	X	X	X	X	
	X	X	X	X	X	X	X	X	X	
	X	X	X	X	X	X	X	X	X	
	X	X	X	X	X	X	X	X	X	X
	X	X	X	X	X	X	X	X	X	X
	X	X	X	X	X	X	X	X	X	X
	X	X	X	X	X	X	X	X	X	X
Percentiles	**1st–9th**	**10th–19th**	**20th–29th**	**30th–39th**	**40th–49th**	**50th–59th**	**60th–69th**	**70th–79th**	**80th–89th**	**90th–99th**
No. of Students	15	13	13	25	17	15	17	16	10	4
	Total: 145									

Note: Each mark represents an individual student.

population are performing. This takes us back to the analysis of the characteristics and demographics of our student population described in Tables 1–6 in Figure 4.1. Since we are working with reading at the elementary school level, it's especially vital to look at the achievement of students by gender, special program participation, and ethnicity.

For example, let's look at what happens when we take the scores of the students represented in Figure 6.4 and display them by gender. In Figures 6.5 and 6.6, I have plotted the male and female distributions on the "Reading Comprehension" subtest so you can see what the school "average" 50th percentile and an NCE of 54 can mask about the achievement of these 80 boys and 65 girls.

You can see that the male distribution is skewed toward the lower-performing end of the distribution and the female toward the higher-performing end. When broken down this way, it becomes apparent that the scores of the higher-performing girls pulled the grade level mean up to around the 50th percentile. Around 13 percent of the boys are performing above the 60th percentile, while around 57 percent of the girls are performing at that level. Of course, not all girls are performing well; the female average is around the 57th percentile. But the male average is around the 36th percentile, and 25 percent of these 4th grade boys are really struggling as readers. Gender distributions that look like these are common in many 3rd, 4th, and 5th grade groups when you disaggregate reading achievement data.

Take another look at the School Average Report in Figure 6.3. Neither exceptional students who participate in special programs nor ESL students are included in these averages. The total 4th grade population is 191 students, so 46 students were not included in the "school average." Of these 46, 8 students were not tested; 38 exceptional and ESL students were. *This means the 4th grade in this school had a test participation rate of 96 percent, but only 76 percent of their students are represented in their summary reports.*

The scores of the 38 exceptional and ESL students were included, along with their special needs codes, on the "Percentiles High to Low Report." I did not include these scores in plotting the male and female distributions because they were not included in the school averages. However, I'm sure it won't come as a surprise that of these 38 students, 27 of them scored below the 20th percentile, so they are also struggling readers.

Let's look at the achievement of different ethnic groups in this same school. Figure 6.7 displays summary statistics or "averages" for the total 3rd grade and for five ethnic subgroups. The total 3rd grade population is 198: 167 students are represented in the school averages in Figure 6.7, and 31 students are not represented. Of these 31, 5 did not take the achievement tests, and 26 were exceptional or ESL students. These 26 students took the tests, but their special needs codes were used to exclude them from the summary data. *So while the participation rate looks good at 97 percent, only 84 percent of 3rd grade students are represented in the summary data.*

FIGURE 6.5

Grade Level Distribution of Percentile Scores on Reading Comprehension Subtest: Grade 4, Males

Subtest: Reading Comprehension

Percentiles	1st–9th	10th–19th	20th–29th	30th–39th	40th–49th	50th–59th	60th–69th	70th–79th	80th–89th	90th–99th
	X									
	X									
	X			X						
	X			X						
	X			X						
	X		X	X						
	X	X	X	X	X					
	X	X	X	X	X					
	X	X	X	X	X	X				
	X	X	X	X	X	X				
	X	X	X	X	X	X	X			
	X	X	X	X	X	X	X	X		X
	X	X	X	X	X	X	X	X	X	
No. of Students	13	7	8	20	11	11	6	2	1	1

Total: 80

Note: Each mark represents an individual student.

FIGURE 6.6

Grade Level Distribution of Percentile Scores on Reading Comprehension Subtest: Grade 4, Females

Subtest: Reading Comprehension

Percentiles	1st–9th	10th–19th	20th–29th	30th–39th	40th–49th	50th–59th	60th–69th	70th–79th	80th–89th	90th–99th
No. of Students	2	6	5	5	6	4	11	14	9	3

Total: 65

Note: Each mark represents an individual student.

—————————————— FIGURE 6.7 ——————————————

Results from "School Average Report: By Ethnicity"
(No Exceptional Students)

	Reading Vocabulary	Reading Comprehension	Reading Total
Grade 3			
Number of Students	167	167	167
Average—All Students			
Mean NCE	47.0	45.0	46.3
Percentile	44th	41st	43rd
Stanine	5	5	5
White			
Number of Students	118	118	118
Average—Mean NCE	49.8	47.2	48.8
Percentile	50th	45th	48th
Stanine	5	5	5
Black			
Number of Students	8	8	8
Average—Mean NCE	29.4	27.1	28.5
Percentile	16th	14th	15th
Stanine	3	3	3
Hispanic			
Number of Students	36	36	36
Average—Mean NCE	42.8	42.0	42.7
Percentile	37th	35th	36th
Stanine	4	4	4
Asian/Pacific Islander			
Number of Students	1	1	1
Average—Mean NCE	59.9	66.5	66.3
Percentile	68th	81st	78th
Stanine	7	7	7
American Indian/Alaskan			
Number of Students	4	4	4
Average—Mean NCE	33.7	32.8	33.7
Percentile	22nd	21st	22nd
Stanine	3	3	3

No group is doing extraordinarily well, unless we count the one Asian student. White students have the best scores after that, with an average NCE of 49 and percentile of 48, but about 25 percent of this population are struggling readers. While there are not many black and American Indian students, almost all of them are struggling readers, as are about 40 percent of the Hispanic students. Whatever the student's ethnicity, the reading program in this school is not working for one-half or more of the population. Approximately 80 percent of these students have attended 3rd grade here all year (mid-August to April), and a very strong, well-implemented reading program could have made a lot of difference, even on standardized reading achievement test results.

Analyzing Participation Rate

Because of the effects of participation rates on school summary results, we have to be very careful when comparing test results across classrooms, schools, and districts. A school right next to the one in Figure 6.3 may have a participation rate of 94 percent, with 94 percent of their students also represented in their school summary data. We've come back to the beginning of this section on reviewing the data needed for assessing reading program effects: know the population, know how many and who they are, and know who is being included and who is being excluded when student achievement is being discussed. This information about the students represented by the data is critical for accurately interpreting classroom, school, and district achievement scores.

The table "Participation Rate" is a useful tool for clarifying the picture of participation rate in your school, whether you are analyzing norm-referenced achievement test results or the results of up-close measures of reading performance (Figure 6.8).

Studying the Distribution of Student Scores

We need to look at frequency distributions so we have a clear picture of how

many of our students are struggling, how many are performing acceptably, and how many are doing well. Results from norm-referenced tests give us a yearly, independent check on student achievement. Across several years, they provide information about how much impact the reading program is having on general reading achievement.

For example, the table in Figure 6.9 can be used to take a closer look at the distribution of reading comprehension scores by gender across several years. In each year, staff members can see the distribution of reading achievement for a grade level group. I've used percentile scores because they concisely display the variance in the population from low to high performance. Similar tables could be used for organizing vocabulary subtest or reading total results, depending on your focus area. When a faculty is working on an in-depth inquiry into their reading program, I suggest using the reading comprehension and vocabulary tests. When other curriculum areas, such as mathematics or science, are taking most of the staff energy and staff development time, then reading total will do.

Of course, the distributions in the table would represent a different group of students each year. If you want to follow the same students for several years, I suggest you sample, drawing at least six students from each class. If 6th grade is the highest grade in your school, select a random sample of three girls and three boys who have attended the school for four years and track their achievement results in 3rd, 4th, and 5th grade. Or you

———————————————— FIGURE 6.8 ————————————————

Table for Participation Rate

On CD-ROM
Table 13

School: _____   Shared with Staff: _____
                                                                    (Dates)
Principal's Name: _____   Grade Level: _____

Name of Test: _____   Time of Year Administered: _____

Name of Academic Area or Subtest Reported
(e.g., Reading Total, Reading Vocabulary, or Reading Comprehension): _____

Participation Rate in Standardized Testing									
		Students Taking Test		Students Represented in the Student and School Averages		Students Excluded from Summaries by Code		Students Absent or Unable to Take Test	
School Year	Grade Level Enrollment	No.	%	No.	%	No.	%	No.	%
2002–2003									
2003–2004									
2004–2005									
2005–2006									
2006–2007									

Date Organized: _____   Data Organized by: _____

———————————————— FIGURE 6.9 ————————————————

Table for Standardized Test Scores: Reading Comprehension by Gender

On CD-ROM
Table 14

School: _____   Principal's Name: _____   Grade Level: _____

Name of Test: _____   Time of Year Administered: _____   Shared with Staff: _____
                                                                                                  (Dates)

Percentile Range		1st–9th		10th–19th		20th–29th		30th–39th		40th–49th		50th–59th		60th–69th		70th–79th		80th–89th		90th–99th		Total No. of Students Tested	Total No. of Students Enrolled	% of Students Tested
		No.	%	No.	%	No.	%	No.	%	No.	%	No.	%	No.	%	No.	%	No.	%	No.	%			
2003	M																							
	F																							
2004	M																							
	F																							
2005	M																							
	F																							
2006	M																							
	F																							
2007	M																							
	F																							

Data Organized by: _____   _____   _____

FIGURE 6.10

Table for Standardized Test Scores: Growth Analysis

On CD-ROM
Table 15

School: _____   Principal's Name: _____

Name of Test: _____   Teacher/Class: _____

Year(s) Tested: _____   Time of Year Administered: _____

Name	M or F	Grade 3 GE	Grade 3–4 Gain	Grade 4 GE	Grade 4–5 Gain	Grade 5 GE	Grade 5–6 Gain	Grade 6 GE
		Grade 3 Average GE	Grade 3–4 Average Gain	Grade 4 Average GE	Grade 4–5 Average Gain	Grade 5 Average GE	Grade 5–6 Average Gain	Grade 6 Average GE

Data Organized by: _____   _____   _____

can identify two high-achieving, two moderate, and two low-achieving students in each class. If you want to start with 3rd grade, I suggest you identify 10 students to follow from each teacher's class so you'll have data in case of attrition. And, again, you should select an equal number of boys and girls.

The table "Standardized Test Scores: Growth Analysis" provides an example of how to organize results for a longitudinal analysis of student achievement (Figure 6.10). I've selected grade equivalent (GE) as the derived score to follow because it's easy to understand as you track the progress of individual students from year to year. The table shell has space for results for up to 10 students,

and a separate table would be needed for each class in a grade level. Following the same group of students across several years provides staff with useful information about how students are developing and often helps answer some of the common questions that surface during collective study.

Think about the normal distribution that was depicted in Figure 6.2 and the 4th grade distributions plotted in Figures 6.4 through 6.6. What we would like to have are students reading so well they "beat" the test design. We'd like a skewed distribution with most scores on the high-achieving end, and if we can't manage that, at least we'd like to move the whole distribution up so its mean is around the 65th percentile or better, depending on where we started.

The Value of Standardized Tests

If we're careful, large-scale standardized tests can provide us with useful information about the performance of groups of students in grades 3 and above. There are a few things we have to fight, such as allowing the tests to control the instructional day through inappropriate test preparation activities, to delay student progress through school, and to operate as the dominant measure of student achievement. It *is* worth knowing how our student population is performing in reading in comparison to nationally normed groups and whether we have some groups who regularly perform less well than other students in the school. These data help us strengthen our cur-

riculum across all disciplines, because if students are having difficulty reading, they are likely to have trouble with all other print-oriented materials and achievement tests, especially those used in science and social studies.

The results of group-administered, norm-referenced achievement tests serve as one indicator of student knowledge and performance in reading and, in part, provide us with an "independent" measure of student achievement because school staff have little to do with the selection of content and skills evaluated or with the assignment of scores and performance levels. But now, let's turn from these high-inference measures designed for group administration and mechanical scoring to up-close measures that allow teachers to examine a student's performance as he works with print, letters, words, sentences, and longer text.

7

Using Results of Up-Close Performance Measures

In your setting, what are the best (most accurate and useful) sources of student performance in reading that grade level teams and the staff as a unit use in studying how well students are progressing as readers?

In this chapter, I'll review the use of up-close, primarily individually administered measures of students' reading development. We use these measures to closely examine how students use print and apply the knowledge and skills identified in our curriculum standards.

Good instruments in this category are designed so that both the assessment process itself *and* its results can be used to guide instruction with greater accuracy and confidence. In contrast to the high-inference, more "objective" assessment instruments described in Chapter 6, with these assessments, teachers interact with students as they sample the reading behaviors that are being taught or will be taught. Teachers ask students about letters of the alphabet and find out how many they know, they hear students blending phonemes, they listen to students read passages, and they analyze the students' comprehension before proceeding to the next task.

For example, if a teacher wants to know how well a student understands the structure and content of a story, she could ask the student to read *Lily Takes a Walk* (Kitamura, 1987) and retell what happened. Then the teacher would record the results on a simple retelling summary and enter the data in a record book or class profile. If the teacher also wants to know if the student can read fluently and with proper expression, she would ask the student to read the story orally while the teacher listens; time the reading; and record accuracy (the percentage of total number of words read correctly), reading rate (time in minutes and seconds), and intonation (probably using a checklist).

Some of you may be thinking, "Oh, yes, this is authentic assessment, measures of real reading." Well, it actually isn't. "*Direct* assessment" would probably be a more accurate term. While instruments in this category do get closer to actual reading and writing performance, in contrast to more indirect measures such as multiple-choice tests, they are also used to assess many en route skills and invisible processes that we would not see if we were to observe highly literate individuals working with text. For example, think about assessing emergent literacy behaviors, such as phonemic awareness in beginning readers. How often have you been asked to count, segment, or blend phonemes lately? Or, for that matter, when were you last asked to retell—in sequence—a story you just had finished reading?

A classroom teacher can use the results of up-close measures to provide reading progress and diagnostic information for planning instruction and grouping students within the classroom. The results also let students know how well they are doing, what they can do, the progress they have made, and areas they need to work on. The staff or team studying student performance in reading throughout the school can use the results to provide information on the reading proficiency of the student population as a whole and on the progress, or gains, being made by students during the time they are enrolled in the school.

For those of you working with the Reading First part of the No Child Left Behind legislation, these instruments serve as both diagnostic reading assessments and as progress monitoring assessments. The assessments can be used to identify a student's specific areas of strength and weakness, to determine the

progress being made during the year, and to improve classroom instruction and intervention strategies.

Before we review the characteristics of up-close measures, let's be clear about which students we assess and why we need these results. *We assess all students whose reading development we are responsible for.* These measures are not used just with struggling readers or for diagnosis when we are concerned about individual student performance or placement. They should be used to study how well *all* students in a class or grade level are developing as readers. The results provide documented evidence about where an individual student stands with regard to emergent literacy, building reading vocabulary, and comprehension of connected text—three of the four dimensions of reading in Figure 2.1. And, when aggregated for groups of students, they provide evidence about the literacy development of the whole student population and subgroups within it, as well as information about the effectiveness of our reading program and of our school and district staff development programs.

In the remainder of this chapter, I'll explain the attributes of good up-close, performance-based measures and provide some technical assistance on how to use them for monitoring progress over time and in different classrooms. You can use the attributes as criteria for selecting, modifying, or designing instruments for use in your setting. And you can use the technical assistance tips to avoid common pitfalls. You won't find many examples of data organization and analysis like those described in Chapters 4 and

6. Instead, I've placed most of the examples for organizing and using the results of up-close measures inside the chapters that address the components of reading development, especially Chapters 10 through 13.

Characteristics of Up-Close Measures for Assessing Student Progress

Using *up-close, standard* measures to understand the effects of reading programs on students is an essential tool in our repertoire. What do I mean by "up close"? *Up close* means we personally and closely examine student knowledge and performance. We focus our assessment lens and strive to accurately capture current levels of reading performance. We observe, listen to, and analyze overt evidence to determine where the student is on various components of the reading development continuum.

Up-close measures are often individually administered (one student at a time). Both teachers and students interact with the assessment materials and with each other in very different ways from when they use group-administered, norm-referenced tests. We use the assessment process, not just the results, to make decisions about what students can and cannot do. Along with observing and listening to reading behavior, teachers may also question student responses or interview them about the reading strategies they used. These assessment tasks may require the teacher to notice how a young student orients his book for reading and attends to directionality of print,

to listen to how a student decodes unfamiliar words, or to interview a student about how he figured out the implicit main idea of a passage.

Up close also means that the results are immediate indicators of student performance, not data that will be returned one to four months later. It means that the results are intended to be used immediately to support student growth in reading. And finally, it means that faculty members have common data—and shared cognition about what these data indicate in terms of student knowledge, skills, and processes in reading—about the current performance and rates of progress of the student population.

To yield useful data about groups of readers, these up-close instruments must be *standard,* or uniform in terms of the reading performance that is being measured, the scoring of the assessments, and the guidelines for administration. Whether these elements of uniformity are part of commercial measures we have purchased, have been added to commercial measures, or are part of locally developed instruments, adherence to them allows us to make comparisons of individual student performance over time and to make comparisons across students and groups, both during a single school year and across several years.

To assess student progress over time and in different classrooms, we standardize the administration of these measures. Without this standardization—public agreement about what and how we are assessing and scoring reading behaviors—our data may yield deceptive results. For example, think about what a lack of standard procedures would mean to the quality of data collected on even very simple behaviors. Let's imagine a faculty is trying to get a picture of students' oral reading fluency in grades 1 through 5, and some teachers have students read familiar books while some have students read unfamiliar books; some have students read fiction while others use nonfiction. The data collected and discussed would provide more information about the teachers than it would about the students' levels of fluency. It does take time for a staff to establish standard procedures for administering and scoring these more direct measures, but they generally find it well worth the effort.

In my experience, *standard* has another very pragmatic meaning in relation to this category of instruments: many of the tests or assessment tasks serve almost like a content standard that clarifies the knowledge, skills, and processes students need to have or demonstrate and often provide us with a performance target in the area being assessed. For example, using the "Concepts About Print" observation task from *An Observation Survey of Early Literacy Achievement* (Clay, 1993) provides us with an overview of the knowledge and skills children need as they come to use the conventions of printed English. For teachers still struggling with pinning down what they need to do to help students build skill in phonemic awareness and what kinds of instructional activities they should include at what time, the "Phonemic Awareness" subtest from the *Emergent Literacy Survey* (Pikulski, 1997/2001) provides a precise overview.

The survey contains six sections covering phonological awareness tasks such as rhyming words and beginning sounds, blending onsets and rimes, and segmenting onsets and rimes and the phonemic awareness tasks of phoneme blending and phoneme segmentation. Slightly different, but very useful for a staff studying student progress in reading, are instruments that include grade level passages accompanied by tables indicating the desired number of correct words per minute for fluency at different grade levels, such as the *Gray Oral Reading Tests* (Wiederholt & Bryant, 2001).

Good up-close measures include both commercially published instruments that provide or specify the material used by teachers and students, the procedures for administration, and the scoring criteria and assessment techniques for which local staff have established standard procedures for selecting content and scoring responses (and in some cases, assessment conditions). Among commercially published instruments, there are three common types of up-close assessments that we can use to support classroom instruction *and* study schoolwide programmatic efforts: (1) instruments and techniques for surveying student knowledge and performance in several components of reading development, such as the *Gray Oral Reading Tests* (Wiederholt & Bryant, 2001); (2) instruments or techniques that focus on one component or dimension of reading development, such as *The Names Test of Decoding* for phonics (Cunningham, 2000; Duffelmeyer, Kruse, Merkley, & Fyfe, 1994); and (3) some of the instruments that accompany basal reading series.

In selecting or developing instruments for assessing student performance up close, make sure they (1) yield student performance data on publicly shared reading curriculum goals that are immediately useful in designing instruction and informing students and parents about progress, and (2) have procedures or criteria for content, scoring, and standard assessment situations that are clear and can be used by others. Ask yourself, "Does this instrument give us reliable information about this component of reading development? Can we use the results to study student performance and rate of progress? Can we use the results to design appropriate instruction today?" And, equally important in selecting up-close measures, "When using this instrument, does the assessment process teach me something about student performance?" If the answer is "No," then the costs outweigh the benefits. Find an instrument that allows you to respond, "Yes!"

Tips for Collective Use of Up-Close Measures

These five tips are included because I have observed "up close" what a gosh-awful mess good people can get into when they begin to examine reading behaviors "up close" and share the results.

Establish Common Assessment Times

For teachers to use these measures to assess student performance within and across classrooms and have meaningful discussions about student progress in reading, they need to establish common assessment times. For the reading com-

ponents addressed in this book (Figure 2.1), each time period for conducting the assessment could range from one to four weeks. For example, all kindergarten teachers would agree to assess concepts of print during the week of August 25–29. Or they could set a broader period, between August 18 and September 12. Grade level teachers working as a team need to set these times at the beginning of the year, if not at the end of the prior school year. These common assessment times facilitate across-class study of student performance as well as the evaluation of progress across the year or years.

In multiple-unit schools, teachers need to assess student performance within specified time periods if grade level summaries are to be used to study and discuss the progress of groups of students, to identify common student needs across classrooms, and to determine common staff development and/or curriculum needs.

Assess Multiple Times During the School Year

For components in the dimensions of emergent literacy, vocabulary, and reading comprehension, I recommend assessment three times a year: during the first month of school, the fourth month, and the eighth month. (I prefer the eighth month instead of the very end of the year mainly because it gives teachers and students time to use the results of the assessment.) For example, in a component such as reading comprehension of narrative prose, teachers in grades 1 through 5 might select the 3rd and 4th weeks of school, the 15th and 16th, and the 29th and 30th as their three time frames. Periodic up-close assessments help us monitor the progress of individuals and groups and provide students and parents or caregivers with frequent, specific updates on student progress. They also let us know if current instructional approaches are working.

Organize Your Results

In order to use the results of these up-close measures to study the progress of and plan instruction for groups of students—whether from a single classroom, a grade level comprising many classrooms, or all K–5 students in a school—they must be organized. Many teachers have folders full of individual student data; many schools have file cabinets filled with dusty reports. A little organization could go a long way in increasing the use of these data. Our intent is to encourage classroom use and staff study of these rich data sources.

Teachers and leadership teams need forms for organizing these results. These forms can be provided to teachers or developed by teachers and school team leaders. The tables in Figure 7.1 are examples of the kinds of table shells teachers and team leaders need for categorizing data and facilitating their use. While these table shells are set up to

---

FIGURE 7.1

Tables for Concepts About Print

On CD-ROM
Tables
16–18

16   Individual Student

School: _____   Teacher: _____   School Year: _____

Student's Name: _____   Age: _____   Grade: _____
                                   (e.g., 9 years/2 months)

Concept	Assessment 1 Date:	Assessment 2 Date:	Assessment 3 Date:	Notes
1. Identifies front of book				
2. Recognizes top-bottom directionality				
3. Recognizes left-right directionality				
4. Identifies that print, not pictures, carries the story or message				
5. Distinguishes letters from words				
6. Distinguishes words from sentences				
7. Connects uppercase with lowercase letter forms				
8. Recognizes the function of simple punctuation marks				
9. Tracks print (matches spoken word with printed word)				

Examiner(s): _____   _____   _____

record data on students' acquisition of concepts about print, the pattern for organizing results about students' knowledge, skills, and process development can be generalized to any of the emergent literacy, reading vocabulary, or comprehension of connected text components.

For any major component of reading development the school is pursuing as a priority, these three levels of data organization are useful:

1. Records of individual student progress (e.g., Table 16);
2. Records of the progress made by groups of students in the same class-

room (a class summary like Table 17); and
3. In multiunit schools, records of progress made by grade level groups (a grade level summary like Table 18).

With components or basic skills that are being taught at multiple grade levels, the faculty can use the grade level summaries to develop schoolwide snapshots of student performance. Figure 7.2 is an example for sight word accuracy and fluency.

To be most useful as instructional tools, classroom summaries need to be organized within a few days to a week

--- FIGURE 7.1 CONTINUED ---

Tables for Concepts About Print

On CD-ROM
Tables
16–18

17 Class Summary

School: _____   Teacher: _____   Grade: _____   School Year: _____

No. of Students in Class: ____   Dates Assessed: _____
Range (e.g., 8/25– 9/12)

Student Name	M or F	1. Front of Book	2. Top-Bottom	3. Left-Right	4. Print Carries Message	5. Letters from Words	6. Words from Sentences	7. Upper with Lower	8. Punctuation Marks	9. Tracks Print	Total
Total for Class											

18 Grade Level Summary

School: _____   Grade: _____   No. of Classes/Teachers: _____   Total No. of Students: _____   School Year: _____

Class/Teacher (No. of Students)	1,2,3 Orientation & Directionality		4 Print Carries Message		5, 6 Letters, Words, Sentences		7 Upper with Lower		8 Punctuation		9 Tracks Print		No. of Students All Est.	No. of Students 7–8 Est.	No. of Students with 6 or Fewer Est.
	1st Ad	Last	1st Ad	Last	1st Ad	Last	1st Ad	Last	1st Ad	Last	1st Ad	Last			
Totals															

Data Organized by: _____   Date: _____   Shared with Staff: _____
(Date)

FIGURE 7.2

Word Accuracy and Fluency During Oral Reading: Mean Words Correct per Minute (WCPM) Across the Grades

School: __Blenheim Elementary__ No. of Classes/Teachers: __23__ Total No. of Students: __517__

School Year: __2002__ Assessment Period (Circle One):   Fall   (Winter)   Spring

Grade 1	67
Grade 2	98
Grade 3	124
Grade 4	135
Grade 5	143
Grade 6	140

after the assessment period ends, and grade level summaries need to be organized soon after. When teams determine the dates for their assessment periods, it's a good idea to go ahead and identify dates for completion of class summaries and submission to team leaders. Also, times need to be built into the school improvement plan (and the school calendar) for faculty members to discuss results in their work groups, plan lessons, and consider instructional or curriculum changes. Time also needs to be set aside for either grade level teams or leadership team members to share data from their grade level with the staff.

Be an Informed Community

Our focus in this book is on identifying or developing and using a common set of assessments that measure student performance and progress in reading, assessments that can be used across classrooms. The dimensions of building reading vocabulary, comprehension of connected text, and reading habits and attitudes are all schoolwide study emphases (meaning all grade levels are involved). Emergent literacy is primarily addressed with K–1, ESL, and some special needs students. However, this does not mean that teachers in grades 2 and above do not need to look at the emergent literacy data that describe where kindergarten and 1st grade students are when they enter school, the kind of progress they are making, and where they are as they exit kindergarten and 1st grade. This is important information for all staff members to know. Remember

Juel's (1992) study: How well students were reading at the end of 1st grade predicted how well they were reading in 4th grade. This is not the case when the school has effective instructional interventions.

Successfully implementing schoolwide initiatives aimed at improving student learning requires us to have continuous information about their effects on students. The results from these kinds of up-close measures— whether we are focusing on reading, writing, science, or mathematics—tell us immediately whether what we are doing is working, for whom, and to what degree. And through our public examination of student results and the level of staff implementation of the instructional and curricular changes, we learn if our initiatives are working. Without collective study and discussion of both student results and implementation results, the modifications we make may not be optimal or widespread enough to affect most of the student population. Credible evidence of positive student effects gives us our warrant for the continuation of current, or pursuit of new, instructional strategies and programs.

Start with Published Instruments

If you and your staff are just beginning to collect, organize, and study the schoolwide results of up-close assessments, I suggest you begin by using some of the published instruments or assessment techniques whose results you have found to be especially useful. Once you have accurate data across classrooms and routines for studying and using the results, you may want to develop different or additional techniques and procedures or make publicly agreed-upon modifications to the ones you've been using.

8

Studying Indicators of Reading Habits and Attitudes

Do many students who can *read choose* not *to* read? *Are we helping students develop a habit of reading? Is our reading program—through its curriculum, our instruction, how we assess performance, and how we organize students for learning—helping students develop positive attitudes about reading and letting them perceive the benefits of literacy?*

Attitude toward reading affects reading habits. Here habit is defined as "a behavior pattern acquired by frequent repetition . . . that shows itself in regularity or increased facility of performance" and as a practice "followed with regularity and usually through choice" (*Merriam-Webster*, 1994, p. 521). If we ask a 2nd grade student if she likes to read, and she responds, "No," and we ask her how much time she spends reading at home, and she responds, "Not much," she is not likely to develop a habit of reading for learning or for entertainment. McKenna, Kear, and Ellsworth (1995) report that the positive attitudes about reading held by kindergartners and 1st graders have disappeared for many students by the time they reach 5th and 6th grades. This is a big concern. Regular engagement with an action or practice—in this case with the act of reading—is necessary for building a healthy reading habit, which in turn will lead to better and more literate readers.

Assessing Attitudes About Reading

In data collection efforts, attitude is often assessed through surveys, questionnaires, observations, and interviews. While it is not easy to gather reliable information about attitude, with care we can collect meaningful data.

We can assess three overlapping aspects of attitude: an *affective* aspect—how someone feels about something (like or dislike, pro or con) and how strongly she feels (very much, somewhat); a *cognitive* aspect—what someone knows or thinks about something; and an *action* aspect—what someone does or is willing to do with regard to something. The action aspect is what we look at when we assess reading habits.

To assess students' attitudes about reading and their reading habits, we want to ask these kinds of questions:

Affective

- How do you feel about reading?
- Do you like to read? Why or why not? (*cognitive*)
- What do you like to read most? Best?*
- What do you like to read least?*
- Who is your favorite author? Why?* (*affective* and *cognitive*)

Cognitive

- What do good readers do?*
- What are some things you have learned from reading?
- How does reading help you learn?*

Action

- How many books did you read this week?
- How much time do you spend reading at home?

Questions such as these can help classroom teachers clarify how students feel about reading and their images of themselves as readers. The questions with an asterisk are especially informative when they are accompanied by group discussions. Individual students may be questioned during informal reading conferences and during book chats. Group discussions can occur during shared reading, literature circles, book club sessions; listening to each other's responses and talking about why they enjoy different authors or what works best for them as learners can be powerful instructional content for students and teachers.

Assessing Affect Across Classrooms and Grades

To study the effects of the school reading program on how students feel about reading, look at group results. A good self-report inventory that covers the kinds of questions asked above about the affective aspect of attitude should be adopted for use across classes and grade levels. You can develop your own or use a published inventory like The Elementary Reading Attitude Survey (McKenna & Kear, 1999), which assesses student attitude toward recreational reading (reading done for pleasure and unrelated to assigned work) and academic reading (reading assigned by the teacher or done as part of classwork, homework, or school projects). The survey has 20 questions with pictorial responses depicting the comic strip character Garfield in poses that represent different reactions ("very happy," "a little happy," "a little upset," and "very upset"). The authors provide explicit instructions for scoring and for converting raw scores to percentile scores. Directions can be read to students.

Here are a few tips for getting started on studying students' attitudes about reading:

- Use an inventory with a limited number of items (around 10, no more than 20).

- Use an instrument with which students simply check or mark responses instead of writing (this helps limit "socially desirable" responses, which reflect what students think the reader wants to see).
- Tell students they do not need to put their names on the inventory, just circle or check grade level, gender, and ethnicity.
- Read items aloud if there are students in the group who might have difficulty reading them.
- Administer the inventory during the first and last months of school.
- Analyze the data for information about subgroups of students (whole classes, grade levels, males and females, socio-economic status).

Assessing Reading Habits of Individuals and Groups (Classrooms, Grades, Schools)

To study habits that are particularly critical to student development—such as extensive reading—we want to move beyond the self-reported affective aspect of attitude and look at the *action* aspect. To do this, we examine what students do by choice. For example, in moving toward a clearer picture of students' attitudes toward and behaviors in reading,

we might ask that they keep a reading log of what they read at home. We may also interview them occasionally about a book they listed on their reading log or note the general circulation of books in our class library. How far we go in clarifying our picture of students' typical response to something (reading, writing, mathematics) and opportunity to engage with it depends on how important it is to the development of student proficiency.

In Chapter 12 of this book, we will concentrate primarily on assessing reading habits—especially whether students choose to read outside of school, how much they read, and what they read. We'll also look at a school and home partnership designed to increase the amount of reading outside of school. One program, called Just Read (Wolf, 1998), which does not require the purchase of special materials, uses an action research approach, asking students to keep weekly reading logs, teachers to analyze these, and teacher teams and administrators to study the results across grades and time. Students, teachers, and school leadership teams end up with frequency distributions that describe how much students are reading and to what degree the school has developed a culture of readers.

9

Developing a Reading
Assessment System

*What is the current state of your school's reading assessment system?
Do your curriculum standards or benchmarks guide the selection of assessment content? Do you have easily accessible data on the reading development of all students, data that are from multiple sources, including up-close measures used across classrooms? Do you have routines for studying the assessment results and working together to make curriculum and instructional changes?*

As you begin to assess the effects of the reading program, do not try to organize and study all the good data at once. Set a steady, determined pace as you inquire into student performance K–2, K–3, K–6, or at whatever levels are present in your school. Set a pace that supports sanity, allows time for staff to discuss and think about the implications of the information for individuals and groups of students, and acknowledges that some data are more critical for the initial assessment and support of student progress in reading than other data.

At the schoolwide level, I suggest you begin by organizing the data on student characteristics and the special programs they participate in, along with the results of group-administered norm-referenced or criterion-referenced tests where available. As you move into the study of results of up-close measures, begin with the dimension of reading you think is most critical for supporting the literacy development of the greatest number of students. Whether this is emergent literacy, reading vocabulary, or reading comprehension, see if there are any data already being collected across classrooms in this dimension. If not, one of your early tasks will be to identify good up-close measures for that dimension. (This is part of the content of Chapters 10 through 12.) What follows are some helpful hints for carrying out your action research.

Establish Assessment Schedules, Routines, and Databases

Three factors will affect your use of data and the kind of system you put together: (1) the presence of a written assessment schedule, (2) the frequency of assessment and study of results, and (3) school and district databases.

To help good intentions become reality, develop a written assessment plan each year. It may be only half a page long, but it will help you think about the multiple data sources that are available and what is missing. It aids almost everyone with self-discipline, scheduling, and providing time to organize and study results as individuals, as grade level teams, and as a faculty. And when it's time to write the school improvement plan, it's easy to identify the best times for collective study and planning. If we want to use data, we need to schedule times into the school calendar to work together, inquiring into assessment results and their implications for curriculum, instruction, and the organization of students.

How often data are collected and studied depends both on the type of data (Figure II.2) and the current needs or emphases of the school. General school data and norm-referenced or criterion-referenced results should be reviewed at least annually. Grades or teacher-assigned indicators of progress should be studied quarterly when faculty members first focus on a curriculum area. After reading grades and their connections to curriculum standards have been studied and the faculty has made any adjust-

ments needed to tighten the relationship, they shouldn't need to be studied schoolwide again for several years, unless gender, socio-economic status, or ethnic differences became visible when the grade distributions were studied.

Once a school has a system for organizing general school data and the results of standardized tests, as well as routines for reviewing information from these sources, these tasks should occupy very little staff time. It's the data from up-close measures of students' reading development and reading habits that need continuous study and use by the staff as they plan instruction and make curriculum modifications.

The results of up-close measures of emergent literacy, reading vocabulary, and comprehension of connected text that help us take a closer look at students' reading behaviors should be given the most attention. These are the data that help groups of teachers work together in support of students' literacy development. They deserve the bulk of our attention and need to be analyzed by the staff three times a year (September/October, December/January, and March/April). Data on students' reading habits also need to be looked at regularly—monthly is best until extensive reading becomes part of the school culture.

School and district databases can help us also. At first, we can use manual databases (where data are organized without computerized assistance). This will help us understand what we need and will use. But eventually, a simple computerized database that consists of individual student records will be needed for handling large amounts of data across several years. This will allow us the flexibility to manipulate data and look at any of the combinations of variables discussed in this book.

Many districts, and some schools, already maintain databases that include student demographic information, student attendance, and standardized test data. And, of course, student results from standardized achievement tests are available on disk by request from most test companies. Some schools have also developed databases for entering the results of up-close measures, such as reading rate and writing assessment scores.

If you are just beginning to set up a computerized database for consolidating data from multiple sources to make them easier for staff to use, *get good help*. This assistance may be from your district office, intermediate service agency, business partners, or parents. You want a system with software that is easy for faculty members to use, has the ability to combine information from other databases, and is compatible with most computer operating systems. Most importantly, you want the database to yield the information you want for studying student performance and progress. This includes many of the analyses of groups addressed here, as well as the ability to have this same information (see Figure II.2) attached to individual student identification numbers. If a 5th grade teacher wanted to see a profile of Sam L. Gamboa, he should be able to tap his name and ID number into a computer and look at a cumulative data picture describ-

ing Sam and his levels of attainment on multiple measures.

Establish and Change Benchmarks and Performance Targets

Think back to Chapter 2 on building a reading curriculum and tightening the curriculum/assessment connection. A reading curriculum is derived from our current knowledge of how language works, how literacy develops, how people learn to read, and what good readers do. In schools and districts, we see the synthesis of this knowledge set forth in curriculum standards that teachers can use as they select content and design instructional activities to support students' reading development from grade to grade. Increasingly, benchmarks are added to tighten the connection between curriculum and assessment content and make it easier to monitor student progress on the reading development continuum. Worthy standards and benchmarks can strengthen your reading program.

At the most basic level, curriculum standards describe what students need to know and do to become good readers. Benchmarks, which are derived from curriculum standards, describe measurable behaviors that can be used to determine if students are making good progress on the reading development continuum.

Faculties can use benchmarks to describe what they expect students to be able to do at different grade levels on each curriculum standard. For example, a school may have "Reading extensively" as one of their K–6 curriculum standards.

Their benchmarks for kindergarten through 6th grade may pin down that somewhat vague criterion by describing different genres and different numbers of books that students should be reading at each grade level to be considered extensive readers. (See Chapter 13 for an example.)

Another example of standards and benchmarks can be found in the New Standards (New Standards Primary Literacy Committee, 1999): Reading Standard 2, "Getting the Meaning," includes the following benchmarks in the dimension of Comprehension; by the end of 3rd grade, students are expected to

- Capture meaning from figurative language (for example, similes, metaphors, poetic images) and explain the meaning;
- Cite important details from a text;
- Compare one text to another they have read or heard; and
- Discuss why an author might have chosen particular words. (p. 198)

If refining or establishing benchmarks in reading is one of the tasks that need to be done in your school, here are a few process suggestions. Form a team that has a teacher from each grade level. Take your major curriculum standards (for example, the dimensions of reading development) and have teachers think about and describe what good readers know or do in relation to each standard. Then, after a description of the top-of-the-scale performance has been put together, have teachers describe what good readers at their grade level do in relation to each standard. Put together a rough draft continuum for all teachers to think about as they observe and work with students. Then provide time for

teachers to compare these draft lists to curriculum content and to results from up-close assessments of student performance. This will lead to a description of current expectations of good reading performance in your school. Don't stop there; in some schools, these expectations are far below students' potential.

Take time to compare your draft lists to grade level recommendations from external sources, such as pages 80–83 in *Preventing Reading Difficulties in Young Children* (Snow, Burns, & Griffin, 1998), *Reading and Writing Grade by Grade: Primary Literacy Standards for Kindergarten Through Third Grade* (New Standards Primary Literacy Committee, 1999), and the *Performance Standards: Elementary School English Language Arts, Mathematics, Science, and Applied Learning* (Learning Research and Development Center at the University of Pittsburgh & National Center on Education and the Economy, 1997). Make modifications if needed. Teachers will need several months to try the lists and make the descriptions of student knowledge and performance more explicit. Then establish a tentative set of grade level benchmarks to try out with your classroom assessments and across-class, up-close assessments of reading performance.

If you need to establish performance targets for your population (identify the levels of achievement that indicate locally acceptable levels of knowledge or skills), develop a performance profile of how many students at each grade level are meeting or exceeding each benchmark. Use these data as you set your targets. If you are in a situation in which you have to designate an amount of improvement in results on norm-referenced tests to get out of the "buzzard group" or to meet state or district guidelines on your comprehensive school improvement plan, you may write a performance target that is as meaningless as "Improve the school mean in reading vocabulary by 2 percentile points." This says a lot more about the district or state than it does about student progress. Do what you need to do, but put your energy into strengthening the reading program schoolwide. (Of course, if you are working on this task, Chapters 10 through 13 will be especially useful as you develop curriculum standards to map a path to reading proficiency.)

Monitor for Equity

In a republic that depends on an educated citizenry to keep democracy and opportunity alive, schools are the treasure houses. And yes, we need to make them better than they are. Studying the progress students make while in school—the gain or value-added difference between entry and exit knowledge and skills—is a fine beginning. Whether students are with us for three months, one year, or seven years, we are always looking at our student assessment results to determine how effective our reading program has been in helping them become highly proficient readers.

Because failure to learn to read has such devastating emotional and financial consequences, we must try to monitor equity of learning opportunities and the progress being made by individual students and groups of students. We need to organize our results to keep an eye on every child, especially those who are at

risk because of demographic characteristics or their placement in categorical programs.

We should regularly ask ourselves these questions about equity and educational opportunity in our classroom and school:

- Is gender a factor in predicting a student's success or failure?
- Is ethnicity a factor in predicting a student's success or failure?
- Is native language a factor in predicting a student's success or failure?
- Is socioeconomic status a factor in predicting a student's success or failure?

To respond, we must gather information from multiple sources: placements in special programs, grade and retention data, standardized test results, results from up-close measures of students' reading development, and indicators of reading habits and attitudes. If we don't like the picture represented in our responses and our data, we need to make changes in the curriculum and instructional opportunities being provided to students.

Report Publicly and Celebrate When Possible

It's better to report students' progress and levels of achievement to our stakeholders—faculty, parents, students, school board members, and the larger community—too often than not enough. When I work with schools and districts, I encourage them to report group results at least twice a year, and sometimes quarterly. I also encourage them to report progress using multiple measures.

———————————————— FIGURE 9.1 ————————————————

Green Valley Elementary School Basic Reading Inventory Results

Percent of Students Who Are Independent at Grade Level in Comprehension

Spring 2001	Spring 2002
N/A	1st Grade—65%
N/A	2nd Grade—79%
2nd Grade—65%	3rd Grade—82%
3rd Grade—80%	4th Grade—74%
4th Grade—60%	5th Grade—81%
5th Grade—89%	N/A

Figures 9.1 and 9.2 are examples from one elementary school. Figure 9.1 displays the percentage of students who were reading independently at grade level based on their comprehension scores from the *Basic Reading Inventory* (Johns, 1997). The leadership team for the school developed fall, winter, and spring reports as well as this Spring 2002 report. Figure 9.2 displays the percentage

———————————————— FIGURE 9.2 ————————————————

Green Valley Elementary School *Iowa Tests of Basic Skills* Results

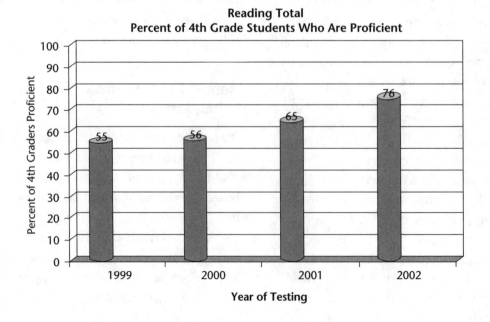

Reading Total
Percent of 4th Grade Students Who Are Proficient

of 4th grade students who are proficient at grade level based on their scores from the *Iowa Tests of Basic Skills*. (Each state's definition of proficiency may vary.)

If your school has data on how much children are reading and how many books they have read, include those in your regular reports. This type of information provides parents and faculty with very overt evidence of whether students are building a reading habit or not.

Reach Out for Support

Get help if things aren't going well. Get help when the faculty need greater expertise to move forward or if you're uncomfortable with a decision that's about to be made, especially if it's one that will affect many students and staff. This human help with tasks may be obtained right around the corner at the district office, from the research and evaluation division at the state department of education, at your local university, or from a consulting firm. In developing a good assessment system, as in most things in life, some people have more competence and experience than others. Use them.

Along with reaching out to people, you can reach out for good print resources. Here are some that support the organization and use of data.

Short List of Resources

General School Data

➤ Johnson, R. S. (1996). *Setting our sights: Measuring equity in school change.* Los Angeles: The Achievement Council.

This handbook provides rationales and tools for using data to study what is happening in elementary, middle, and high schools. It's an excellent general resource filled with tools (forms) for studying student populations. It is written with clarity and passion. A more recent edition is also available.

Teacher- or School-Assigned Indicators of Student Performance (Grades)

➤ Wiggins, G. (1998). Grading and reporting. In *Educative assessment: Designing assessments to inform and improve student performance* (pp. 241–288). San Francisco: Jossey-Bass.

This chapter explains what staff need to consider if they wish to improve how grades are given and reported. Several approaches are presented, but some of the real strengths of this resource include the section on standards-referenced and expectations-referenced reports, the examples and explanations of what schools and districts have done, and the emphasis on making the reports useful to parents.

Norm-Referenced or Criterion-Referenced Measures

➤ Calkins, L., Montgomery, K., Santman, D., & Falk, B. (1998). *A teacher's guide to standardized reading tests.* Portsmouth, NH: Heinemann.

The authors of this easy-to-read book emphasize becoming informed about standardized tests, especially large-scale, norm-referenced measures, so that we can help our students and "take our place at the policy table." The five chapters on test preparation are especially useful in helping us think about how to integrate daily instruction in strategic reading with test-taking tasks, such as reading passages on the test, understanding format, and figuring out what the question is really asking. Many of the processes literate persons use in everyday life are embedded in the discussions about appropriate test-preparation minilessons, from author's purpose to analyzing evidence to predicting responses.

Up-Close Measures of Reading

➤ Caldwell, J. S. (2002). *Reading assessment: A primer for teachers and tutors*. New York: Guilford Press.

If you are most concerned with helping individual teachers and paraeducators assess the reading performance of individual students, this is the resource I would begin with. In fact, this is my top recommendation if you are a teacher working alone or with a few colleagues. It is theoretically well grounded and filled with easy-to-use assessment techniques. And the author writes beautifully!

➤ Mariotti, A. S., & Homan, S. P. (2001). *Linking reading assessment to instruction: An application worktext for elementary classroom teachers* (3rd ed.). Mahwah, NJ: Lawrence Erlbaum.

Chapters 3–8 of this book address methods for assessing emergent literacy, word recognition, reading rate, and reading comprehension. Explanations and examples of assessment instruments are included. Chapter 9, "Grouping and Instructional Decision Making," is espe-

cially useful if you are working on grouping students for instruction using multiple sources of information.

➤ McKenna, M. C., & Stahl, S. (2003). *Assessment for reading instruction*. New York: Guilford Press.

If you are looking for a comprehensive overview of classroom assessment techniques and instruments, this is the book for you. It includes sections on assessing emergent literacy, fluency, word recognition skills, comprehension, and attitude. The authors describe many public-domain instruments and include examples and scoring criteria. A good resource for individual teachers and school teams.

Attitude and Affect Toward Reading

For those of you interested in systematic assessment of the affective component across classrooms and grade levels, here are several good sources:

➤ Anderson, L. W., & Bourke, S. F. (2000). *Assessing affective characteristics in the schools* (2nd ed.). Mahwah, NJ: Lawrence Erlbaum.

If you really want to work on measuring affect regularly and carefully, this textbook is an excellent resource. The authors provide explanations, rationales, and examples for gathering, organizing, and interpreting data on student affect. They consider the study of affective characteristics as "means to ends. The ends in this case are [student] attentiveness, persistence, lack of disruptiveness, and learning" (p. 9).

➤ Popham, W. J. (2001). *Classroom assessment: What teachers need to know* (3rd ed.). Boston: Allyn and Bacon.

See especially the chapter on affective assessment and Popham's rationale for and examples of confidence inventories (used to gather information about how confident students feel in performing certain skills). As the author states, there are some good "stealable examples."

Additional resources that focus on a range of reading assessment options are available. They range from Harp's (1996) *The Handbook of Literacy Assessment and Evaluation* to two resources compiled by Kameenui and colleagues (2002), *A Practical Guide to Reading Assessments* (available from the International Reading Association), and *Analysis of Reading Assessment Instruments for K–3* (provided online to support Reading First, available at http://idea.uoregon.edu/assessment/index.html).

PART THREE

Assessing Your Reading Curriculum

The chapters in Part 3 serve as a content guide for inquiring into four dimensions of reading development. While these dimensions need to be taught in an integrated way, I have addressed them separately in an attempt to make it easier for you to analyze how each one is nurtured and monitored in your particular setting. Emergent literacy is addressed in Chapter 10, reading vocabulary in Chapter 11, reading comprehension in Chapter 12, and reading habits in Chapter 13.

Each of these chapters includes an explanation of the dimension and its components; recommendations for up-close assessment of student development; illustrations for organizing student results at the classroom level and across classrooms; a list of questions that can be used to guide further inquiry; and a short list of recommended resources. As you read each one, think about how the dimension being discussed is represented in the reading curriculum and assessment process in your classroom or school.

In terms of our Action Research Matrix and tasks (Figure 1.1), these four chapters represent Cells 2 and 5—what we can learn from the external knowledge base about student learning and optimal learning environments. As you read, compare this external information to what your students can do (Cell 1) and what you would like them to be able to do (Cell 3). Think about your reading curriculum, instruction, assessment, and organization for learning (Cell 4), and see if you can identify any promising modifications or lines of inquiry (Cell 6).

10

Emergent Literacy

When you think about emergent literacy, what concepts and skills come to mind? What assessment techniques and tools for organizing data help you determine whether students have acquired these concepts and skills?

Children need to engage in many language experiences to develop conventional literacy. Conversations, listening to books being read, pretend reading and writing, and oral language all help children to display and continue to develop knowledge and skill about how language works. While most of them could not define communication, they demonstrate it at work and show the value they place on it. Depending on their age and interests, their attention spans may be short or long, but they learn how to use words to get others to listen when they speak and to find out things. Whether at home or in preschool, they notice print and they notice that other people can make sense from it, whether it's used on a grocery list, in a television schedule, or in a book.

As children begin to use print to comprehend or produce written language, they go through many successive approximations on their way to conventional literacy, defined here as being able to use the English alphabetic system as proficient readers and writers. They may call all uppercase *Ms* "McDonalds." Because Terry's name begins with a *T*, when he sees "Tommy," he may read it as "Terry"; likewise, Angie may interpret "Andy" as her own name. Do they know a lot about how the English language works in print? Yes! Are they conventionally literate? Not yet. As they move from drawing to scribbling to their early attempts to use letters, "Dad" may just look like a *D* on its side. They eventually straighten that *D* and now we may have "DAAD." Eventually, if all goes well, they'll soon decode "Dad" as /dad/, not /da/, and they'll encode it conventionally as "D-a-d."

Reviewing the Components Recommended for Collective Study

In kindergarten and 1st grade, three knowledge and skill components of emergent literacy that are predictors of successful reading development need systematic attention: concepts about print, letter recognition, and phonological and phonemic awareness. These three components enable children to begin to use the written language code.

Many early primary teachers work on concepts about print, letter recognition and use, and phonological awareness throughout the day and the year, if needed. What is sometimes missing, which would make their work much more effective, are tools to support the systematic assessment of student progress.

Periodically assessing these components allows us to study current student performance and the progress students make. For example, how many of our entering 1st graders can track print (current status)? Three months later, how many more students have acquired this skill (gain or progress made)? We can use the results to select the curriculum and design lessons that are just right for moving our students along the literacy continuum.

Most classrooms have variability in levels of student development—often three to five years of achievement difference by 3rd grade—and the range continues to expand as students progress through school. In kindergarten, while the achievement differences aren't so large, the variety of literacy experiences the students have prior to schooling makes the kindergarten teacher's task intimidating and a challenge for many school staff. Students who come to us with several thousand hours' worth of literacy experiences in the home need a different curriculum part of the day than those students who come to us not knowing the front of the book from the back. What we try to do in kindergarten and 1st grade is provide a literacy program strong enough to move those students who are in the bottom of this range into the middle or higher.

Knowing students' performance and progress on something as basic as letter recognition is a big deal if you're teaching emergent literacy. Kindergarten and 1st grade students who recognize all their letters are at a very different point on the literacy continuum from those students who can only recognize a few. While some instructional activities— such as reading and working with alphabet books like *Animal Action ABC* (Pandell & Wolfe, 1996) or *A Prairie Alphabet* (Bannatyne-Cugnet, 1992)— can be used productively with students who vary widely in literacy development, both groups will need a different curriculum for part of the day if they are to make optimal progress. Also, students who lack just a few letters need activities that will help them master those quickly. We don't want them to lose months of *using* letters, a major key to unlocking the print code for both reading and writing, because we follow a "letter of the week" curriculum. And, as is often the case with young students still working on letter recognition, there will be several students having difficulty discriminating those "tricky" letters, such as *b* and *d, g* and *q, e* and *a,* and the print and typeset variations of *a, q,* and *g.* Working with magnetic letters to make words and writing words with these letters are needed to help students focus on the differences.

There's much we can do to close the achievement gap early. We just need to shape our precious instructional time more accurately so that we can provide additional instruction for students who enter kindergarten with little knowledge and skill in emergent literacy. Hopefully, if this instruction is intensive enough and provides students with connections to the print and sound codes of the English language, we can prevent reading difficulties. Like Clay (1987) and Vellutino and Scanlon (2001), I believe that many reading difficulties could be avoided through adequate literacy instruction.

Of course, we don't assess only to prevent reading difficulties. We also want to avoid boring students by spending too much time "teaching" them what they already know and can do. The results of assessment are also used to accelerate progress for students who are more advanced in literacy.

Let's review content and rationale for keeping a close eye on concepts about print, letter recognition, and phonological and phonemic awareness and take a look at assessment considerations for each component.

Concepts About Print

Fundamental concepts about print include knowing that print carries a message, that print represents the sounds in spoken language, and that there are units of print and rules for writing the English language. While students' knowledge of concepts about print does not seem to be as powerful a predictor of success in learning to read as knowledge of letter identification and phonemic awareness (Snow, Burns, & Griffin, 1998; Vellutino & Scanlon, 2001), some understanding of how print works is necessary before students can name letters, discriminate phonemes within words, and understand how the alphabetic system works. Having students value print and helping them develop an appreciation of its many uses are important components of early literacy curriculum and instruction.

Teachers commonly observe and record students' use of the following concepts about print: that print, not the pictures, carries the story or message; that the message is made up of letters, that letters make words, and that words make phrases, sentences, and longer communications; that what we say can be written down and what is written down can be read; that in the English language, reading and writing go from left to right and top to bottom; that spaces separate words; and that punctuation marks have meaning and indicate different actions for the reader. This is not an exhaustive list of all concepts about print, but it does represent essential characteristics of how print works that children need to acquire to support their use of text.

Becoming literate takes time, and the development of these concepts about print begins very early in the life of a child. By the time a child is in kindergarten and 1st grade, her understanding and use of these concepts provide a foundation for learning to read. If that understanding is missing or has not been developed adequately enough to support interaction with printed words and extended text, intensive instruction that includes rich interactions with books, storytelling, and much wordplay is needed.

Assessment Considerations. Teachers may assess these concepts about print during instruction or in special reading events with individual children. Kindergarten and 1st grade teachers—along with special education and English-as-a-second-language teachers—may establish an assessment schedule and routines for data collection and review. For example, they could decide to review where students are on certain concepts the first month of school and the last week of each quarter, using the records they have been keeping as they observe students applying the concepts during daily work. A review of student results, discussions about areas of concern, and the planning of lessons need to be regularly scheduled events during staff development or study group time. (See Clay, 1989, 1993; Purcell-Gates & Dahl, 1991; and Teale, 1989, for more in-depth information on concepts about print.)

Letter Recognition

Can students name the letters of the alphabet, lowercase and uppercase, when they are presented out of sequence? Whether we look at the United States Office of Education 1st grade reading studies from over 30 years ago (Bond & Dykstra, 1967/*Reading Research Quarterly*

reprint 1997) or more recent studies that allow us to evaluate the contribution of emergent literacy skills to success in reading achievement (Vellutino & Scanlon, 2001), letter identification at school entry remains a major predictor of success in learning to read.

What are some of the reasons alphabet knowledge predicts later reading success? When we read and write, we see every letter in the word. Knowledge of the alphabet is a way to begin "breaking the code" of how print works. It is essential for beginning to understand the alphabetic principle, and it appears to play an influential role in the development of phonological awareness (Stahl & Murray, 1998). Beginning readers and writers use this letter knowledge as they work on decoding (Ehri, 1994, 1998a) and writing (Read, 1971; Treiman, 1993). Of course, skill in letter recognition is undoubtedly a surrogate for a number of literacy experiences children have had; nonetheless, knowing the names of letters is an access key to using the English language.

Learning the names of the letters of the alphabet generally occurs over time and is quite a complex task. Learning to identify letters consistently requires that students learn to discriminate among them, learn what we call them in English, cope with the lowercase and uppercase forms, and cope with numerous fonts. As they notice and work with letters in context, students encounter many letter and sound complexities, such as the differences between Oak Street and Maple Street. In Oak, there is a match between the name of the initial letter and its phoneme, but not so in Maple Street. And why can you hear *a* or /ā/ in "Maple" but not in "Oak"? But the most marvelous thing is how easily most students break this print code!

Assessment Considerations. When measuring student knowledge in this component, we need to assess the naming of both uppercase and lowercase letters out of sequence. Sometime during the first few weeks of kindergarten, we need to know which letters students recognize and which ones they do not. For students without mastery, we probably need to assess again around November or December, and for those students still struggling, again around March or April. In this component of emergent literacy, we want mastery, developed appropriately (that is, not skill and drill), as quickly as possible. However, we should not hold up students' instruction, waiting to work with words and text until all letters have been learned, because—among many other reasons—working with words can facilitate students' recognition and naming of letters.

Phonological and Phonemic Awareness

Over the past 25 years, knowledge has continued to accumulate about the importance of phonological awareness to a child's success in learning to read, especially the importance of phonemic awareness (Adams, 1990; Liberman, Shankweiler, Fischer, & Carter, 1974; National Reading Panel, 2000; Stanovich, 1986; and Vellutino & Scanlon, 2001). Phonological awareness, which refers to all levels of awareness of the sound structures of oral language (Torgesen &

Mathes, 2000), includes phonemic awareness (perceiving and manipulating single sounds within words). It also includes many other aspects of spoken language important in literacy development: hearing the different words within a sentence, identifying and making oral rhymes, identifying and working with syllables in spoken words, identifying and working with onsets and rimes, recognizing alliteration, and recognizing intonation and stress.

In *Preventing Reading Difficulties in Young Children,* phonemic awareness is defined as "the insight that every spoken word can be conceived as a sequence of phonemes" (Snow, Burns, & Griffin, 1998, p. 52). This "insight" is often determined by asking students to identify, say, and manipulate phonemes, the individual sound segments in words. For example, can the students tell us that "hat" has three different sounds—/h/, /a/, /t/—and that if they take off the first sound they will have "at"?

In phonemic awareness, the focus is on the sound system—specifically the sound units within words—in contrast to phonics, where the emphasis is on simultaneously building print decoding and encoding skills at the word level and on teaching students to deal with letter and sound correspondences (grapheme/phoneme relationships). While there is an overlap between skill in phonemic awareness and skill in phonetic analysis since they both have a "sound" component, the current belief of many scholars is that traditional phonics instruction often ignores a necessary knowledge and skill step:

children's ability to identify and manipulate the different individual sounds that make up words.

Instruction in phonemic awareness includes teaching students to notice, think about, and work with phonemes. Explicit instruction should help students understand that "book" has three different sounds—/b/, /oo/, /k/—and that "band" has four—/b/, /a/, /n/, /d/. Developing a conscious awareness of the sounds represented by phonemes will help students understand the relationship between oral language and print.

Currently, there's much dissension about how to teach phonemic awareness, who needs the instruction, and when. I and many of my colleagues believe that developing skill in phonemic awareness is part of good emergent writing instruction in which students are encouraged to sound out the words and write them "phonetically"; that it is part of good phonics instruction that teaches students to sound out and blend letters to decode words; and that students' learning of the alphabetic code and the phoneme/grapheme correspondences is strengthened by working on the print system and the sound system simultaneously. The good news is that appropriate up-close assessment can identify those students who need extensive explicit instruction in phonemic awareness and those who do not.

Assessment Considerations. At the kindergarten level, I would assess some of the more gross sound discrimination tasks first and use student performance on these to help me determine if students should be assessed on phoneme

blending and segmenting. These easier phonological awareness tasks include recognizing and generating rhymes, recognizing when words begin with the same sound, and blending and segmenting onsets and rimes. When phonemic awareness is assessed, students are generally given tasks that require them to isolate or segment one or more phonemes in a spoken word; to manipulate the phonemes in a word by adding, taking away, or rearranging phonemes to make a new word; and to blend a sequence of phonemes into a word.

While instruction in phonemic awareness should occur as part of language play and discussions in kindergarten, initial formal assessments on blending and segmenting phonemes can wait until 1st grade. Because phonemes are co-articulated—the sounds blend together and are not discrete as we say words and syllables—it's not easy to tell that "sent" has four sounds and what each one is. Segmentation, especially, can be difficult for some students. Of course, if your kindergarten students are ready based on the results of the easier phonological awareness tasks, go for it. Just don't get uptight or let your students get stressed if they don't have phonemic awareness yet, because there appears to be a connection between students' skill in phoneme segmentation and their formal instruction in decoding and reading in 1st grade (Adams, 1990). You will want to hold this in mind as you decide when to assess phoneme segmentation and manipulation. (See Torgesen & Mathes, 2000, for more in-depth information about phonological and phonemic awareness, and see Armbruster, Lehr, & Osborn, 2001, for a concise overview of phonemic awareness skills and instructional suggestions.)

Assessing Student Progress

Let's think about assessing student development in these components as if we were a school team studying our reading program effects. In this section, I will review instruments you can use to measure student progress and procedures for organizing data at the individual student, class, and grade levels.

We use standard, up-close measures to assess emergent literacy. As discussed in Chapter 9, *standard* means we use instruments or techniques that are uniform in terms of the performance that is being measured, how it is scored, and how many of them are administered. *Up close* means we closely examine student knowledge and performance; we observe, listen to, and analyze overt evidence to determine where the student is in using concepts about print, letter recognition, and phonological and phonemic awareness. We assess periodically, at least every three months or until the student has reached a level of performance that ensures future success. These periodic assessments answer our questions about students' rates of progress and the effectiveness of our instruction. We organize the results immediately so that we have a current summary of individual and group performance. And we use the assessment process itself *and* its results to target instruction and guide student actions with greater accuracy and confidence.

Most of the measures I include as examples are commercially published as assessment instruments. And some, such as the *Yopp-Singer Test of Phoneme Segmentation* (Yopp, 1995b), have been published as part of articles or books on reading, so they are easy to retrieve. The use of these published instruments is not meant to imply that other instruments or locally developed measures lack quality. It's simply that we need a few good, easily accessible examples to use as we think about monitoring the development of emergent literacy throughout the student population.

Instruments designed for assessing several emergent literacy components are presented first, followed by those that assess a more limited range of emergent reading behaviors.

Assessing Multiple Components: Published Surveys of Emergent Literacy

These instruments are used to identify the presence of a range of beginning reading and writing skills. This range generally includes concepts about print, letter identification, phonological and phonemic awareness, word recognition of high-frequency words, and word writing. Sometimes reading of connected text and sentence dictation are included. Most of these instruments are designed for use at kindergarten and 1st grade (sometimes also 2nd grade) and with students in special needs and intervention programs. I'll address the characteristics that make these surveys useful, give examples of two of them, and then focus on how we could organize and use their results beyond the individual student level.

The *Emergent Literacy Survey/K–2 with Phonemic Awareness Screening* (Pikulski, 1997/2001) assesses student knowledge and skill in six areas of beginning reading and writing: concepts about print, letter identification, phonological and phonemic awareness, word recognition, word writing, and sentence dictation. Text reading is not assessed. Except for the assessments of word writing and sentence dictation, the survey is designed to be individually administered. It takes approximately 30 minutes and includes guidelines for omitting and discontinuing tasks.

An Observation Survey of Early Literacy Achievement (Clay, 1993) also assesses student knowledge and skill in six areas of beginning reading and writing: concepts about print, letter identification, word recognition, word writing, sentence dictation, and text reading (oral reading). Phonemic awareness is assessed with the sentence dictation task. The observation survey is designed to be individually administered. While different subtests and tasks of the survey can be used to assess student performance in one area, such as letter identification or sentence dictation, *An Observation Survey of Early Literacy Achievement* is designed for systematic observation of student performance across literacy tasks. In most cases, it is used to provide a tight assessment-instruction connection. Its administration time varies considerably depending on how the teacher, school, or district is using the survey.

The results from both of these surveys yield information about student acquisition of critically important early reading skills. Results from both instruments can be used by the classroom teacher to design individual and group instruction and create appropriate learning experiences. And their results can be aggregated and used by leadership teams and staff for program evaluation. Beyond this, though, these two instruments serve very different purposes.

The *Emergent Literacy Survey* is primarily an assessment instrument. The material used to assess each area is part of the instrument. It is a quick and efficient tool. In contrast, *An Observation Survey of Early Literacy Achievement* is almost a training manual on the systematic observation of students who are learning to read and write. Clay provides rationales for the literacy tasks and areas assessed (and taught) and encourages users to administer the tasks as assessments, record the data, summarize their meaning, and discuss questions and reflections about student performance with colleagues. Because of the amount of freedom in selecting the content with which students engage during the literacy tasks and its close link with instruction, some would not consider this survey as a standard measure. With some agreements established among teachers, I do.

Instruments and Techniques That Assess Primarily One Component

The assessment instruments you purchase or develop depend on the student literacy knowledge and processes you wish to assess and on how you wish to use the results. If your focus is on assessing one component, there are instruments designed for measuring only one skill area of emergent literacy. As with the examples of emergent literacy surveys, this will not be an exhaustive list, but will simply present some good examples.

For concepts about print, the Klesius-Searls (1995, in Mariotti & Homan, 2001, pp. 15–22) "Modified Concepts of Print Test" is a structured observation instrument. The authors adapted Clay's (1993) "Concepts About Print" for use with any picture book. Six concepts are assessed: front and back, print carries the message, left to right, first and last, top and bottom, and word and letter boundaries. This would be fine for prekindergarten and early kindergarten, but I would add a few concepts for mid-kindergarten and 1st grade.

I have seen some excellent local assessments of concepts about print that were adaptations of Clay's instrument, using most or all of the concepts and modifying the directions slightly because of the different books used. In these cases, teachers used sets of picture books in which they had selected and identified pages to correspond with each set of directions.

One of the more comprehensive of the several tools that target student performance in phonological and phonemic awareness—and one I feel relatively comfortable recommending for those who are especially concerned—is "The Assessment Test" (Adams, Foorman, Lundberg, & Beeler, 1998). This instrument has six subtests, with five items each for assessing the following performance tasks: detecting rhymes, counting syllables, matching initial sounds, counting phonemes, comparing word length, and representing phonemes with letters. The tests for these performance tasks are included in *Phonemic Awareness in Young Children: A Classroom Curriculum.*

For a quick check on phoneme segmentation, the *Yopp-Singer Test of Phoneme Segmentation* (Yopp, 1995b) has standardized instructions and is free. The *Yopp-Singer* is especially useful with 1st grade students who have been successful in demonstrating the easier phonological awareness tasks and who were assessed with the *Emergent Literacy Survey* or a similar one in kindergarten.

I have seen only a few locally developed instruments for assessing phonological and phonemic awareness that could be included in this up-close, standard measures category. In each case, the staff had to work on standardizing directions and scoring procedures for use from one assessment period to the next and for use across classrooms. Once this was done, and probably because of the increased discussion of this component and its content, the assessment/instruction/assessment loop was enhanced. One of the more effective cases had teachers assign a plus or a minus to different tasks as they observed students during classroom activities. Two pluses indicated a student did not need to be assessed on that task again.

Organizing Emergent Literacy Results at the Student, Class, and Grade Levels

There are three keys to successfully organizing results of up-close measures of emerging literacy:

1. Study student results at the individual student level, the class level, and the grade level (multiple

classes) when focusing on school-wide improvements in student performance.

2. Use up-close measures regularly to assess student performance and progress (for example, for components such as concepts about print and letter recognition, we assess at least three times a year or until the student demonstrates successful performance). This is called *formative assessment.*

3. Select or design forms that help you organize student data so that you can see how individuals within a group are performing and how groups of students are performing.

Most commercial instruments have individual student record forms. However, many do not include forms that help teachers assemble individual student results into class profiles, nor do they include grade level summary forms. We need these class profiles to plan lessons and select activities for students with similar needs, and we need grade level summaries to help teams study student performance and the effects of the reading program within and across grade levels.

Periodic, up-close assessments to monitor the progress of individuals and groups and to provide students and parents or caregivers with frequent, specific updates on this progress are imperative. I recommend that for kindergarten and some 1st grade groups, we assess students' letter recognition and concepts about print during the first month of school. A student's performance in rec-

ognizing the letters of the alphabet not only represents letter knowledge, but informs us about his previous literacy experiences. And the sooner students can name the letters, the sooner they have a language for talking about print. The results from assessments of concepts about print tell us much about how to organize our classroom environment and student activities. But how can we make these results easy to find and easy to use?

In most schools, much useful data are collected but remain largely ignored because they aren't organized to meet the needs of the faculty. Simple table shells are handy tools for this task. Once we have entered the results of our assessments into these tables, we have both descriptive data about our student population and diagnostic information.

The table shells I include in this book are blank forms designed for recording individual student data and group data. The examples in Figure 10.1 match the curriculum and student-learning content discussed earlier. Beyond that, they are generic and can be easily modified if you wish to add items from your curriculum standards. Their purpose is to support staff in organizing data for studying student progress in a single classroom and across several classrooms. And the student > class > multiple-class formats will work no matter what instrument you use.

I have selected phonological and phonemic awareness as the component to illustrate data organization procedures. This is not because I believe it's the most important literacy component, but because it's the one creating the most angst at the moment. I have used one section of the *Emergent Literacy Survey* (Pikulski, 1997/2001) to provide data organization examples because it is a survey that is easy to use for anyone who wants a quick assessment.

Table 19, "Phonological and Phonemic Awareness: Individual Student," is used to record the responses of individual students in six categories of sound-related discriminations: rhyming words, providing words that begin with the

---

FIGURE 10.1

Tables for Phonological and Phonemic Awareness

On CD-ROM
Tables
19–22

19 Individual Student

School: _____   Teacher: _____   School Year: _____

Student's Name: _____   Age: _____   Grade: _____
(e.g., 9 years/2 months)

Phonological Awareness	Assessment 1 Date:		Assessment 2 Date:		Assessment 3 Date:	
1. Rhyme		___/8		___/8		___/8
2. Beginning Sounds		___/8		___/8		___/8
3. Blending Onsets and Rimes		___/8		___/8		___/8
4. Segmenting Onsets and Rimes		___/8		___/8		___/8
Phonemic Awareness						
5. Phoneme Blending		___/8		___/8		___/8
6. Phoneme Segmentation		___/8		___/8		___/8

20 Class Summary

School: _____   Teacher: _____   Grade: _____   School Year: _____

No. of Students in Class: ____   Dates Assessed: _____   Date: _____
Range (e.g., 8/25 to 9/12)

Student Name	M or F	1. Rhyme	2. Beginning Sounds	3. Blending Onsets & Rimes	4. Segmenting Onsets & Rimes	Phonemic Awareness 5. Phoneme Blending	6. Phoneme Segmentation	Total No. 1–4	No. 5–6
Totals									

(continues)

—————————— FIGURE 10.1 CONTINUED ——————————

Tables for Phonological and Phonemic Awareness

On CD-ROM
Tables
19–22

21   Grade Level Summary

School: _____   No. of Classes/Teachers: _____   Total No. of Students: _____

School Year: _____   Grade: _____

Class/Teacher (No. of Students)	1. Rhyme		2. Beginning Sounds		3. Blending Onsets & Rimes		4. Segmenting Onsets & Rimes		Phonemic Awareness				No. of Students Working on 5 or More Tasks
									5. Phoneme Blending		6. Phoneme Segmenting		
	1st Ad	Last	1st Ad	Last	1st Ad	Last	1st Ad	Last	1st Ad	Last	1st Ad	Last	
Total													

Data Organized by: _____   Date: _____   Shared with Staff: _____
                                                                      (Date)

22   Phonemic Awareness Only: Grade Level Summary

School: _____   No. of Classes/Teachers: _____   Total No. of Students: _____

School Year: _____   Grade: _____

Class/Teacher (No. of Students)	Demonstrates Phoneme Blending		Does Not Demonstrate Phoneme Blending		Demonstrates Phoneme Segmentation		Does Not Demonstrate Phoneme Segmentation	
	M	F	M	F	M	F	M	F
Total								

Data Organized by: _____   Date: _____   Shared with Staff: _____
                                                                      (Date)

same sound, blending onsets and rimes, segmenting onsets and rimes, phoneme blending, and phoneme segmenting. Space has been provided for the results of up to three assessments.

I put a subheading over the two phonemic awareness categories (phoneme blending and phoneme segmentation) for several reasons: to high-

light them as the more advanced skills in this component; to help readers who are still working on the relationship or distinctions between phonological awareness and phonemic awareness tasks; and to emphasize once again not to worry if kindergarten students have not yet developed skills in these two categories. Instruction during the first half of 1st grade can go a long way in building enough skill in blending and segmenting phonemes to easily support the development of literacy, especially for those kindergarten students who are successful with rhyming words and beginning sounds.

The ____/8 in each column is provided as a reminder of the number of items used in assessing each task, with 7 of 8 or 8 of 8 items considered a successful demonstration. If you are using a different instrument, simply enter the number of total items available for assessing each phonological and phonemic awareness task and designate the number that represents successful performance. The two numbers together help us think about the definition of successful performance.

You'll notice that space has been provided to record the date of each assessment. The dates allow teachers to study a student's rate of progress. If someone other than the classroom teacher—para-educators, collaborating teachers, or tutors—is conducting the assessment, have her sign the bottom of the column.

Table 20, "Phonological and Phonemic Awareness: Class Summary," allows the teacher to consolidate the results from individual student response forms into a class profile indicating which students have successfully demonstrated performance in each category and which students are still struggling to develop a basic level of skill. Teachers can use the data in the "Total" column and the "Total" row to group students and select appropriate curriculum content for lessons.

Once we become skilled in studying the results of classroom summaries of student performance, many useful patterns appear. Some patterns will include many students in the class; others only a few students. In either case, these patterns help direct our next instructional moves. For example, it's not unusual in a class profile on these phonological and phonemic awareness tasks to find a small group of students who are skilled in rhyming, beginning sounds, blending onsets and rimes, and phoneme blending, but who haven't developed basic skills in segmenting either onsets and rimes or phonemes. For these students, clapping and counting syllables, add-a-letter or add-a-sound games, and writing activities (when they spell words phonetically, students represent phonemes with the letters they select) are among many of the instructional activities that provide a scaffold for helping students discriminate the separate sounds that make up words.

Table 21, "Phonological and Phonemic Awareness: Grade Level Summary," is used to study student performance in several classrooms. Either the classroom teachers or whoever compiles across-class data can use the class summaries to complete this form. When these data are organized, teams and staff will have a grade level profile of the number of students with basic skill in each task and across tasks and the number of students still working on phonological and phonemic awareness.

Look at the body of the table. After the column for identifying the teacher and class size, there are six pairs of columns for recording student performance results. These six pairs of columns have numbers that match the performance tasks on the individual student record form (Table 19) and the class summary form (Table 20). The teacher, or whoever is organizing these data, can use Table 20 and count the number of students who successfully demonstrated performance in each area on the first assessment administration (1st Ad), then count the additional number of students who were successful on the last administration (Last). When teachers enter or provide data for Table 21, a student's successful performance should be represented in either 1st Ad or Last, but not both. By comparing the total number of students in each class with the sums of the 1st Ad and Last columns, it's easy to see how many students still need instruction in each phonological or phonemic awareness task.

Some students may demonstrate successful performance on the first assessment. For those students who need to be assessed a second or third time, the staff can study gain during the instructional times between the first and second administration, the second and third, and the first and third, providing an excellent up-close look at the effectiveness of instruction.

I have emphasized the "Total" numbers in the last column "No. of Students Working on 5 or More Tasks." We want all of our kindergarten students represented in the rhyming and beginning sounds totals and none in the final column total for students still working on five or six tasks. For 1st grade results, I would change the heading of the last column to "No. of Students Working on

2 or More Tasks," and of course, we'd like the total to be "0."

For grade level summaries to be most useful in looking at student progress in multiple-unit schools, teachers need to agree to assess student performance during a specified time period. For an emergent literacy component such as phonological and phonemic awareness, the period could range from one to four weeks. For example, all 1st grade teachers would agree to check on student performance in this component from January 5 through 9. Or they would set a broader period, between January 5 and January 30. In this component, it is important not to assess the more advanced tasks (such as phoneme blending and phoneme segmentation) if students have not been successful with at least two of the earlier tasks.

For those of you working with 1st grade or ESL students, or supporting teachers who are, organizers such as Table 22 can be used to summarize performance across grade levels on the advanced tasks of phoneme blending and phoneme segmentation. I added gender as a variable to keep an eye on, just in case.

We assess so that we can accelerate literacy learning and prevent reading difficulties by designing learning experiences that move students forward on the reading development continuum. Because these early emerging literacy skills affect reading success later on, school teams and staff need to look at the progress students make in kindergarten and 1st grade. As your team reviews reading program components, ask, "Are we prepared for all of these students, those making good progress, the high achievers, and those students still at risk?" And, "Are we using our student assessment results to identify staff development needs and evaluate the effectiveness of our staff development activities?"

Questions to Explore for Early Literacy Programs (K–1 and Primary Special Needs Classes)

Success in reading is accelerated when students come into formal literacy smoothly and rapidly. Thus, we strive to provide strong literacy programs at every grade level, including kindergarten.

The list of questions in Figure 10.2 (page 113) about the reading program—especially the materials used, the instruction provided, and the organization of students for learning—is provided to help you think about how reading development is supported in kindergarten, 1st grade, and special needs classrooms in your school. The questions address inquiries and actions in Cell 4 of the Action Research Matrix, "Information About Your School's Learning Environment." This is not intended to be an exhaustive list; instead, it addresses areas that often need to be strengthened and some of the common omissions in literacy programs at these levels.

A Short List of Recommended Resources

If you are concerned about accelerating student development in concepts about print, alphabet recognition, and phonological and phonemic awareness, the fol-

lowing items are useful resources about instruction in these components:

➤ Hiebert, E. H., Pearson, P. D., Taylor, B. M., Richardson, V., & Paris, S. G. (1998). Early concepts: Concepts of print, letter naming, and phonemic awareness. In *Every child a reader: Applying reading research in the classroom* (Topic 2 of series). Ann Arbor, MI: University of Michigan School of Education, Center for the Improvement of Early Reading Achievement. (Available at http://www.ciera.org.)

This short, six-page resource suggests instructional strategies for teaching three early literacy components.

➤ Cunningham, P. M. (2000). *Phonics they use: Words for reading and writing* (3rd ed.). New York: Longman.

This is an easy-to-read resource loaded with specific strategies for teaching the alphabet, phonological and phonemic awareness, phonics, and vocabulary (especially high-frequency words), as well as for teaching reading and writing together to help students accelerate their literacy learning.

➤ Bell, D., & Jarvis, D. (2001). Letting go of "Letter of the Week." *Primary Voices K–6, 11*(2), 11–24.

In this article, two kindergarten teachers share their experiences as participants in Reading Initiative, a three-year professional development experience sponsored by the National Council of Teachers of English. What is most relevant to our topic is how these two teachers used the professional knowledge base, competent and caring external technical assistance, and colleagueship to study student learning and increase reading and writing among their kindergarten students. This piece gives readers a chance to hear the teachers' voices as they discuss their inquiry into classroom instruction and where it took them.

➤ Yopp, H. K. (1995a). Read-aloud books for developing phonemic awareness: An annotated bibliography. *The Reading Teacher, 48,* 538–543.

This is a handy resource to have. Young students enjoy and can learn from read alouds that focus on rhymes and alliteration.

For a more in-depth inquiry into research, see the *Handbook of Early Literacy Research* (Neuman & Dickinson, 2001), especially the chapter by Vellutino and Scanlon called "Emergent Literacy Skills, Early Instruction, and Individual Differences as Determinants of Difficulties in Learning to Read: The Case for Early Intervention." And for a fine essay on the development of emergent literacy prior to school and the linguistic assumptions embedded in most kindergarten through 2nd grade literacy programs, see the article "Growing Successful Readers: Homes, Communities, and Schools" in the *Journal of Reading Behavior* (Purcell-Gates, 1998).

—————————— FIGURE 10.2 ——————————

Questions to Explore for Early Literacy Programs

Curriculum Materials

1. How print-rich are kindergarten, 1st grade, and special needs classrooms? Do they include all the typical signs and labels and charts with work words, plus trade books and magazines? Allington recommends "at least 500 different books in every classroom with those split about evenly between narrative and informational books" (2001, p. 55), and indicates that even more are needed in the primary grades.

a. Do classroom libraries contain a range of types of books? Classroom libraries should include the following:

• Picture concept books that focus on a theme through pictures, such as Byron's *Wheels* (1981).
• A variety of alphabet books at different reading levels, beginning with those that have familiar pictures and not too many words and ranging to those that have a science or social studies theme. Examples include *Dr. Seuss's ABC* (Seuss, 1963), *Paddington's ABC* (Bond, 1996), *The ABC Bunny* (Gág, 1961), *Animal Action ABC* (Pandell & Wolfe, 1996), and *A Is for Africa* (Onyefulu, 1993).
• Easy-to-read books that include repetition and rhyme as part of text predictability, such as *The Cat in the Hat* (Seuss, 1957) and *Brown Bear, Brown Bear, What Do You See?* (Martin, 1967).
• Picture storybooks in which text and illustrations work together in developing the story, such as *Sunday Morning* (Viorst, 1968/1993) and *Do You Want to Be My Friend?* (Carle, 1976).
• Traditional children's literature—nursery rhymes, fairy tales, and fables—such as *The Random House Book of Mother Goose* (Lobel, 1986), *The Gingerbread Boy* (Galdone, 1975), and *Henny Penny* (Galdone, 1968).
• Poetry and poetic texts such as *Where the Sidewalk Ends* (Silverstein, 1974) and *Welcome to the Sea of Sand* (Yolen & Regan, 1996).
• Manipulative or participation books such as *Dear Zoo* (Campbell, 1982) and the *A to Z Sticker Book* (Pienkowski, 1995).

b. Does the nonfiction portion of the collection contain informational books that are richly illustrated and that support students' general interest in the world around them as well as the science, social studies, and mathematics concepts being developed in the primary grades? Examples include the following:

• *Bugs! Bugs! Bugs!* (Dussling, 1998)
• *The Reason for a Flower* (Heller, 1983)
• *Extra Cheese, Please: Mozzarella's Journey from Cow to Pizza* (Peterson & Upitis, 1994)
• *Tools* (Morris & Heyman, 1992)
• Nonfiction big books, such as *Growing Pumpkins* (Berger, 1994)

c. Does the collection include books written by students, by the teacher, and by present and earlier classes?

(continues)

—————————— FIGURE 10.2 CONTINUED ——————————

Instruction

2. Look at language arts modes at work in the classroom. How are they being used to support students' entry into the literacy community?

   a. How is listening taught and what do teachers do to explicitly support students' practice of listening as a learning and participatory act?
   b. How is oral language being developed and what do teachers do to explicitly support students' use of oral language?
   c. How is writing being taught and what do teachers do so that students are practicing communicating and recording information via print? Examples of such communication could include writing messages to family and friends or describing the turtle in the terrarium. The use of writing to support reading development is just as important in kindergarten, and for many special needs students, as it is for students in 1st grade and beyond.
   d. What instructional activities occur regularly that require and support students' integration of reading, talking, listening, and writing processes?

3. Do teachers have an instructional process for teaching concepts about print following or accompanying read-alouds? (Big books are especially useful for this.)
4. Is shared reading of predictable books (those with repeated pictures, rhymes, patterns, or refrains), especially predictable big books, a regular part of instruction?
5. Does the daily schedule include time for choral reading of simple things like nursery rhymes, in which students follow along with the text in big books?
6. Is the alphabet taught in multiple ways through reading activities and students' writing activities?
7. Are alphabet books and rhyming books (such as *Moose on the Loose,* Ochs, 1991) used extensively to support the development of letter recognition, phonemic awareness, and phonics?
8. Is phonological awareness taught through rhyming activities, both recognition and generation of rhymes; through clapping the syllables in spoken words; and through wordplay that involves the identification of beginning and ending sounds? Is phonetic spelling encouraged to support students' development of phonemic awareness and phonics skills?
9. Is the academic content of instruction rich throughout the day (not too much of what Schmoker [2001] calls the "Crayola Curriculum")? "Developmentally appropriate" does not mean "academically empty"; it means providing students with curriculum content they are able to learn and providing instruction that serves as a scaffold for their learning.

Organizing for Learning

10. While literacy applications should take place throughout the whole day, are there approximately two hours dedicated to focused instruction in beginning reading and writing? In 1st grade classes with large numbers of at-risk students, you might want to think about three-hour blocks.
11. Are there procedures for providing additional assistance for students with oral language deficits? These would not be students with speech difficulties, but those who just need more opportunities for conversation and verbal interactions. For example, community volunteers or upper-grade student buddies in kindergarten could provide these students with more discussion and interaction over books and other class activities. In 1st grade, are there tutors to intervene and provide additional instructional support for students who are not making satisfactory progress by mid-year?

11

Reading Vocabulary and Word Analysis Skills

When you think about how people build large reading vocabularies, beginning in early childhood and continuing as adults, what do you think of? Which aspects of your curriculum address the development of reading vocabulary? What assessment techniques are used to inform teachers, students, and the school community about student progress?

Words are used to communicate ideas. The more words you "own," the better you can communicate, and the better you are at acquiring words, the more control you have over your own learning processes and educational progress. Thus, in the dimension of building reading vocabulary, we think about students' knowledge of and progress in acquiring sight vocabulary and using word analysis skills (decoding, using meaningful word parts, and using context). Whether as beginning readers or as highly proficient readers, students use these word-level processes (and taught explicitly or learned inductively) in recognizing words, understanding their meanings, and making print make sense.

Reviewing the Components for Building Reading Vocabulary

I've divided the dimension of Building Reading Vocabulary into four components focused on seeking meaning from printed symbols at the word level: acquiring sight words, using phonics and decoding skills, using meaningful word parts, and using context. In cognitive action, these components represent vocabulary acquisition processes that support each other and probably have reciprocally facilitating relationships. It may seem strange that I made sight words a separate component—knowing that the three skill-oriented components help build sight words—but there are two main reasons for giving them such prominence. One is that automatic word recognition is so critical to developing reading proficiency that I did not want to risk its being lost in the word analysis skills. The other is that how we store and retrieve words in our mental storehouse includes how words are spelled, how they sound, *and what they mean*; therefore, I include the development of vocabulary knowledge (what words mean) in the sight word and using context components.

Sight Words

Sight words are words students do not have to decode or figure out. They are recognized immediately from how they are spelled. This is called automaticity; the pronunciation and meaning of the word are retrieved automatically from memory. Because the mind can attend to only a limited number of processes at any one time, the larger a student's sight vocabulary, the more attention he can devote to comprehending larger units of text and relating them to current knowledge.

The work of Linnea Ehri (1991, 1995, 1999) has done much to advance our understanding of how children learn to read words and how they acquire sight words. In Ehri's definition of sight words, she "suggest[s] that any word which is read sufficiently often becomes a sight word" (1999, p. 2). Students learn to read sight words by establishing "connections between the letters seen in the spelling of the words and the sounds detected in the pronunciation of the words" (Ehri, 1998b, p. 108). These "graphophonemic connections provide a powerful mnemonic system that bonds written words to pronunciation in memory" (Ehri, 1999, p. 3).

For example, as fluent readers, we see every letter in a word and connect our letter-pattern knowledge and our sound-pattern knowledge rapidly and unconsciously. These automatic connections are why we would rarely misread "label" as "libel," "then" as "thin," or "cognitive" as "cognition," even when reading a word list. It's why we can catch spelling errors when we proofread our writing. Talk about a reading-writing connection! How words are spelled allows them to be instantaneously retrieved from memory. Because we've had many experiences and have read widely, we have multiple meanings attached to many words. But as soon as we recognize the word "label," whatever meaning we have attached to it is available. We don't have to work on meaning unless the word is used in an unusual or different context, such as the first time we encountered "label" as a company that issues commercial recordings under one or more brands, for instance: "Has Diana Ross spent her entire recording career under that one *label*?"

In terms of general academic success, vocabulary knowledge is one of the best predictors of overall verbal ability, yielding correlations of around .80 (Anderson & Freebody, 1981; Sternberg & Powell, 1983). Basically, each new word a student can comprehend and use appropriately adds to her cognitive processing capacity. Approaching this conversely, "one of the most consistent findings of educational research is that having a small vocabulary portends poor school performance" (Anderson & Nagy, 1992, p. 14). And, especially relevant to our inquiry, an extensive sight vocabulary promotes reading comprehension development (Beck & McKeown, 1991). A strong vocabulary-building curriculum is needed to bring about the good effects of an extensive sight word vocabulary—increasing cognitive processing capacity and promoting reading comprehension development—and decrease the dismal ones of a poor vocabulary.

How is sight word vocabulary expanded? By wide reading and interaction with print, through vocabulary instruction, and by the application of word analysis skills.

Acquiring Words While Reading. Think about the relationship between wide reading and building sight vocabulary. This vocabulary acquisition process, often called "incidental word learning while reading," refers to moving a word into one's sight vocabulary through a single print exposure while reading and through multiple exposures to the word while reading connected text. It also relates to increasing one's depth of knowledge about word meaning through multiple exposures in different texts and from different perspectives.

Some sources say the probability of moving an unfamiliar word into one's sight vocabulary from a single exposure while reading is around 5 percent (Nagy, Anderson, & Herman, 1987). Other sources say it's around 15 percent (Swanborn & de Glopper, 1999). Even at these rates, the average growth in vocabulary size during elementary school is around 2,000 to 3,000 new words a year (Nagy & Scott, 2000).

There is relatively widespread agreement that a large storehouse of sight words and their meanings is acquired simply from reading extensively (Nagy, Anderson, & Herman, 1987; Nagy, Herman, & Anderson, 1985; Stahl, 1999; Stanovich, 2000; Sternberg, 1987; Swanborn & de Glopper, 1999). And beginning around 3rd grade, amount of reading is the "major determinant of vocabulary growth" (Nagy & Anderson, 1984, p. 327). Just reading words in context builds sight vocabulary and knowledge of word meanings.

While there are few experimental studies demonstrating causal effects for quantity of reading on reading development, there are many studies indicating strong correlations between amount of reading and reading growth (see, for example, Cipielewski & Stanovich, 1992; for reviews see Allington, 2001; Anderson, 1996; Krashen, 1993).

In learning words while reading, better readers are advantaged. Better readers read more than poorer readers, thus developing their vocabularies more rapidly and enjoying more intrinsic rewards from the act of reading, which encourages them to read even more. Children who do not read well read less and with less enjoyment, thus limiting their development of sight vocabulary and their opportunities for reading practice, which further constricts their progress in reading and reduces their ability to use school texts. This puts them in a continuous downward spiral as they advance from one grade level to the next and into ever more complex reading materials. The popular label for this advantage/disadvantage is the "Matthew effect," from the Gospel according to Matthew: "For unto every one that hath shall be given, and he shall have abundance: but from him that hath not shall be taken away even that which he hath" (25:29). And the scholar who has done the most to study these reciprocal processes and clarify how reading volume has a "rich get richer" effect on reading development is Keith Stanovich (1986, 2000).

In some schools, the reading program actually widens the gap between poor readers and good readers. This happens when students who are struggling the most in reading are provided with more, and then even more, instruction on the lowest level subskills, focusing on letters and words out of the context of meaningful reading and writing experiences, while good readers are provided with many more opportunities to read, to discuss what they've read, and to use reading and writing as communication (Allington, 1983, 1991; Applebee, Langer, & Mullis, 1988; Johnston & Allington, 1991; Pearson, 1992).

Vocabulary Instruction. While extensive reading supports the acquisition of sight vocabulary, there are two types of words that may need to be taught directly as part of our reading curriculum: *high-frequency words* and *teacher-selected vocabulary words*.

We want students to move high-frequency words—the most common words in print—into their sight vocabularies as rapidly as possible. Many of these words are abstract and are more difficult for readers to attach meaning to. For example, how would you define "of," "the," "was," and "about"? The good news is that just 10 high-frequency words account for around "20 percent of the words students will see in continuous text": *the, of, and, a, to, in, is, you, that,* and *it* (Gunning, 1996).

There are a number of word lists available that rank words according to their frequency of occurrence in specified text (Dolch, 1936; Fry, 1999; and words from *The American Heritage Word Frequency Book,* Carroll, Davies, & Richman, 1971). Often these lists are included in basal reading series, reading textbooks, and resource books, along with an estimation of the percentage of words in written text accounted for by the list. While the percentages vary a little, what is consistent is that a relatively small number of words make up a large percentage of the words students will encounter when reading. For example, Fry (1999) indicates that the first 100 Instant Words on his list make up 65 percent of written text. The first 100 words of the Carroll, Davies, and Richman (1971) list, compiled from school books and materials that students are likely to read in grades 3 through 9, make up about 60 percent of the words in continuous text. Figure 11.1 lists the 100 most frequent words from the latter list.

It's easy to see from looking at this list how many of these words are present in the books we read to children and in the books they choose to read. It's easy to include these high-frequency words in compositions developed as part of whole-class curriculum activities in sci-

---

FIGURE 11.1

100 Most Frequent Words in Written English

the	not	out	its
of	or	then	who
and	by	them	now
a	one	she	people
to	had	many	my
in	but	some	made
is	what	so	over
you	all	these	did
that	were	would	down
it	when	other	way
he	we	into	only
for	there	has	may
was	can	more	find
on	an	two	use
are	your	her	water
as	which	like	little
with	their	him	long
his	said	time	very
they	if	see	after
at	will	no	word
be	do	could	call
this	each	make	just
from	about	than	new
I	how	first	where
have	up	been	most

Source: Adapted from *The American Heritage Word Frequency Book* by J. B. Carroll, P. Davies, & B. Richman, 1971. New York: American Heritage Publishing.

ence and social studies and in language experience activities. Much exposure to and use of these words in writing will help students move them into their sight vocabulary, not just onto the word wall.

Teachers and students may *select vocabulary words* that need to be taught or learned immediately. We may want students to know these words because they have wide utility across many contexts; because they are in text materials students will be using; because they represent concepts that students have, but have not yet encountered at their current reading levels; or because they are unfamiliar words representing unfamiliar concepts (concepts that are needed for expanding students' understanding of the world).

These words might be taught as part of language arts, social studies, science, or fine arts curriculum. We may "teach" these words before or after a reading selection, or we may develop a series of vocabulary lessons that include multiple exposures (8 to 14) to them and student use and discussion of their meanings. When we want students to learn a particular word, such as "emergency" or "phototropism," we teach it, even if it's introduced in the text. Content area textbooks contain many key words and terms. However, they generally do not include enough repetitions or exposures to these words for students to learn them immediately. And in many school texts, such as basal readers (Beck, McKeown, & McCaslin, 1983) and social studies and science texts, there is not enough information provided for students to learn the meaning of the word.

Let's look at how Darlys and her students are working on building reading vocabulary, both word recognition and meaning. Darlys, a 1st grade teacher, has her students investigating animal characteristics during their unit on animals. She has read them many nonfiction books about animals, and they have books available at a range of reading levels, from picture books and alphabet books to illustrated juvenile literature such as Amanda O'Neill's *Cats.* The books are in cartons, some arranged by

animal species (bears, cats, birds, fish) and some by environment or region (desert, Africa). Students have also been keeping journals that describe an animal they have at home or a neighbor's pet, and recording their observations of behavior. The students have access to several videotapes, such as National Geographic's *Animal Babies,* and can visit two Web sites to further observe animals. The class's 4th grade Book Buddies, who come in two afternoons a week, bring in additional books. When the Book Buddies are visiting, 1st graders share their journals and read their buddy a page or two from their favorite book.

As students collect information and generate questions from their observations, teacher read-alouds, and independent reading, Darlys records their findings on chart paper. There have been a number of class compositions and many individual student ones. Here's one of their class compositions:

> Polar bears <u>are</u> carnivores. <u>They</u> eat meat. <u>Their</u> long, strong necks <u>and</u> legs help <u>them</u> swim. Polar bears <u>are</u> <u>the</u> best swimmers of <u>all</u> bears. <u>And</u> <u>they</u> <u>are</u> <u>the only</u> bears <u>that</u> live <u>in the</u> Arctic, near <u>the</u> cold North Pole. <u>Their</u> thick fur <u>and</u> layers <u>of</u> fat help <u>them</u> stay warm.
>   <u>When they</u> <u>are</u> hunting <u>in the</u> snow, <u>they are</u> camouflaged. <u>Their</u> white coats <u>make</u> <u>them</u> almost invisible.

As you can see, Darlys and her students are working on a science benchmark: "knows that plants and animals have features that help them live in different environments." But they are also working on building sight vocabulary for reading and writing. This vocabulary includes both high-frequency words (Figure 11.1 and underlined in the composition) and concept words such as "carnivore" and "camouflaged." Darlys knows that her students need to read a lot and write a lot to secure the spellings and pronunciations of words in memory.

Where is building sight word vocabulary in your curriculum? Have you established benchmarks about reading quantity across the grade levels as reminders? Are your students reading and writing extensively enough to support the development of a reading vocabulary? What portion of each school day do students spend reading? Allington (2001) "suggest[s] that one and one-half hours of daily in-school reading would seem a minimum goal" (p. 33). What portion of each day do your students spend in meaningful writing activities, which also support the acquisition of sight vocabulary and the consolidation of language skills such as spelling patterns? How do you teach "vocabulary words"—those words that students need to know to understand science, social studies, mathematics, and other texts, and those words that mature language users have in their vocabulary?

Assessment Considerations. There are several ways to assess student performance and progress in developing sight vocabulary. Some of them are integrated with instruction, and some are more like word recognition tests. If teachers are keeping running records (coded notations of text reading), word reading accuracy in text is easy to analyze, as is the nature of words that are causing difficulties for students.

For example, select a passage from an informal reading inventory (IRI) or any set of passages with grade level designations. As a student reads the passage orally, mark all reading errors. Then, using the number of words in the passage, calculate a percentage score for word identification accuracy. Let's say a 4th grader is reading a 3rd grade passage with 212 words, and she makes eight errors. Her accuracy score is 96 percent. Generally, an accuracy score of 98–100 percent represents a student's independent reading level; 90–97 percent, the instructional level; and below 90 percent, the frustration level. Our 4th grader's score of 96 percent word identification accuracy means this passage is at her instructional level. In terms of assessing progress in sight word acquisition, a score below 90 percent would indicate that the student does not adequately recognize the words at the grade level represented by the passage.

If teachers are using IRIs, leveled books or passages, or similar measures *across grade levels* to assess word analysis and comprehension, word accuracy scores as students proceed from one level to the next can provide data about student progress in acquiring a sight word vocabulary and their knowledge of high-frequency words. For example, students who can read primer level text (end of first semester of 1st grade) usually have the 100 highest-frequency words in their sight vocabulary (Hiebert, Pearson, Taylor, Richardson, & Paris, 1998). If a student is struggling at this level, it's also a good idea to immediately check her recognition of the 10 highest-frequency words. We can also make a justified assumption that if students are answering 90–100 percent of reading comprehension questions correctly, they understand the meanings of the words in that level of text. For reading words out of context, many IRIs include graded word lists that can be used to provide an indication of students' growth in vocabulary.

We also want students involved in assessing their own progress in acquiring sight words. Kindergarten and 1st grade students can keep vocabulary boxes of "Words I Can Read," and older students can keep vocabulary logs of words they need to know and "Words I Like" from science, social studies, and independent reading.

If you want to extend your inquiry into students' knowledge of word meanings, there are several promising avenues. Knowledge of word meaning "falls along a continuum" from no knowledge to established, automatic knowledge (Beck & McKeown, 1991, p. 796). Consider a word such as "relief." A student may be able to pronounce it as a sight word but have little or no understanding of its meaning; may be vaguely familiar with it; may have understanding of one meaning of the word; or may have the full range of denotative and connotative meanings and can, out of context or with just a phrase, correctly explain its various meanings.

If such routines are not already in place, you can begin involving students in self-assessment of their levels of

knowledge about word meaning and in developing conscious awareness of when their levels of knowledge are impeding comprehension. (See Stahl, 1999, pp. 29–30, for a brief description of knowledge rating checklists for students.) You can explore how those words that represent key concepts in science, social studies, and mathematics are taught and assessed as part of the content of those subjects. And you can periodically ask word-meaning questions following oral or silent reading of passages and books. (This also helps sensitize students to their level of word knowledge.)

If your school administers reading achievement batteries, you will get some indication of progress in vocabulary knowledge from student scores on the Vocabulary subtest of norm-referenced, multiple-choice tests. These results indicate how a student's word knowledge compares with that of other students and often include a grade equivalent score. However, the shelf life of these results is short, and we need more frequent assessments to determine progress during the year and plan lessons accordingly.

Other than wide reading with its multiple exposures to words and instruction on troublesome high-frequency words and key concept words, what other curriculum emphases help students build reading vocabulary? Both while they are learning to read and later when they are proficient readers, students will encounter words they do not recognize automatically. When this happens, we want them to have a toolkit of word analysis strategies ready for figuring out pronunciations and meanings. This toolkit includes three components, often labeled word analysis or word recognition skills. The first component is phonetic analysis: decoding words by using letter-sound correspondences—or larger units such as rimes, familiar letter combinations, syllables, and analogies—and blending these individual or larger sound units together into recognizable words. The second is morphological analysis: using root words, prefixes, and suffixes in determining the pronunciation and meanings of words. And the third is contextual analysis: mining the surrounding text and illustrations to gather information about word meaning.

Of course, these three word analysis components are not discrete. In some cases, more than we are probably aware of, there is overlap in using phonics, morphology, and context to understand what we are reading. Let's review these three components and think about why we need to study student progress in their development.

Phonics and Decoding Skills

A quote from Linnea Ehri (1999), one of the authors of the National Reading Panel report (National Reading Panel, 2000), provides a nice introduction for our review of phonics and decoding skills:

> Skills taught in phonics instruction are tools to build a mature sight vocabulary. Beginners need to learn to decode so that they can acquire a sight vocabulary well secured in memory, but our goal is the sight vocabulary, not the decoding skill. (Ehri, 1999, p. 12)

We use phonics, or knowledge of letter-sound correspondences, when we are reading or writing words that are not in our sight or spelling vocabularies. When we ask students to apply their phonics skills to reading a word that is unfamiliar to them in its print form, we are actually asking them to use an array of language knowledge and processes: knowledge of the alphabetic principle and how it works (spoken words are represented by written spellings); knowledge and use of letter-sound correspondences; skill in blending graphemes into phonemes; knowledge and use of syllable division and accent if the word is multisyllabic; and use of metacognition to compare the word to real words. If the word is in connected text, we also want them to use context cues to see if it makes sense in relation to the surrounding words and ideas. While it is far beyond the scope of this book to analyze the phonological, orthographic, and metacognitive processes listed above, just think about the complexity of one of them, using letter-sound correspondences, when there are somewhere between 44 and 52 phonemes represented by more than 200 forms—some say as many as 250 graphemes (Adams, Foorman, Lundberg, & Beeler, 1998; Morris, 1997). This reminds me what powerful language learners most students are.

Students' use of phonics while writing can strengthen their decoding skills, so along with using phonics as a reading tool, today we encourage students to use it as a spelling and writing tool. When we do this, we often say our students are engaging in phonetic spelling or invented spelling as they "write it like it sounds." Students who are using phonics to spell words use their knowledge of the alphabetic principle as they listen to a word, repeat the word for themselves to identify the phonemes, then convert these phonemes to graphemes as they spell the word. Of course, knowledge of conventional spelling includes more than skill in phonemic awareness and knowledge of letter-sound correspondences, and with all the various combinations of graphemes that represent phonemes in the English language, students don't always end up with the conventional spelling, but we can often read their phonetically spelled prose. For example, few of us would have any difficulty understanding the message of a student who writes, "C th duks." This application of the alphabetic principle and awareness of phonemes as students encode words whose spelling they have not mastered is why we can use their spelling of words or dictated sentences as an indicator of skill in phonemic awareness.

In applying their phonics skills, good readers use analogies to familiar words and segment unfamiliar print words into useful chunks, such as roots, prefixes, suffixes, phonograms, and syllables (Gaskins, Gaskins, & Gaskins, 1991; Gaskins et al., 1988). As students become more and more knowledgeable about English orthographic units and move beyond single letters and phonemes and individual letter-sound correspondences to using larger units such as rimes or phonograms (word families), syllables, or analogies to known words, the speed with which they can decode and encode unfamiliar words increases rapidly.

Let's look at these phonics skills that move beyond letter-by-letter decoding. The major phonological speech unit is the syllable. Syllables contain a vowel sound or a consonant-vowel combination. In linguistic terms, many one-syllable words are made up of an *onset* (initial consonant or consonants) and a *rime* (the vowel and any consonants that follow it). In the single syllable word "can," the onset is /c/ and the rime is /an/. In "scan," the onset is /sc/ and the rime is /an/. For years, I have called these rimes that have the same spelling "word families" or "phonograms," and my 1st graders greatly enjoyed playing make-a-word games with them. When students can use these consistent spelling patterns to figure out words, it's a nice addition to their phonics toolkit. They see "pan" and realize the "an" is the same as in "can," and can read it as /pan/ instead of letter by letter, /p/, /a/, /n/. When they can use their knowledge of common patterns in figuring out multiple-syllable words such as "eating," they've picked up another tool. And when they know the word "belief" and use that knowledge to read the word "relief," they've added the use of analogies to their toolkit. All of these techniques are much faster than letter-by-letter or grapheme-by-grapheme decoding.

Figure 11.2 is a list of 37 phonograms or rimes that allow students to read and spell 500 commonly used words. It is a useful curriculum resource for primary and special needs teachers. The more opportunities students are given to attend to and use these consistent

---
FIGURE 11.2

Thirty-Seven Rimes That Can Be Used for Deriving
500 Common Primary Woods

-ack	-eat	-ip
-ail	-ell	-it
-ain	-est	
-ake		-ock
-ale	-ice	-oke
-ame	-ick	-op
-an	-ide	-or
-ank	-ight	-ore
-ap	-ill	
-ash	-in	-uck
-at	-ine	-ug
-ate	-ing	-ump
-aw	-ink	-unk
-ay		

Source: From Wylie, R. E., & Durrell, Donald D. (1970). Teaching vowels through phonograms. *Elementary English, 47,* 787–791. Copyright 1970 by the National Council of Teachers of English. Reprinted with permission.

spelling patterns as readers and writers, the faster their sight vocabularies will grow. While this list from Wylie and Durrell (1970) has been around a while, just like the word frequency list from Carroll and colleagues, it is still useful in teaching phonics and decoding. And while *rime* does not mean the same as *rhyme* (words that sound the same at the end), each rime will yield between 14 and 26 rhyming words.

Recent syntheses of studies of phonics instruction and its effects on students yield these findings to consider as we think about our curriculum and when we need to assess students' development of phonics decoding skills:

> The impact of phonics instruction on decoding, word reading of regularly and irregularly spelled words, reading text orally, comprehension of text, and spelling is greatest at kindergarten and 1st grade, for both normally developing and at risk students. (Ehri, Nunes, Stahl, & Willows, 2001; National Reading Panel, 2000)

In kindergarten and 1st grade, and into 2nd grade as needed, we need to teach students how to blend graphemes into phonemes to form words, how to use common spelling patterns such as phonograms and suffixes, and how to use analogies to known words to figure out unfamiliar words. We need to identify the most useful phonic generalizations (Clymer, 1963/1996) and the spelling patterns that have the greatest utility (for example, the 37 phonograms) and see that they are included in our curriculum and embedded in our instruction. We won't argue here about the nature of the "one best way" of phonics instruction, because there are numerous forms of systematic phonics instruction (Ehri et al., 2001). We do need guidelines about the sequence for introducing phonics generalizations and spelling patterns, but they should not be rigid.

Assessment Considerations. As we support student development in this area, we need to study students' knowledge and skill in using letter-sound correspondences and larger units such as phonograms and analogies in decoding words. We need to know what word-reading strategies they can use.

First grade teachers often analyze students' word reading and note what students can and cannot do and where they are making good progress and where they are struggling in the following subskill areas: initial consonant sounds, final consonant sounds, short vowel sounds in consonant/vowel/consonant patterns, initial consonant blends and digraphs, final consonant blends and digraphs, final "e," vowel diphthongs, "r" control vowels, and syllabication.

Other 1st grade teachers focus more on assessing students' word reading processes. They observe and record how well students are sounding out words and whether they are checking the pronunciations they come up with against their knowledge of real words or the meaning of the text. They note where students are on the phonics knowledge and application continuum: whether they are relying on a few letters and configuration as they decode words; blending all the letters; blending graphemes into known words; or beginning to use larger patterns such as phonograms, syllables, or analogies to known words.

In both assessment orientations, teachers may collect their data informally, simply keeping notes about each student; evaluate students more formally through running records or assessments that accompany the basal series or other commercial reading programs; or check student progress at regular intervals using word lists, graded passages, or leveled books. And, of course, some teachers assess both subskills and how students approach and try to figure out unfamiliar words.

You and your team or staff will have to decide which grade levels to evaluate and which assessment focus to take. I prefer a combination, with an emphasis on how students are learning to read words and use the spelling patterns and generalizations in written English. Daily lessons would include opportunities for students to apply their knowledge of letter-sound correspondences, phonograms, common letter combinations, and analogies as readers and as writers, allowing me to continuously assess progress. More formally, at 1st and 2nd grade, I would continue assessing until the student has built a basic sight vocabulary and can decode multisyllabic words easily.

What about kindergarten? The kindergarten curriculum already includes the phonological awareness knowledge and skills addressed in Chapter 10, which entails much work with consonant and short vowel sounds. If students' up-close assessment results indicate they are ready to move beyond that in their word study, just keep going.

Morphological Analysis

Nagy and Anderson (1984) estimate that the meanings of as many as 60 percent of English words can be predicted from the meanings of their parts. I find this a compelling reminder of the value of this component. Understanding how suffixes, prefixes, and compound words work will help students build vocabulary rapidly.

In English, there are many common patterns in the structure of words and in how words are formed. One kind of pattern has to do with how words are built by adding parts. In morphology, these parts are meaning units, called *morphemes,* and their addition relates systematically to changes in word meaning. As a skilled English language user, your recognition and use of morphemic relationships is automatic. For example, little mental energy is required in using suffixes to change the tense and number of a regular verb such as "talk" to "talks," "talked," or "talking," or in making most nouns plural or possessive as in changing "girl" to "girls" or "girl's." Whether concentrating on word meaning or on decoding skills, when you look at

"talked," you see "talk" as the root or base word and the main meaning unit and you automatically pronounce it as /tok't/, not as /tol ked/.

Think about how knowledge of meaningful word parts helps with decoding and pronouncing multisyllabic words. Apply your knowledge and skills to the nonsense word "reriguration." My guess is that you did not decode it grapheme by grapheme. My guess is that you identified /re/ as a prefix and pronounced the first syllable as /re/, not /rer/, and that you noticed the suffix /ation/ at the end and pronounced the last two syllables as /ra shen/, not /rash en/. Or maybe you decoded it by analogy to "reconfiguration," with its base word "configure," its prefix "re-" and its suffix "-ation." Even with a nonsense word, your knowledge of word parts and relationships was probably applied almost automatically. While *morphological analysis* is the more accurate term, many of us call this recognition and use of meaningful word parts *structural analysis.*

When readers apply their phonics skills, they are dealing with units of pronunciation (letter-sound correspondences and larger sound units such as phonograms); when they apply their structural analysis skills, they are dealing with units of meaning. While the single sound units within a single word are labeled as *phonemes,* and the print units representing these single sounds are labeled *graphemes,* the individual language meaning units within words are labeled *morphemes.*

Morphemes are divided into two categories based on how they are used in spoken and written language. *Free morphemes* can stand alone as a word, and are often called root or base words. *Bound morphemes* cannot stand alone; they are added to root or base words as prefixes or suffixes, changing the form or function of the original word. For example, the root word "works" has two morphemes: the root word "work" is the main meaning unit, and the suffix "-s" is a meaning unit that signals a change in number, which means a change in word form but not in the function of the word. And when free morphemes or root words are combined with other free morphemes, as in "workshop," the result is a compound word.

In oral language, children begin using correct morphemic variations very early. When they see three dogs, they are soon saying "three dogs," not "three dog." Or if you ask them what they are doing, they say "playing," not "play." By the time they reach kindergarten, many of them have quite an expansive listening/speaking vocabulary, if we count all the root words and the inflections, derivations, compound words, and contractions they use.

In current reading research and current practice in schools, much attention is being given to helping students develop phonemic awareness and phonics skills, but much less attention is given to helping students use structural analysis in building reading and writing vocabulary. Yet thousands of words students need to know, read, and spell are inflected and derived forms of root words.

Nagy and his colleagues (1994) open their chapter on structural analysis and its role in reading with these estimates: the average 5th grader encounters about 10,000 "new" or low-frequency words a year. More than half of these 10,000 new words are familiar words with prefixes and suffixes added.

And there is more good news: four suffixes account for approximately 72 percent of suffixed words: "-s/-es," "-ed," "-ing," and "-ly"! And these few prefixes account for 58 percent of prefixed words: "un-," "re-," "in-" (as well as "im-," "ir-," and "il-," meaning "not"), and "dis-." Figure 11.3 lists the 20 most common suffixes and prefixes in written school English, accounting for approximately 93 percent of suffixed words and 97 percent of prefixed words. (This paragraph and Figure 11.3 are derived from White, Sowell, & Yanagihara, 1989; and Graves, 1992.)

The sequence for curriculum and instruction progresses from familiar words with the most common suffixes and prefixes to the use of those suffixes and prefixes in unfamiliar words and more complex derived forms of words. I would focus first on suffixes, because the simple inflected and derived forms are part of students' vocabulary when they enter school, and their recognition is a handy decoding tool. Looking at the list of common suffixes in Figure 11.3, the first five— -s/-es, -ed, -ing, -ly, and -er/-or—stand out as items to work on in kindergarten and 1st grade. The others can be addressed in 2nd through 4th grade, or as they begin showing up in what students are reading.

While knowledge of prefixes also helps with decoding, they are especially

FIGURE 11.3

20 Most Common English Suffixes and Prefixes Arranged by Frequency

Suffixes	Prefixes
-s, -es	un-
-ed	re-
-ing	in-, im-, ir-, il- (not)
-ly	dis-
-er, -or (one who)	en-, em-
-ion, -tion, -ation, -ition	non-
-ible, -able	in-, im- (in or into)
-al, -ial	over- (too much)
-y	mis-
-ness	sub-
-ity, -ty	pre-
-ment	inter-
-ic	fore-
-ous, -eous, -ious	de-
-en	trans-
-er (comparative)	super-
-ive, -ative, -itive	semi-
-ful	anti-
-less	mid-
-est	under- (too little)

Source: White, Thomas G., Sowell, Joanne, & Yanagihara, Alice. (1989, January). Teaching elementary students to use word-part clues. *The Reading Teacher, 42*(4), 302–308. Reprinted with permission from the International Reading Association.

helpful in determining word meaning. While prefixes will occur in what we're reading to students and what they are reading at kindergarten and 1st grade, I would not build formal study of them into the curriculum until 3rd or 4th grade. Instead, as words like "unhappy," "disappear," and "replace" appear in 1st and 2nd grade, we would have mini-lessons on how the prefixes "un-," "dis-," and "re-" work.

In the elementary school curriculum, at the more advanced end of the structural analysis continuum, we work with students on English root words with many common derivatives, then move to those that are less common but important in understanding the curriculum concepts we're teaching. For example, we teach students to recognize and use common derivatives that show up in social studies, like those from "colony" ("colonial," "precolonial," "colonize," "colonist," and "colonization"). We also teach less common derivatives as they appear, like derivatives from "conserve" that represent concepts in science, social studies, music, and law ("conservation," "conserving," "conservative," "conservatism," "conservator," and "conservatory").

Skill in structural analysis helps students understand the meanings of many related words, how to pronounce them, and how to spell them. If we teach students to use meaningful word parts, they can build their sight vocabulary more rapidly. By the time our students reach 3rd or 4th grade and begin encountering the increased use of prefixes and suffixes common in content area textbooks, we want them to recognize the systematic relationships between changes in word form and changes in meaning that they already use in their listening and speaking vocabularies. Plus, they have been working with these variations in word form and meaning in spelling, grammar, and usage from at least 1st grade onward. Learning morphological analysis will help them see the similarities in the structure of the English language, whether they're reading, writing, listening, or speaking.

Assessment Considerations. Our assessment of structural analysis should probably lean toward what Anderson and Nagy term *word consciousness*, "a concept that includes understanding how the parts of words contribute to their meanings." (It also includes "a sense of curiosity about word meanings" and "appreciation of nuances of meaning," Anderson & Nagy, 1992, pp. 46–47. For the moment, let's stay with word parts.)

If teachers are using graded passages, running records, or leveled books to assess students' progress, it is relatively easy to note how students use meaningful word parts and to ask questions that assess students' development of word consciousness. Teachers can ask young students in 1st and 2nd grade how they are able to tell one form of a related word from another and what the differences in meaning are. For example, they can ask, "How did you know that word was 'cats' and not 'cat'?" "How did you know that word was 'warmer' and not 'warm'? Tell me. Show me." "What is the difference between 'warm' water and 'warmer water'?" "What does 'closed' mean?" They can also ask about the meaning of compound words: "What do you think a 'railcar' is?"

For older students, teachers can select sentences with prefixes and suffixes and ask them to explain how the prefixes and suffixes relate to word meaning and the meaning of the sentence or passage as a whole. For both younger and older students, I would use the word in the context of a sentence most of the time instead of using single words or word lists.

Student development in using word parts in spelling and pronouncing words (as when a known root, prefix, or suffix is used as a decoding tool) will be visible in their writing and when decoding and spelling errors are analyzed. Neither letter-sound relationships nor structural patterns are 100 percent reliable for any single word, but across many words both have ample consistency to make them necessary word analysis tools.

Using Context

Let's think about how readers intentionally use context—surrounding words, phrases, and sentences—to clarify or determine word meaning. Using contextual analysis as a problem-solving tool requires that the reader focus her attention on a word and mine the text for clues to its meaning.

Good readers are continuously monitoring for meaning. They realize when they do not understand a word well enough to support comprehension, and they are skilled in analyzing the surrounding text and illustrations for information. This self-monitoring includes an awareness of when one does not know the meaning of a word or its antecedent, attention to whether a word that is being decoded phonetically or analyzed structurally makes sense in the larger context of the sentence or passage, and an awareness of when the understanding of a word's meaning is essential to comprehending the major message. Monitoring for meaning is part of word consciousness.

Imagine you are interested in learning more about biogeography, the study of where plants and animals are and are not found and what they coexist with. These sentences are part of the introduction of a major concept:

> P. J. scoops up a handful of wood shavings. He cradles them toward his nose. He spreads his fingers. Wood shavings fall. "No. Wait. Here now." He scoops again. Finally, success and relief: In his palm is a tiny mammal.

> Face like a carrot, dark little eyes, gray fur; it resembles a shrew. It isn't a shrew. It's a member of the species

Geogale aurita, otherwise known as the large-eared tenrec. "He's a termite specialist. . . ."

Every species of tenrec (except for those anomalous African otter-shrew forms) is endemic to Madagascar—meaning, native to this island and nowhere else. (*The Song of the Dodo,* by David Quammen, 1997, pp. 42, 45)

If you did not already know what a tenrec was, these paragraphs* are loaded with context clues. You may have speculated about what some of its characteristics—mammalian, located on only one island, termite-eating—have to do with the study of patterns of distribution of species. The author, knowing that many of his readers might not have a full grasp of the word "endemic," and knowing that this word was important to the larger concept, threw in a context clue for that word also. As a proficient reader, you had no trouble gathering information about the meaning of "tenrec" or the adjective "endemic."

Learning to use context is about learning to use content. Just as you did with the paragraph about tenrecs, students need to learn to read and think about the content and where the author is trying to take them, to be word conscious, and to mine the text for information about word meaning. Contextual analysis is about good information tracking, or as I used to say to my students, being good word detectives.

To use connected text and illustrations to determine word meaning, students first have to realize there is a problem and then have to tools for

---

resolving that problem. The good news is that students are quite accurate in identifying words that they know and do not know (White, Slater, & Graves, 1989). They have more trouble recognizing when they need to know more about a slightly familiar word or a word that is used in a different way. In my experience, many struggling older readers are not skilled in using context to clarify antecedents, possession, time using verb tense, sequence, and relationships among words or concepts. But with concentrated instruction on knowing when and where to look, it doesn't take them long to learn how to use these kinds of context clues.

Why should contextual analysis be in the curriculum if just reading widely will build vocabulary? Because many students cannot use context to help them solve problems with words and word meaning, and many students never develop a reading habit that fosters vocabulary development.

Both expert readers and poor readers can use context to gather information about word meanings. However, less skilled or poorer readers are at a disadvantage once again. In using context to figure out the meaning of a word, better readers make better use of context (Adams & Huggins, 1985; Jenkins, Stein, & Wysocki, 1984). This difference in ability to use available context makes sense: better readers generally have a larger sight vocabulary as a base, far more world knowledge, more concepts, and a deeper understanding of written language and how it works to bring into play when deriving word meanings. This does not mean that poorer readers fail to use con-

textual analysis; in fact, there is evidence that poorer readers rely on context for word recognition and meaning more frequently than skilled readers, possibly attempting to compensate for their poorer decoding skills and more limited sight vocabulary (Stanovich, 2000). What probably happens when poorer readers try to use context to derive word meaning is that their vocabulary development toolkit is lighter in terms of breadth of sight vocabulary and meaningful concepts to use in making connections, and possibly lighter in decoding and structural analysis, so when they do rely on context, it is less useful for them.

Why not simply send students to dictionaries, glossaries, thesauri, and other external sources to work out word meaning? Many of us use these regularly when we run into words that we're not sure about. Most school reading programs have "uses reference sources" as a student-learning outcome. However, using dictionaries and formal definitions to understand the meaning of a word in context does not work for many students (McKeown, 1993; Miller & Gildea, 1987; Nagy & Scott, 2000). Maybe it's because they are written in a "secret code" (Nagy & Herman, 1987, p. 29) or because of students' inability to understand the structure of definitions or take syntax into account when they try to apply them (Nagy & Scott, 2000, pp. 277–278). But once again, for those highly motivated and skilled readers who encounter words in context and seek clarification through reference sources, definitions are more useful than they are for less skilled and struggling readers.

From kindergarten on, students need explicit instruction lessons in monitoring word meaning, finding and using contextual clues, and going beyond the text to other sources, such as dictionaries. These processes must be explained, modeled, and practiced until they are part of the students' vocabulary building and problem-solving toolkit. If we want students to be able to use dictionary definitions, we have to model—many times—how this can be done, and students need to practice until they can easily and accurately use these resources.

Contextual analysis helps students add words to their sight vocabulary and supplements decoding and structural analysis skills by either confirming or casting doubt on the word decoded or the meaning derived.

Assessment Considerations. As always, you and your team have to decide how this component of building reading vocabulary should be supported and assessed. It's obvious where I come down. I would engage in frequent informal assessment of students' use of context. Across all grade levels, I would work on students' development of word consciousness: consciousness about when they do not understand a word, when a word's meaning is essential to comprehending the larger message of the text, and when they need to go to external resources to identify the meaning of a word. In addition, students would be engaged in their own self-assessments of vocabulary building and strategy use.

From 1st grade on, I would want students to apply contextual analysis strategies such as Sternberg and Powell's

(1983) three-step cognitive process in using context clues:

1. What information is available in the sentence and in earlier and later sentences that is helpful in figuring out the meaning of this word?
2. When I think about what I am reading and all the available information, what does the word seem to mean?
3. What do I know from my own experiences that will help me figure out the word?

I would also add a fourth: When do I need to seek external resources, such as tapping the word into the *MacMillan Talking Dictionary*, listening to the pronunciation, and reading the definition or asking someone else for an explanation? And as I work with students, I would periodically interview them about the strategies they are using.

The results of these assessments can be used to analyze what students are doing to facilitate sight vocabulary acquisition and whether they are using the information that is available in the text to determine word meaning and aid comprehension. In the primary grades, the more formal assessments would occur when I am using graded passages, running records, or leveled books to assess oral reading accuracy, fluency, and comprehension. At the upper elementary grades, I would make sure that some of the passages used to assess comprehension required most students to use context to clarify word meaning.

Looking at word analysis from a developmental perspective, it seems as if during our first few years of reading, we practice using phonetic, structural, and contextual analysis as skills for working with words that are not in our sight vocabulary but are often in our listening and speaking vocabularies. Then, as we read more and more and develop a larger sight vocabulary, these skills we have practiced become part of our problem-solving toolkit of strategies that are automatically available for figuring out the pronunciation and/or meaning of unfamiliar words. Our word consciousness and reasons for reading the material may activate the search for additional clarification of pronunciation or meaning. If so, we turn to friends, to print or electronic resources such as dictionaries and thesauri, or to more extensive references such as encyclopedias or technical resources.

Assessing Student Progress

Consider what school staff can learn when they work together using up-close measures to assess sight word acquisition, decoding and phonics skills, and structural and contextual analysis. Other measures, such as norm-referenced achievement tests, that are less affected immediately by daily instruction were discussed in Chapter 6. When we study students' progress in building reading vocabulary, we look at the progress they are making in expanding the size of their sight vocabulary and the progress they are making in using vocabulary building strategies—phonics and decoding skills,

structural analysis, and contextual analysis. We want to see growth in the number of words students read with automaticity and growth in students' knowledge of word meanings. We also want to see improvements in decoding skills and increases in the number of strategies students use to decode and understand unfamiliar words. Fluent reading depends on having a large sight vocabulary; skilled reading depends on being able to deal effectively with new words.

If your current assessment system already does a good job of providing data for monitoring individual student progress, all you need to do is organize these data so the staff can routinely—at least three times a year—study the progress of the student population. For example, if staff have identified sets of leveled books for assessment purposes and use students' oral reading of these books for measuring students' sight vocabulary acquisition and word analysis skills, or if staff members are using the error analysis records from published programs such as *Word Matters: Teaching Phonics and Spelling in the Reading/Writing Classroom* (Pinnell & Fountas, 1998), the task becomes one of organizing these results so the school community can use them routinely for studying the performance of the student population and identifying areas of the reading program that need to be strengthened.

Instruments and Procedures for Assessing Multiple Components

Students' oral reading of grade level word lists or leveled passages can be used to assess sight vocabulary and progress in sight word acquisition. What students do when they encounter unfamiliar words in these lists or passages can be used to assess their word analysis skills.

If time is pressing, or if staff members do not have time to study an informal reading inventory or select passages and standardize administration procedures across classes—and the school leadership team needs relatively reliable results immediately—they can select a commercial instrument such as the *Gray Oral Reading Tests* (Wiederholt & Bryant, 2001).

The *Gray Oral Reading Tests (GORT-4)* is an example of a commercially published measure for assessing word accuracy in context, oral reading rate (fluency), and comprehension of connected text. The *GORT-4* is individually administered and has two parallel forms, each with 14 leveled passages for use in grades 1 through 12. Its administration materials include a spiral-bound book with large print for students to read, individual booklets for the teacher to use in recording student responses, and a scoring and interpretation manual.

I've often recommended the *GORT-4* when teams ask for something they can use immediately to give them a school-wide profile of student performance in reading for the following reasons:

- It has a good content validity (measures what it says it will) and appears to do a good job in assessing growth.
- It's not a complex instrument. With about three hours of training, inter-rater reliability is usually satisfactory.
- The administration procedures eliminate many decisions that have to be

made when less standard measures are used.
- Depending on how it is used, it provides student results in two to five components of reading development.
- It has national norms and grade equivalents, which are especially useful in some settings.

Figure 11.4 displays *GORT-4* results for 4th grade students in a school that has six 4th grade classes. The staff that collected this information were especially interested in looking at grade level equivalents and student growth between the fall and spring assessments. Using the scoring procedures in the *GORT-4* manual, the staff converted students' raw scores on word accuracy, fluency, and comprehension to norm-referenced scores. Figure 11.4 displays the average, or mean, grade equivalent for each class in September and May, as well as the average gain.

What do you first notice about the results? I hope it was the excellent gains the students made. Many of them are much better readers, and many more of them enter 5th grade able to use the upper elementary texts as instructional materials. It's nice to celebrate progress and confirm that instruction really does work!

How did teachers and students change this picture of performance? Teachers increased their modeling of comprehension strategies, not just by a little, but by three to four times. Their modeling was followed by student practice of these strategies. They provided more discussion time for students, more

—— FIGURE 11.4 ——

Gray Oral Reading Tests Results for Six 4th Grade Sections: Grade Equivalent Means and Mean Gains

Class	Accuracy			Fluency			Comprehension		
	Sept.	May	Gain	Sept.	May	Gain	Sept.	May	Gain
A	4.0	5.9	1.9	4.0	5.7	1.7	3.3	5.3	2.0
B	3.9	5.1	1.2	3.7	4.9	1.2	3.5	4.9	1.4
C	4.4	5.7	1.3	3.9	5.7	1.8	3.2	5.7	1.5
D	3.5	5.2	1.7	3.5	5.1	1.6	3.1	4.9	1.8
E	3.9	5.2	1.3	3.2	4.9	1.7	3.5	5.1	1.6
F	4.8	6.7	1.9	4.3	6.1	1.8	3.5	5.4	1.9
School Average	4.1	5.6	1.6	3.8	5.4	1.6	3.4	5.2	1.7

time for paired reading, and added reciprocal teaching (Palinscar & Brown, 1984) to the cooperative learning models they were using with students. They worked to extend the amount of reading and discussions about reading into the home environment (Wolf, 1998). For the students who had the lowest fluency scores, they added repeated readings to their Book Buddy work and tutorials. And for their 18 students who were having difficulties with decoding, teachers provided explicit instruction lessons and inductive lessons (including word sorts) (Duffy, 2003; Bear, Invernizzi, Templeton, & Johnston, 2000; Calhoun, 1999).

Now, let's analyze these results, focusing especially on what they tell us about building reading vocabulary. Look at the September results in accuracy, fluency, and comprehension. What do you notice? Word accuracy (meaning sight word recognition and correct decoding) was the strongest, followed by fluency, or reading rate. The comprehension performance was the weakest component. These results surprised many staff members. They thought reading comprehension was the strongest dimension for their students. In fact, one of their worries—based partially on external pressures and demands—was that students were weak in word recognition skills.

Compare the accuracy and fluency scores for September. Notice that in no case is fluency higher than accuracy. While it's possible for students to have a good sight vocabulary and not be fluent, it's not possible to be a fluent reader without a good sight vocabulary. Look especially at Classes B, C, E, and F. This is a very common pattern of results: these students are good at decoding but their reading rate is lagging slightly behind, and their reading rate (fluency) is probably affecting their comprehension.

Of course, we do not have to look at comprehension when we're focusing on sight words and word recognition skills, but it's a good idea for at least two reasons. First, there may be—and often is—a relationship between a student's performance on one component and his performance on another. And second, good decoding is not the same as good reading. If students have excellent decoding skills but do not comprehend what they are reading, they are not likely to become good readers or gain enough satisfaction from the reading act to sustain continued engagement, learn from reading, or develop a reading habit. So, while it's a good idea to focus attention on components we're trying to improve, we also keep our eyes on other components of development. Reading is a multidimensional process.

When a staff is seeking measures for monitoring progress three times a year, in multiple classes and from kindergarten through 6th grade, I make the following recommendations. The first year they should use the *GORT-4* or a similar, already standardized measure. The results will yield a profile of student performance for grades 1 through 8, and the staff will have an opportunity to learn to work together on developing assessment schedules, planning lessons for students with common needs, and making across-classroom interventions. Routines need to be put in place for scheduling the administration of the tests, analyzing the

results and considering their implications for individual students and groups of students, and considering modifications in the reading program. When these routines become scheduled tasks in the school action plan, teachers will have time throughout the year to study, reflect, and take action.

In the second year, the *GORT-4* should be used as the outcome measure for the end of the year, and grade-level-designated passages should be used for the first two assessments. These passages can be taken from published informal reading inventories, from the assessment packages in some basal readers, or from designated "real" books. I'm going to concentrate on what we can get from informal reading inventories, but the methods used to assess student performance are similar regardless of the source of the assessment text.

Informal reading inventories and IRI processes (Caldwell, 2002) can be used to assess students' sight vocabulary and word analysis skills, text reading level and fluency, and reading comprehension. IRIs are rich sources of assessment content and procedures. Like Clay's (1993) *An Observation Survey of Early Literacy Achievement,* they can function as an assessment manual and a teaching manual, strengthening teachers' clinical skills in analyzing students' reading behaviors. Staff members can select components of reading development they are most concerned about and assess them with sections of the IRI; they do not have to administer the whole thing to have useful results. (Chapter 12 includes a description of two published

IRIs: *Qualitative Reading Inventory-3,* Leslie & Caldwell, 2001; and the *Basic Reading Inventory,* Johns, 1997.)

Most of the commercially published inventories are designed for use across a range of grade levels, generally 1st through 8th grade or higher. They are individually administered and generally include word lists and sets of graded passages. The word lists are used to assess the accuracy of word identification, as well as automaticity or speed sometimes, and to determine the starting point for reading the graded passages. The sets of graded passages are used to determine oral reading rate and fluency; a student's independent, instructional, and frustration reading levels; reading comprehension level and strategies; and word recognition strategies. Since passages provide more information about students' reading development than word lists, let's consider them first.

Using Passages. To assess sight word vocabulary and word recognition skills in context, students are given a grade-level-designated passage to read orally. It should be an unfamiliar passage. The examiner times the reading and records miscues such as mispronunciations, omissions of words, insertions, and substitutions. These errors and miscues are used in calculating accuracy and analyzing the students' word recognition strategies. After the oral reading, examiners can ask students to tell about what they read (retelling) or ask questions to determine if they understood the passage content.

Figure 11.5 displays the examiner's copy of a passage read by Alex, a beginning 3rd grader. This is the second passage Alex was asked to read. Because of the staff's interest in sight word vocabulary, Alex's reading rate (fluency) results are calculated in words correct per minute (WCPM), not just words per minute (WPM). His word accuracy, counting all errors, is 91 percent. He also answered four of the five comprehension questions correctly. So for both word accuracy and comprehension, this 2nd grade passage is at his instructional level. His reading rate is a little below average for a beginning 3rd grader.

Alex is on his way to building a sight vocabulary. He knows many words. He used analogies, prior knowledge, and context to figure out "chrome" and "motorcycle." We'd prefer that he not omit words (4 words omitted). With several of his errors, it seemed as if instead of reading the text, he "read" it as he would say it, for example, reading "Sam said" instead of "said Sam"; "buy me one like it" instead of "buy me one just like it"; and "long enough for this one" instead of "long enough for this one yet." While his replacement words for "biked" ("rode"), "shouted" ("said"), and "mother" ("mom") were semantically and syntactically correct and did not affect his understanding of the story, he was not attending to each word in the text as good readers do. Dropping or omitting the /ed/ doesn't appear to be dialect because he pronounced "looked," "slowed," "stopped," and "called" correctly. Along with trying to ensure that Alex reads a lot of easy books at his independent level, and some choral reading followed by repeated oral reading, I would want Alex writing frequently.

──────── FIGURE 11.5 ────────

Marked-Up Examiner's Copy

A Bike for the Future

One morning Sam was playing in the yard. He looked up and saw a policeman riding a bicycle. Sam wav(ed) and yell(ed) "Hello!"

The policeman slowed down and stopped right in front of the yard. His bike was black and ~~chrome~~ (*cōme*) and (very) shiny.

"I really like your bike," said Sam. "I wish my mom would buy me one (just) like it."

The policeman smil(ed) and said, "Well, maybe you can buy yourself one when you're (a little) bigger. Your legs aren't long enough for this one yet." Then he wav(ed) goodbye and ~~biked~~ (*rode*) on down the street.

Sam ran inside. "Mom," he ~~shouted.~~ (*said*)

"I'm on the computer," she called.

Sam ran into the room. "Mom, Mom, I saw a policeman riding a fast black bike. He was on our street."

"You mean a motorcycle, don't you?" said his ~~mother.~~ (*Mom*) (*sikecl*)

"No, Mom, a bike, the kind you pedal. I want one just like it for my birthday!"

"Well, we'll see," said Mother. "You are becoming a big, ~~busy~~ (*big*) boy. On Saturday, you'll be five years old."

Word Accuracy: _15_ errors in 176 words	**Accuracy Rate:** _91%_	**WCPM:** _73_
Comprehension: _1_ error in 5 questions	**Comprehension:** _80%_	

The examiner administered the 3rd grade passage next. Alex's word accuracy and comprehension scores were at a frustration level with this text. His reading rate dropped to 51 WCPM, approximately one grade level below average, which may have affected his comprehension. However, the examiner was as concerned about Alex's personal behaviors while reading the 3rd grade material as she was about his scores. On the first two passages, Alex was cheerful and eager to read. When reading the 3rd grade passage, he missed only a few more words, but he became irritated when his self-corrections did not make sense.

If this is regular behavior for Alex—frustration and irritation when he

—————————————— FIGURE 11.6 ——————————————

Table for Sight Words and Word Analysis Skills: Class Summary

On CD-ROM
Table 23

School: _____   Teacher: _____   Grade: _____   School Year: _____

No. of Students in Class: _____   Dates Assessed: _____   Date: _____

Range (e.g., 8/25 to 9/12)

Student Name / Special Ed. or ESL Code	M or F	Sight Word Vocabulary				Word Analysis Skills Used					
		Passage Level	% Accurate	WCPM	Comp. Level	Decoding Letter by Letter	Spelling Patterns, Chunks	Analogy	Prefixes, Suffixes, Base Words	Context Predict	Check
		Mean WCPM:									

encounters more than two or three unfamiliar words—he needs instruction that will help him develop a toolkit of strategies for coping with these words. He needs to see demonstrations of how skilled readers resolve word recognition problems by looking for meaningful word parts such as base words, prefixes, and suffixes; making analogies to known words; looking for familiar spelling patterns; mentally rehearsing the decoded word to see if it makes sense; and trying the word out in context. He also needs practice using these strategies. And again, I would encourage Alex to use some of these same strategies when he is trying to spell words that are in his listening and speaking vocabulary but not in his writing vocabulary.

Individual student results like Alex's can be compiled into class summaries.

The table in Figure 11.6 is an example of a class summary form for organizing results on student progress in the dimension of building reading vocabulary. It can be used to provide teachers with a description of current student performance and with diagnostic information on sight word acquisition, phonics and decoding, structural analysis, and contextual analysis.

In the first column, along with student names, teachers can indicate whether students are participating in categorical programs such as special education, Title I, or English as a second language. The purpose of most of these programs is to assist students academically, so up-close assessments of student performance provide evidence of how successful these programs are. The second column is for indicating gender. Because young males tend to have greater difficulty in learning to read than females, gender is also a variable for teachers to study in relation to student performance.

The table has two sections for recording student performance results. The columns under "Sight Word Vocabulary" provide space for recording results on passage level, the percentage of words the student read accurately, the number of words read correctly per minute, and comprehension level. The cell at the bottom of the WCPM column can be used to record the class average. The columns under "Word Analysis Skills Used" provide space for teachers to mark off skills and jot notes or examples about the way they are used by students. As students build larger sight vocabularies, fewer notes are needed. If teachers are studying students' use of strategies, they can ask students about a few words after they have finished reading the passage and responding to the comprehension questions.

As they build a large sight vocabulary, we would like students to quickly move beyond letter-by-letter decoding into more rapid techniques, such as using spelling patterns, analogies, word parts, and combinations of these. And, of course, we prefer they use context to confirm word accuracy and meaning, not just as clues to support a good guess.

Staff members can decide what information is most useful for them in thinking about their students as a group. They may want to organize results in different categories or fewer categories. The ones in the class summary table match the components in this dimension of reading development and provide information on fluency and comprehension. The categories under "Word Analysis Skills Used," combined with the use of sight words, are similar to Ehri's (1999, p. 1) five different ways students read words:

- By decoding; that is, by sounding out and blending graphemes into phonemes to form recognizable words.
- By pronouncing common spelling patterns, a more advanced form of decoding.
- By retrieving sight words from memory.
- By analogizing to words already known by sight.
- By using context cues to predict words.

In using class summaries such as Figure 11.6, which consolidates results from several components of reading development, teachers need to establish some rules if they want to study student progress across the year and aggregate the results for studying the effects of the reading program. For example, since this dimension focuses on sight words and word analysis skills, it's important that the passages students read be unfamiliar. It would not be a standard assessment if some students had an opportunity to read the passages silently first and other students did not. For "Sight Word Vocabulary," teachers need agreement about which passage level to record; for example, students' "highest independent level" in word accuracy and at least 70 percent comprehension could define the passage level recorded. To record notes about students' word analysis skills,

——————————— FIGURE 11.7 ———————————

Table for Building Reading Vocabulary—Fluency

On CD-ROM
Table 24

School: _____   No. of Classes/Teachers: _____   Total No. of Students: _____

School Year: _____   Grade: _____

Class/Teacher (No. of Students)	Dates of 1st Assessment		Dates of 2nd Assessment		Dates of 3rd Assessment	
	Mean WCPM	Class Range	Mean WCPM	Class Range	Mean WCPM	Class Range
Grade Level Mean						

Data Organized by: _____   Date: _____   Shared with Staff: _____

(Date)

anything a student used to resolve word problems at whatever level of passage difficulty could be recorded, not just skills used at the independent reading level.

The table in Figure 11.7 is for grade level teams and school staff working as a community to improve student performance. It can be used to organize class means on word accuracy in context (reported as words correct per minute during oral reading) into a grade level profile. Space has been provided for recording results for up to 10 classes. Using copies of the table, team leaders can record the mean words correct per minute (WCPM) and the class range for each group of students. The mean is a summary statistic for each class, and the range shows the variance for that class. When recording range, simply enter the lowest and highest WCPM scores. Data

from three assessment periods can be recorded so that staff can study changes across the year.

Look back at Figure 7.2, "Word Accuracy and Fluency During Oral Reading: Mean Words Correct per Minute Across the Grades." It's a snapshot of Blenheim Elementary's results from their second assessment. By just scanning the results, it's easy to see that students at each grade level have acquired more sight words and can read them at a faster rate than students in the lower grades, with the exception of 6th grade. However, unless you are used to studying fluency, reported in words correct per minute instead of words per minute, you may wonder what these results mean in terms of "average" grade level performance.

As is true with many questions about literacy, the external knowledge base is a rich source of information. Figure 11.8

FIGURE 11.8

Oral Reading Rates for Students in Grades 2 Through 5

Grade	Percentile	Fall WCPM	Winter WCPM	Spring WCPM
2	75	82	106	124
	50	53	78	94
	25	23	46	65
3	75	107	123	142
	50	79	93	114
	25	65	70	87
4	75	125	133	143
	50	99	112	118
	25	72	89	92
5	75	126	143	151
	50	105	118	128
	25	77	93	100

Source: From Hasbrouck, Jan E., & Tindal, Gerald (1992). Curriculum-based oral reading fluency norms for students in grades 2 through 5. *Teaching Exceptional Children, 24,* 41–44. Copyright 1992 by Council for Exceptional Children. Reprinted with permission.

presents the median oral reading rate for students in grades 2 through 5. (The median indicates the score of the student in the middle of each distribution.) These norms are based on the reading results of over 7,000 students and were shared with other educators in an article by Hasbrouck and Tindal (1992).

When we compare Blenheim's mean results (Figure 7.2) with these median scores, it's easy to see that many students at Blenheim are doing well in word accuracy and fluency. Of course, means, because they are averages, can hide information about students. Not all of Blenheim's students are doing well. For example, the 2nd grade range was 31 WCPM to 176 WCPM. So if you use Figure 11.8 to think about the 2nd grade student who read at an accuracy rate of 31 words correct per minute during the winter assessment, you'll see that student places below the 25th percentile for 2nd graders. This student needs to read a lot of books that are easy (at his independent level) and needs instructional strategies such as the picture word inductive model (Calhoun, 1999) to help build sight vocabulary and apply word analysis strategies.

Using Word Lists. Now, let's look at the word lists included in most IRIs and think about how they are developed and why we might use them.

In general, we can gather much more information about our students' reading skills when we have them read grade-level-designated passages. But there have been times when I've advised school teams to use the word lists as a starting point, especially when they wanted immediate information about students' reading vocabulary and levels. A student's results on a graded word list are a good predictor of whether she can read the words in texts at that grade level.

These graded word lists are usually developed by using word frequencies, especially the frequency of words in printed school materials. The Standard Frequency Index from the Carroll, Davies, and Richman (1971) *The American Heritage Word Frequency Book* is a common source. Figure 11.1 included the 100 most frequent words from this book, like *the, it, which,* and *him.* The more frequent words are found in the word lists (and passages) at lower grade levels. The less frequent words are found in the word lists at higher grade levels, words such as *stringent, pungent, instigate,* and *delusional.* Other common sources of word frequency in school materials include the *EDL Core Vocabularies in Reading, Mathematics, Science, and Social Studies* (Taylor et al., 1979) and *The Living Word Vocabulary: The Words We Know* (Dale & O'Rourke, 1976).

In developing these graded word lists, some authors use a sample of current school texts to double-check word frequency and the grade level(s) in which the words appear. Then the word lists are field-tested with groups of students until the authors are comfortable with the accuracy of each list as an indicator of a student's grade level performance in word recognition. These word lists, with their designated grade levels, serve multiple purposes. As a student reads the words, the examiner records which ones are recognized as sight words and which ones are decoded correctly. If the word is recognized and pronounced automatically (within one-half to one second), it is recorded as a sight word. And whether the word is decoded accurately or inaccurately, the examiner can note the decoding strategy used. For example, the examiner can note whether the student is using letter-by-letter blending predominantly, focusing primarily on initial consonants, using or not using word parts, or having difficulty with sight words he has seen many times. Figure 11.9 displays the results from one 4th grade student in May.

Roberto read the first seven words very rapidly, possibly making the first three errors carelessly. However, several words that were included in his social studies and science curriculum during his 4th grade year—*prairie, meadow,* and *voyage*—still had not made it into his sight vocabulary. His reading of this list places him at the frustration level. However, he did read 65 percent of the words as sight words and self-corrected his misreading of two other words. He has several strategies (use of syllables and analogies to known words). To further Roberto's reading progress, I would encourage extensive reading at his independent level along with repeated oral

FIGURE 11.9

Graded Word List: Student Responses

Student Name: "Roberto"   **Teacher:** Carter   **Word List: Grade 4**

	Sight Word	Decoded Correctly	Incorrect/ Not Attempted	Decoding Strategy Used
1. passenger	✓			
2. tropical			✓	"topical"
3. wrecked	✓			
4. adventurer			✓	"adventure" -er
5. announce	✓			
6. interrupted		✓		"interrupt" then ted
7. islands	✓			
8. prairie			✓	made several attempts
9. meadow			✓	mē dō, syllables & analogy
10. decided	✓			
11. energy	✓			
12. voyage			✓	voi āge, syllables & analogy
13. famous	✓			
14. settlers	✓			
15. signs	✓			
16. nervous	✓			
17. centered	✓			
18. wrong	✓			
19. expert		✓		syllables
20. ocean	✓			

Total Sight Words 13 /20   65 %

LEVELS		
Independent 18–20 90–100%	Instructional 14–17 70–85%	Frustration Below 14 Below 70%

reading, and I would also occasionally have Roberto audiotape his reading of a few paragraphs and then play back his reading as he followed along. If Roberto displays similar errors while reading connected text, he would benefit if his 5th grade teacher involved students in assessing their knowledge of key words in science and social studies units and in collecting related words and forming connections between these words.

Listening to students read isolated words, one by one, is not an authentic reading task; however, this measure does allow examiners to focus on the phonics and decoding skills students have.

Student results on automatic word recognition also serve as an indication of how far students have progressed in building a sight word vocabulary. For instance, using the highest independent level (usually 90 to 100 percent for word lists) as a criterion score, we can find out how many 1st grade students place at the preprimer, primer, or 1st grade level, and proceed up the grade levels until we know how many 5th graders are at the independent level on the 5th grade list or beyond. In this instance, we would be using each list to "stand in" for reading vocabulary at that grade level. And from 2nd grade up, we can check understanding of word meaning by identifying about 5 words from each list of about 20 words and ask students for explanations of these words. Some good possibilities include the following: from Figure 11.9—*passenger, tropical, prairie, voyage,* and *expert*; from the *Qualitative Reading Inventory-3* 2nd grade list—*noticed, clue, hatch, promise,* and *trade*; and from the *Basic*

Reading Inventory 5th grade list—*blush, marvelous, grace, nugget,* and *balcony*.

The table in Figure 11.10 is a class summary form for organizing sight word recognition results from word lists. Such summaries are useful for selecting instructional materials, determining how many students can read the classroom texts, and pairing students for partner reading. If a student's score in Column 1, "Sight Word Level," is on or above her appropriate chronological grade level placement that is good. As students move up the elementary school grades, if their scores begin to fall below their appropriate chronological grade, they may begin having problems using grade level texts. The wider the gap, the more serious the reading problem is.

We could also use the table for organizing class results from other instruments used in measuring word recognition, such as the *Word Identification Test* and *Word Comprehension Test* of the *Woodcock Reading Mastery Tests—Revised* (Woodcock, 1987).

If staff are focusing on building students' sight vocabulary and fluency, and they are already measuring these components during oral reading of passages, then assessing all students using graded word lists would not need to be done. However, there are a number of cases in which word lists can prove useful:

- When school staff have been using the same assessment instrument for several years, they may want another source of information about student progress in sight word acquisition and students' reading levels.

—————— FIGURE 11.10 ——————

Table for Sight Word Recognition: Class Summary

On CD-ROM
Table 25

School: _____   Teacher: _____   Grade: _____   School Year: _____

No. of Students in Class: _____   Dates Assessed: 1st _____   2nd _____   3rd _____
                                              Range (e.g., 8/25 to 9/12)

Student Name/ Special Ed. or ESL Code	M or F	1st Assessment		2nd Assessment		3rd Assessment		Notes
		Sight Word Level	Meaning No./% Correct	Sight Word Level	Meaning No./% Correct	Sight Word Level	Meaning No./% Correct	

- When teachers have students they are working with extensively on building sight vocabulary and decoding skills—whether these students are in the regular classroom, Title I, ESL, or special needs classes—they may use these graded lists more frequently to check progress.

- When teachers are concerned about a student's overreliance on context to figure out words, then having the student read isolated words provides additional diagnostic information. Since the research base indicates that poorer readers rely more on context as an aid to word recognition, it's useful to check the reading performance of struggling readers both with and without context.

- When a teacher or tutor has no information about a student's reading level and wishes to place stu-

dents into instructional materials or reading groups immediately, word list assessments can be handy.

Instruments and Procedures That Assess Primarily One Component

For any of the word analysis components we are especially concerned about for a single student, the entire student population, or subgroups within that population, we may select or develop a measure that primarily targets that component. A few examples follow.

Phonics. *The Names Test of Decoding* (Cunningham, 2000; Duffelmeyer, Kruse, Merkley, & Fyfe, 1994) is an easily administered test of phonics. Cunningham used names that sound like their spellings to assess students' decoding of unfamiliar words out of context. Her premise was that children often have many more names in their listening vocabulary than they do in their sight vocabulary and that asking students to read a list of names was far better than asking them to read lists of nonsense words. I especially like *The Names Test* because no "nonsense words" are used. My experience is that struggling readers I've worked with often have trouble with nonsense words, since they are often encouraged to "check and see if the word you figured out makes sense" when they are reading. Duffelmeyer and colleagues took Cunningham's (1990) original list of 25 names and added 10 more to increase the number of instances certain phonics elements were assessed, thus increasing the reliability of the instrument. In reading the list of 35 first and last names, a student's use of the following common phonics elements are assessed in multiple instances: initial consonants, 37 instances; initial consonant blends, 19; consonant digraphs, 15; short vowels, 36; long vowels/vowel consonant plus final "e," 23; vowel digraphs, 15; controlled vowels, 25; and schwa, 15. The article includes a sample protocol for recording student responses and a scoring matrix.

The Names Test is especially useful for assessing the phonics skills of struggling readers in grades 3 and 4. At times, I have also recommended that upper grade staff who believed that phonics was a problem for their students use it to check out their hypothesis.

Word Meaning. From the *Woodcock Reading Mastery Tests* (Woodcock, 1987), we might use the *Word Comprehension Test* to assess students' understanding of word meaning and the progress they are making in building a reading vocabulary. This test requires students to identify synonyms, antonyms, or an appropriate analogy for test words. Four "types" of vocabulary words are represented: general reading, science and mathematics, social studies, and the humanities.

Develop Good Standardized Up-Close Measures and Tend to Word Consciousness

Some readers will consider the procedures and instruments described in this section as nonstandardized measures that are most useful to the individual classroom teacher in determining student reading levels, grouping students for instruction, and planning instruction. My colleagues and I have found that using the results of the measures described here to look at the performance and progress of groups of students within a single class, in multiple classrooms, and across several years gives staff a much more accurate picture of student performance in their school than most collective measures in current use. However, for this to happen, staff have to take time to study the instruments, use them, discuss student responses and their own questions, decide which sections they will use as a collective body, and standardize some of the administration procedures.

Sight word acquisition and the use of word analysis skills never end. Probably as long as we continue to learn, we will continue to learn more words and more about words. It's a rare week that I do not learn more about some word or words—and feel the need to know more. And I still add words to my vocabulary that I have to decode—usually by analogy, syllables, and spelling patterns—or figure out through structural analysis and use of context. Then, if I'm not comfortable with my "phonological recoding" of the word, I often look it up in my *American Heritage Talking Dictionary*. I also have many words whose meaning I know but whose pronunciation I'm not comfortable with, even phonetically regular words such as "cicadas." We want our students to develop curiosity about words and the desire to use them well. Our assessments should provide knowledge for us and for them.

Questions to Explore for Building Reading Vocabulary (K–6)

Note: If you have not read the "Questions to Explore" in Chapter 10, begin there. Many of the recommendations for supporting emergent literacy apply to supporting students as they build reading vocabulary.

The list of questions in Figure 11.11 (page 151) about your reading program—the materials used, the instruction provided, the use of self-assessment by students, and the organization of students for learning—is provided to help you think about how the dimension of building reading vocabulary is supported in kindergarten through 6th grade and in special needs classrooms in your school. It is not an exhaustive list; instead, it addresses areas that often need to be strengthened and some of the com-

mon omissions in programs. (Your inquiries and responses to these questions are Cell 4 actions.)

A Short List of Recommended Resources

If you want to learn more about how to help students build reading vocabulary, the following items are useful resources:

➤ Ehri, L. C. (1998). Essential processes in learning to read words. In P. D. Pearson (Ed.), *New York State Reading Symposium: Final Report* (pp. 39–58). Albany, NY: New York State Education Department.

This paper is an easy-to-read synthesis of the research on how students learn to read sight words and the phases of acquisition in learning to read words (pre-alphabetic, partial alphabetic, full alphabetic, and consolidated alphabetic). It's an excellent resource to use in analyzing the instruction you are providing students and the assessment used to analyze their word learning.

➤ Gaskins, I. W., Ehri, L. C., Cress, C., O'Hara, C., & Donnelly, K. (1996/1997). Procedures for word learning: Making discoveries about words. *The Reading Teacher, 50*(4), 312–327.

This article describes how the Benchmark Word Identification Program was improved by incorporating Ehri's theories and research on sight word learning. This article is an excellent example of continuous action research on student progress and program quality.

➤ Stahl, S. A. Duffy-Hester, A. M., & Stahl, K. A. D. (1998). Everything you wanted to know about phonics (but were afraid to ask). *Reading Research Quarterly, 33*(3), 338–355.

Teachers can use this article to self-assess their current phonics instruction and review different approaches to teaching phonics.

➤ Johnston, F. R. (1999). The timing and teaching of word families. *The Reading Teacher, 53*(1), 64–75.

This article provides a good overview of why and how to teach students to decode words by using rimes and phonograms.

➤ Cunningham, P. M. (2000). *Phonics they use: Words for reading and writing* (3rd ed.). New York: Longman.

This is an easy-to-read resource loaded with specific strategies for teaching the alphabet, phonological and phonemic awareness, phonics, and vocabulary (especially high-frequency words), as well as for teaching reading and writing together to help students accelerate their literacy learning. The chapter on decoding and understanding big words includes instructional techniques for teaching students to use prefixes and suffixes. If you are worried about the quality of phonics instruction, this is the book I recommend.

If you are working on expanding vocabulary, these next two books are essential to your professional library. If it's a schoolwide effort, every teacher and paraeducator should have his own copy.

➤ Beck, I. L., McKeown, M. G., & Kucan, L. (2002). *Bringing words to life: Robust vocabulary instruction.* New York: Guilford Press.

The authors present techniques for selecting highly utilitarian and engaging words for study and multidimensional strategies for teaching word meaning. It includes lists of words from 80 popular children's books. This book is most appropriate for elementary teachers.

➤ Stahl, S. A. (1999). *Vocabulary development.* Cambridge, MA: Brookline Books.

This short book (59 pages) provides a review of the research on vocabulary knowledge. Two chapters, "General Principles for Teaching Words" and "Procedures for Teaching Word Meanings as Concepts," are especially useful in helping teachers strengthen their vocabulary (word meaning) instruction. This is a good K–12 resource.

—————— FIGURE 11.11 ——————

Questions to Explore for Building Reading Vocabulary (K–6)

Curriculum Materials

1. To have students continuously practicing their word analysis skills and adding to their sight vocabularies, you need lots of books in every classroom. What is the size of your classroom collections? Around 1,000 is a good average for a print-rich learning environment for each K–3 classroom, then about 500 for each grade 4 through 6 classroom. Check your fiction/nonfiction balance. Is it approximately 50/50? Do the collections cover a range of grade levels from picture books to juvenile literature to resource books? Does the content cover a range of interests? Do most of the informational books develop or expand on the science, social studies, mathematics, and fine arts content of the elementary school curriculum?

2. How are your classroom libraries organized to support easy access to a range of appropriate texts? Are books organized in boxes or shelves by topic, by genre? Are there some boxes of "easy practice" books with reading levels indicated?

3. Does each classroom have a computer dedicated to running talking dictionary software (any old one that takes a CD-ROM and has speakers will do) available for students to use when they are reading independently? The CDs for the *American Heritage Talking Dictionary* and *MacMillan Talking Dictionary* cost about $12.00. In classes with students who are learning to speak English as a second language, is there a dedicated computer with a translator program available? CD-ROMs with 10 to 50 languages range in cost from $20 to $50, and some of the simpler Spanish to English and English to Spanish programs are even less expensive.

4. Do classrooms in which reading and vocabulary are taught have large vinyl pocket charts for teachers to use to display words during explicit instruction and concept attainment lessons? Do K–1 classrooms and teachers who work with special needs and ESL students have sets of magnetic letters for students to use in spelling words and practicing their phonics skills?

Instruction

5. What is being done in every classroom to systematically help students expand their reading vocabulary? This includes actions promoted as part of the reading program, such as extensive reading in and out of school; instructional moves, such as reading aloud to students; and teaching strategies, such as Text Talk (Beck et al., 2002), semantic mapping (Heimlich & Pittelman, 1986), and semantic feature analysis (Pittelman, Heimlich, Berglund, & French, 1991).

6. Have students been taught a technique for determining if books are at their independent reading level? For example, some teachers ask students to use a "three finger" rule of thumb for determining if a book will be easy for them to read. If they encounter more than three unfamiliar words per page on the first page or two, it's probably too difficult for them to use to easily build reading vocabulary.

7. For K–1 students, some 2nd grade students, and older struggling readers, does daily instruction include choral reading with big books and repeated oral reading?

(continues)

——————————— FIGURE 11.11 CONTINUED ———————————

8. How much demonstration of word analysis skills is occurring? Whether it's blending syllables or using analogies for decoding words phonetically, recognizing and using prefixes, or using context for confirming word meaning, are there enough demonstrations by the teacher, and enough massed then distributed practice by students, for them to become highly skilled and transfer these actions to their independent reading? It's difficult to specify the number of demonstrations and practices needed because the complexity of content and skills vary, as do student populations and individuals. However, more are generally needed if students are just beginning to learn the skill or are having difficulty applying it. For any content and skill sets students need to master, teachers will need to provide at least three or four demonstrations, three or more guided practice examples, and three or more independent practice examples just to get students started. By observing what students can do during their practice, teachers can determine the content and emphasis of the next demonstrations and how many are needed. For example, a 1st grade teacher working on blending onsets and rimes may teach one or two short (around 15 minutes long) explicit instruction lessons a day for 10 days or until most of the students have some level of skill with the task. The teacher would probably begin with the most common phonograms, such as "an," "at," "in," and "it." Then, she would help students apply these skills as they engage in daily reading and writing activities. Throughout the year, lessons would be taught that required students to apply this skill—recognizing and blending onsets and rimes—to more complex spelling patterns, such as "fl-ew," "bl-ew," "thr-ew," and "scr-ew."

9. How is discussion used to support vocabulary development? Students need opportunities to practice using new words, especially students with limited vocabularies. Both open discussions among students about word meanings and guided or directed discussions among teachers and students are needed. When teachers design lessons and cooperative group work so that all students prepare responses covertly, more students are more actively engaged in processing word meaning, and they have additional opportunities to rehearse their responses and use of the word(s) being discussed.

10. How is word consciousness being taught? Many teachers use a "word of the day" approach, beginning with teacher-selected words and then moving to student-selected words. These minilessons on words include a definition and explanation of the word, its use in various contexts, why it was selected, and how it relates to the lives or work of students. As the year progresses, do students as well as teachers "teach" words to the class? Some teachers share words that made them pause or phrases that are particularly arresting, and some model and explain how they recognize and figure out unfamiliar words they encounter in text.

11. How is phonics taught? What is important is that instruction is provided that helps students develop skill in using letter/sound relationships. First grade is a crucial year. This does not mean that teachers do not work on phonics skills in kindergarten and 2nd grade, just that most students need to exit 1st grade able to phonetically decode regular short words and be on their way to decoding multisyllabic words.
In digesting the Report of the National Reading Panel (2000), many policymakers and educators have reacted as if synthetic phonics (sounds are taught first, then children read words with those sounds) is the only successful route to helping students learn letter/sound relationships. They need to take a closer look at the nature and quantity of studies that made it through the National Reading Panel screen and at what some of the lead scholars of the report have to say outside of the constraints of the federally funded report (see especially Ehri, Nunes, Stahl, & Willows, 2001; Camilli, Vargas, & Yurecko, 2003).

—————— FIGURE 11.11 CONTINUED ——————

I think this statement from Ehri and her colleagues summarizes the guidelines for instructional approaches we can use from the NRP:

> The effectiveness of two types of approaches for teaching phonics systematically was examined in our analysis, a synthetic approach teaching students to decode grapheme-phoneme units, and a larger-unit approach teaching students to blend subsyllabic units such as onsets, rimes, and phonograms. . . . Findings indicated that the two approaches did not differ in their impact on reading, with both producing effects close to moderate in size. (Ehri, Nunes, Stahl, & Willows, 2001, pp. 429–430)

12. How is structural analysis taught and what is taught? Is enough time allocated for students to develop skill? Does instruction in using meaningful word parts begin in kindergarten?

13. To develop phonics, structural, and contextual analysis skills, students need both explicit instruction lessons that explain, demonstrate, and provide practice with these skills *and* inductive concept formation lessons that engage them in analyzing words and texts and identifying patterns, forming and testing their hypotheses about these patterns, and applying them as they read and write. Are your students provided with an instructional balance that gives them opportunities to learn by listening, observing, and practicing (explicit instruction and direct instruction lessons), as well as by analyzing, forming hypotheses about how language works, and applying tested generalizations to literacy tasks (inductive concept formation lessons)?

Assessment

14. Are students asked to self-evaluate their use of word analysis skills? Even 1st grade students can keep a log of what they do when they need to figure out an unfamiliar word. Items such as these show up on their lists:

- Is there a rhyming pattern I know?
- Do I know the beginning sounds or the ending sounds?
- Does it sound like a word I know?
- Does it make sense?
- Is there a picture clue?
- Reread the page and use what I know.
- Skip the word and come back later.
- Ask someone.

Organizing for Learning—Grouping and Scheduling

15. Word analysis skills can be taught effectively to both small groups and whole-class groups. The results of up-close assessments identify students who can be productively grouped for ad hoc skills work, either because they are struggling with a skill or because they are more advanced than most of their classmates. How are students grouped to maximize instructional time?

16. Are students provided with the instructional *time* and *opportunity* to develop a large sight word vocabulary and skill in phonics, structural analysis, and contextual analysis? To develop sight word vocabulary, they need to read a lot of books at their independent reading level (where they recognize 98 percent or more of the words). Part of each day needs to be dedicated to students reading books of choice. How much time do students spend reading easy-to-read books (books that are at their independent reading level)?

12

Reading Comprehension

Think about reading comprehension. How do you know when it occurs? What does it look like for good 1st grade, 3rd grade, 5th grade, or 8th grade readers? For highly proficient adult readers?

Most of us read because we can comprehend what we read. Reading helps us satisfy our needs for knowledge and understanding. As we interact with the printed ideas and stories of others, our responses vary widely, ranging anywhere from conceptual annoyance when our beliefs contrast harshly with the author's to great emotional pleasure when we are immersed in a grand tale. Our skill in comprehending text allows us to develop new knowledge, confirm current understanding, apply new or different ideas, and enjoy the stories, poetry, and perceptions of others. These results are always there for us because we learned to read proficiently. But how did we move from reading and understanding the word "tree" to reading and understanding *A Tree Is Growing* (Dorros, 1997); from understanding *Go, Dog, Go!* (Eastman, 1961) to *The Call of the Wild* (London, 1903/2000)? Practice in reading, application of our current knowledge, and seeking to understand the ideas of others as presented in text are part of the answer.

In this chapter, I will examine reading comprehension and processes that support comprehension. We'll first focus on how the act of reading comprehension is defined. We'll also review some of the characteristic behaviors of highly skilled readers. Then we'll look at the differences between expository nonfiction text and narrative, primarily fiction text, and think about what these differences mean for curriculum and assessment. Finally, we'll pull it all back together as we think about what to teach and assess in our elementary school reading program and how to organize student results for individual and collective study.

Describing Reading Comprehension and Good Reader Behaviors

Reading comprehension is often defined as understanding what has been read. A more accurate and scholarly definition would be that *reading comprehension is constructing meaning from and interacting with text,* generally using prior knowledge as well as the information in the text.

When I was teaching reading comprehension, it was useful for me to think about interaction with text almost on a continuum from less personal and minimal engagement to more personal and more in-depth engagement. The degree of engagement depended on the purposes for reading. These three questions represented points on the continuum:

- What does the print say?
- What does this mean to me?
- What does this mean to me for my purposes at this time?

The first question, "*What does the print say?*" requires the reader to literally translate sets of symbols that are put together to stand for objects and beings, actions, and ideas (real or imaginary), and the relationships among them. The second question involves the reader in filtering the information provided in the text through her own personal experiences; knowledge of the topic or events; and knowledge of the syntax, forms, and functions of written English. The external printed text and internal prior

knowledge work together in short-term memory, yielding responses to "*What does this mean to me?*" When proficient readers engage with longer or more complex text, they have an array of more consciously controlled "smaller" processes and strategies they use. The printed text, their automatic use of internalized prior knowledge, and the conscious application of appropriate processes and strategies answer the question, "*What does this mean to me for my purposes at this time?*"

Figure 12.1 is my current synthesis of the cognitive processes proficient readers use fluidly as they comprehend text. The first column lists cognitive processes that skilled readers use automatically, with little conscious effort. The second column lists cognitive processes and strategies that readers are more aware of and bring to bear flexibly, as needed. Proficient readers selectively apply these more conscious comprehension processes before, during, and after reading: they may use them as they seek to follow text and understand the ideas presented; they may use them to help recall and connect ideas and concepts; and they may use them when composing as reminders of what needs to be done to make stories or messages coherent and easy for their readers to understand. They appear to coordinate their use of these processes and strategies with great mental agility.

Of course, there may be movement across the first (automatic processes) and second (conscious, less automatic

--- FIGURE 12.1 ---

Reading Comprehension: What Proficient Readers Do as They Construct Meaning and Interact with Text

Automatic Processes

Use text/graphic information and prior knowledge

- Use word knowledge and sight vocabulary

- Use world knowledge

- Use knowledge about the English language and how it works

- Use knowledge about how communication works in print

- Read fluently and vary rate according to purpose and nature of the text

Conscious, Less Automatic Processes

Use a range of processes as needed

- Be aware of purpose or goals for reading

- Make predictions about content and ideas

- Determine importance (including main idea) and read selectively

- Figure out the meanings of unfamiliar words that are important to overall meaning

- Use text and prior knowledge to connect and generate ideas, mental models, or images

- Connect ideas in text to develop a coherent message (follow the message or story)

- Use organizational structure and discourse knowledge

- Consolidate, compare, and synthesize text/graphic information

- Use multiple sources of information

- Evaluate author's purpose and quality of text/graphic presentation

Monitoring for Meaning

- Continuously monitor for meaning and rationale of text/graphic presentation: literal, inferential, personal, application, and reasoning of author/self

The Results of Comprehension Processes

Knowledge: Adding to, confirming, or revising one's personal knowledge

Application: Providing support for performing everyday tasks, solving problems, and engaging in more intellectual tasks

Intellectual and Emotional Affect: Engagement with the ideas and experiences presented in text

Generating New Knowledge and Applications: Going beyond what is "known" and generating hypotheses for testing experientially or theoretically

processes) columns as a reader brings more or less conscious attention to the use of a process. Monitoring for Meaning is placed across both columns because sometimes it happens so rapidly and integratively that it's more automatic, and at other times it requires much more attention. The results of these automatic processes and more conscious comprehension processes and strategies are summarized at the bottom under knowledge, application, intellectual and emotional affect, and generating new knowledge and applications.

Figure 12.1 helps me "see" what we are trying to develop through our reading program. All of the processes listed make up the macroprocess of "reading comprehension." They represent the good reader behaviors we want students to exhibit.

Let's try a simple example that primarily requires the use of the more automatic processes described in the first column. Read the two sentences in italics. Think about what they say in print and what they mean:

> She looked at the daisy on the windowsill and thought about how it was reaching for sunlight. Was she like the daisy?

Now, what were some of the comprehension processes that occurred?

- *Use of word knowledge and sight vocabulary.* You knew all the words. If you were not familiar with "windowsill," it was relatively easy to figure out using structural analysis and context.
- *Use of world knowledge.* Among other points, you were aware that the daisy was a live plant, not a silk one. You

understood that it probably has its leaves or flowers turned toward the sun, an example of phototropism, as it fulfills one of its basic needs for survival (water, food, and *light*).

- *Use of knowledge about the English language and how it works.* The order of the words and ideas made sense and let you know that the experience (viewing of the daisy by a female) was happening and that the female was comparing herself to the daisy. Much is omitted but understood because you are familiar with the syntax and order of reflection.
- *Use of knowledge about how communication works in print.* Someone is sharing an experience, a personal analogy about needs, and a reflection with others.
- *Fluent reading.* You probably read the sentences quickly, with good phrasing and appropriate intonation and expression.

To comprehend those two sentences and connect the ideas between them, you used conceptual knowledge stored in your long-term memory: knowledge about the meanings of the words, knowledge about plants and the needs of living things, linguistic knowledge of how the English language works, and discourse knowledge. Your skill in reading the text fluently and your working memory supported your quick grasp of the message being shared.

Let's think about an example that would require most readers to move beyond the rapid blending of printed text and prior knowledge used to understand the two sentences about the daisy.

The task described next requires greater use of the less automatic processes listed in the second column.

Imagine you're reading dense text on genome research and its implications. You're trying to think about your personal position and understand the author's. You stop regularly to rethink and connect ideas or to jot down implications as you think of them. You find yourself paraphrasing several key points, then rereading the text to check your accuracy of interpretation. You make a list of unanswered questions—your metacognitive skills are in high gear. You are striving to accurately derive author-based meaning, interpret it in terms of your own life and belief system, and then decide on your position or actions in relation to genome research.

Why should we pay so much attention to these invisible cognitive processes? Because your conceptualization of what happens during reading comprehension—which may be different from mine—guides your curriculum, instruction, and assessment decisions. What is important is that it includes somewhere, in some form, many of the processes addressed here. The degree to which one can utilize the literal information in the text almost simultaneously with information that resides in the mind has much to do with the development of reading comprehension. Of course, much remains to be learned about how we use connected text as a meaningful chain and how our prior knowledge interacts with the links in that chain to yield ideas, concepts, stories, and affect. But much progress has been made in the last 10 years.

As the results of previous and current research on reading comprehension continue to be synthesized, new conceptions are generated. Pressley's (2000) concise analysis of "processes above the word level" and how good readers automatically apply some processes and more consciously apply others helps us understand the complex interplay of cognitive processes that yield reading with comprehension. The emphasis on the "outcomes" of reading comprehension by the scholars who generated the RAND report (2001) has great promise for providing instructional and assessment knowledge that we can use to support student progress in reading. The good news for us right now is that knowledge and research are available about what skilled readers do. And, as Pressley (2000), Duke (2001), and others remind us, the processes and strategies used by proficient readers can become goals in our reading program.

Comprehension of Connected Text: Curriculum Content and Assessment Emphases

As we think about our K–8 curriculum and what to assess in reading comprehension, let's go back to the short list of components in Figure 2.1, "Dimensions of Reading Development Recommended for Study," under "Comprehension of Connected Text." One component addresses engagement with expository, nonfiction text and graphic information. One addresses engagement with narrative, primarily fictitious text and illustrations. And one addresses basic processes that support reading with comprehension and the accumulation of knowledge:

fluency and monitoring for understanding. With these three components, I can work on anything I want from Figure 12.1. I can decide at which grade levels processes will be emphasized and which aspects of these processes will be assessed.

Of course, automatic and conscious comprehension processes used by proficient readers apply to any genre. Most of our school and district language arts programs include a range of genres from nursery rhymes and folk tales to editorials. However, for exploring reading comprehension development from grade to grade in the elementary school, I recommend beginning your study with students' understanding of exposition and of narrative.

Why give such prominence to comprehending nonfiction, informational text? In many classrooms and schools, we have much work to do in improving the curricular and instructional balance between expository nonfiction and narrative fiction. Research from the United States and England (Duke, 2000; Millard, 1997) indicates there is a major imbalance in reading and sharing quality nonfiction, informative prose with students, especially at the primary level (kindergarten through grade 3). The emphasis on fiction, especially narrative fiction stories, along with lack of instruction about how to comprehend and compose expository, informative text, may affect students' attitudes toward reading (especially in boys) and their ability to comprehend nonfiction, informative prose as well as their skill in writing it.

Many of us have taken reading courses and studied books and articles that focused solely on the use of fiction and narrative in kindergarten through 3rd grade, but we know this does not make sense in terms of what our students enjoy and can experience. My 1st graders took pleasure in both storybooks and informational, nonfiction books. In fact, many of them liked writing "expositions" about their bean plants more than they enjoyed writing creative stories.

In the last 15 years, several scholars have addressed the fiction-nonfiction imbalance in schools. Hiebert reminded us in 1991 that "expository text should consume a substantial portion of the elementary literacy and language curriculum" (p. 482). The work of Langer (1986) and Pappas (1991a, 1991b, 1993) has shown "that young children can understand and use nonfiction texts very well—if they're given the chance" (Pappas, 1991a, p. 449). And Duke (2000, 2002) continues to confront us and make the case for teaching comprehension of informational text with young children. The picture is similar in writing (Kamberelis, 1999; Newkirk, 1989; Wollman-Bonilla, 2000).

We do not know if or to what degree the demands on comprehension and memory vary from one genre to the other. What we do know is that narrative texts and use of fiction have tended to dominate literacy instruction in elementary schools in the United States (Duke, 2000; Stein & Trabasso, 1982). Yet, except for basal reading texts and literary anthologies, expository, nonfiction prose is dominant in the textbooks we give students to use as learning tools, especially in 4th grade and above. Once students leave school, most of the prose they are expected to understand in their daily work is nonfiction expository or procedural text. And "[a]pproximately 96% of the sites on the World Wide Web are expository in form" (Duke, 2002).

Some scholars suggest that the difficulty in reading nonfiction, informative text may be partially responsible for the infamous "4th grade slump" (Chall, Jacobs, & Baldwin, 1990). To make sure that exposition does not get lost in the usual dominance of story, students' development in each genre should be examined. Think about your own curriculum choices when sharing books with kindergarten and 1st grade students. What about students in the upper grades? What is the current balance in your classroom? Your school?

Let's define these two genres and think about their structural differences and how these differences influence reader expectations and affect our daily choices about curriculum and assessment of student performance.

Understanding and Learning from Expository, Nonfiction Text

Well-written expositions are designed to communicate specific information or teach readers about a topic or idea(s). To support the reader's understanding, authors of exposition organize their points to present logical relationships among concepts. Thus, they often organize their text presentations differently from the storylines or sequences found in narratives.

Some of the most common organizational patterns used in exposition include

- comparison and contrast,
- cause and effect or causal analysis,
- problem-solution or question-response,
- attribution (list of characteristics, definitions) or classification,
- sequence (may or may not be chronological or enumerated),
- methodical or conceptual descriptions, and
- combinations of the above.

These organizational patterns used in writing—intentionally selected and used by the author to convey author-based meaning and support the message he is trying to share—are called text structures in reading. Students who can recognize and use these text structures are better able to comprehend and recall the information in the text, probably because these organizational patterns represent conceptual connections among the ideas presented.

Let's look at the macrostructure of some simple examples. Read the following two examples of exposition from informational trade books. Think about how the author has organized her information and how you are processing and interacting with it.

The first is from *What's the Difference? A Guide to Some Familiar Animal Look-Alikes* (1993), written by Elizabeth A. Lacey and illustrated by Robert Shetterly:

Bison or Buffalo*

Especially in North America the terms "bison" and "buffalo" have sometimes been used as if both meant the same thing. Actually, these are different animals.

The animal native to the plains country of North America and the forests of northern Europe is the bison. . . .

All bison are herbivores (plant eaters). . . . All buffalo are grass grazers. . . .

Buffalo are the animals native to Asia and Africa. Some six species are recognized, including dwarf varieties. Buffalo are externally different from bison and internally different as well—bison have 14 pairs of ribs, buffalo have 13. Darker and less shaggy than bison, buffalo are most commonly around 5 feet (1.5 meters) tall at the shoulder. . . .

Thousands of years ago buffalo were domesticated, meaning they were tamed and then bred specifically to serve humans. As a result they are common today, particularly in Europe and Asia. One estimate put the world population of water buffalo at 75 million, with 50 million of those in India and Pakistan. . . .

Did you recognize the contrast and comparison pattern in *What's the Difference?* How many signals did the author provide that helped you organize information about bison and buffalo? Not considering the other contrasts provided, such as between the reduction of bison in Europe and that in North America, there are numerous signals for us, beginning with the title and heading and the use of signal words such as "different," and continuing on to location, sizes, and differences in modern-day population figures, to name the most obvious ones. Now look at the excerpt* from *How Seeds Travel* (1982), written by Cynthia Overbeck with photographs by Shabo Hani:

Source: From How Seeds Travel by Cynthia Overbeck. Text copyright 1982 by Lerner Publications Company, a division of Lerner Publishing Group, Minneapolis, MN. Adapted from *Where the Seeds Go*, copyright 1978 by Shabo Hani; English translation rights arranged with Akane Shobo Company, Ltd., Japan. Used by permission. All rights reserved.

A yellow dandelion appears in the middle of a smooth green lawn. A wildflower pushes its way up through a crack in a city sidewalk. A tiny maple tree sprouts on a rocky hillside. Why are these plants growing in such places? How did they come to sprout and take root so far away from other plants of their kind?

The dandelion, wildflower, and maple tree have been brought to the places where they are growing by traveling seeds. In this book, you will learn about the many fascinating ways in which plant seeds move from place to place. . . . (p. 5)

Sometimes people play a role in helping seeds to grow into plants. They put seeds into the rich earth of gardens or fields, water them, and give them fertilizer and other plant foods. But plants in their natural state do not need human help in order to reproduce themselves. They have many ways of making sure that their seeds get to just the right places so that they will be able to grow.

Some seeds travel by sailing on the wind or floating on water. Others hitchhike on the fur of animals. All traveling seeds have special features and structures that help them to take advantage of the free rides that nature offers. . . . (p. 6)

How about *How Seeds Travel*? Did you identify it as either question/response or problem/solution? What were the clues you used? How did the author help you connect ideas about how seeds travel? Did you find the questions to be good advance organizers? Were the examples both provocative and illustrative? In many ways, this well-written book answers many how and why questions about the movement of seeds from one place to another and how they function in plant reproduction.

If you were to look at *Backyard Birds* (1999), by Jonathan Latimer and Karen Nolting, or *All About Turtles* (2000), by Jim Arnosky, you would find many examples of attribution (characteristics), classification, and the integral use of photographs and drawings to support meaning-making. If you were to read *When Hunger Calls* (1994), by Bert Kitchen, or *Silent Spring* (1962), by Rachel Carson, you would find many examples of cause and effect or causal analysis. Of course, extended text may include many organizational patterns, two major patterns combined, or may not have an identifiable pattern or structure at all. What is important is helping our students recognize when the author has organized information to support learning and assimilation into current knowledge and to use these organizational patterns or text structures as comprehension, learning, and retrieval aids.

Understanding and Relating to Narrative Text (Primarily Fiction)

Narrative is defined as stories composed of event sequences experienced by imaginary or real characters. The primary focus of the narrative is to tell a story that entertains or provokes affect in the reader. Narratives may be only a few sentences long or may be novel-length, but most have a similar structure. This structure is often described as *story grammar* in an attempt to explain the common elements in stories and how these elements function.

Story grammars range from very simple—with a single setting (time and location), a main character with a problem or goal, and a single event with a beginning, middle, and end—to more complex structures that include multiple characters, settings (time and place), problems and major goals of main characters, plots and resolutions, affect patterns, themes and morals, and points of view and perspectives (Graesser, Golding, & Long, 1991). Over time and with much exposure to the typical order and nature of events in stories, readers can predict the literary elements and anticipate the kinds of experiences that will be revealed.

While narrative can certainly be nonfiction, as in historical narratives and biographies, here the emphasis is more on fiction. We can use the genre of the narrative story to teach students the differences between fiction and nonfiction and the complexities authors deal with in attempting to render accurate interpretations of real events and experiences.

To emphasize the differences in structure and reader expectation, let's look at two excerpts from narrative fiction trade books. Try to be conscious of the comprehension processes at work when you read the expository excerpts. See if you can detect and feel any differences between the excerpts in terms of structure, rhythm, affect, and your own expectations based on your knowledge of story grammar.

These are the first three sentences of *Harlequin's Story*:

> Once upon a time on a little island off the coast of Georgia, there lived a young calico kitten whose name was Harlequin. Most of the kittens in the neighborhood liked to sit in windows and watch the world go by or laze contentedly on sunny porches, but not Harlequin. She liked to roam in the marsh and bring special treats back to her owners. One day . . . .

And here are the first few pages* of *Because of Winn-Dixie* (2000), by Kate DiCamillo:

> My name is India Opal Buloni, and last summer my daddy, the preacher, sent me to the store for a box of macaroni-and-cheese, some white rice, and two tomatoes and I came back with a dog. This is what happened: I walked into the produce section of the Winn-Dixie grocery store to pick out my two tomatoes and I almost bumped right into the store manager. He was standing there all red-faced, screaming and waving his arms around.
>
> "Who let a dog in here?" he kept on shouting. "Who let a dirty dog in here?"
>
> At first, I didn't see a dog. . . .
>
> And then the dog came running around the corner. He was a big dog. And ugly. And he looked like he was having a real good time. His tongue was hanging out and he was wagging his tail. He skidded to a stop and smiled right at me. I had never before in my life seen a dog smile, but that is what he did. He pulled back his lips and showed me all his teeth. Then he wagged his tail so hard that he knocked some oranges off a display, and they went rolling everywhere, mixing in with the tomatoes and onions and green peppers. (pp. 1–2)

Did you feel story structure at work—setting, main character, problem, and a hint of a theme or moral—in the excerpt from *Harlequin's Story?* How about in *Because of Winn-Dixie?* Did you identify, almost automatically, setting, main characters, the introduction of the problem and anticipation of upcoming events, point of view and perspective, and a bit of the theme to be developed?

---

*Source: Because of Winn-Dixie, Copyright © 2000 by Kate DiCamillo. Reprinted by permission of the publisher Candlewick Press, Inc., Cambridge, MA.

Did you notice any differences in how you engaged with these narrative stories in contrast to how you engaged with the expository selections? Did you feel differences in the rhythm of your reading, even though you were probably reading silently? Did you find yourself predicting future events or story episodes? Did you find your affect engaged humorously, whimsically, or ominously?

The differences in the characteristics of these two genres can be blurry. Even if we define expository prose as being written to inform, and narrative as having a storyline and being written primarily to entertain or provoke affect, we can all think of good exceptions. Playwrights, novelists, and poets write to inform, just as essayists sometimes write to entertain (see, for example, Benjamin Franklin's satires). But there is enough difference in form and author's purpose for us to productively pursue a more balanced curriculum and assessment of each in our literacy curriculum.

Basic Processes That Support Comprehension of Connected Text: Fluency and Self-Monitoring

Fluency and self-monitoring are two basic reading processes that make our understanding of connected text possible. *Fluency* is the ability to read text with reasonable speed, accuracy, and expressiveness. Readers need a certain level of fluency to support comprehension of extended text and the accumulation of knowledge through reading. As they progress through school, most students' reading rates increase steadily—if they have good oral reading models and many opportunities to practice their oral

--- FIGURE 12.2 ---

Fluency Reading Rates K–12

Grade	Words per Minute (WPM)	Grade	Words per Minute (WPM)
1	60–90	6	195–220
2	85–120	7	215–245
3	115–140	8	235–270
4	140–170	9	250–270
5	170–195	12	250–300

"Reading rate guidelines must be applied with caution because a number of factors will influence rate. For instance, oral reading is slower than silent reading. The reading rates for younger children are typically established from oral reading activity while the rates for older children are established from silent reading activity. But younger children may exhibit little difference in oral and silent reading rates, while for older students that gap should be quite substantial." (p. 72)

Source: From Richard Allington (2001). *What Really Matters for Struggling Readers.* Published by Allyn and Bacon, Boston, MA. Copyright © 2001 by Pearson Education. Reprinted by permission of the publisher.

reading in appropriately difficult texts (at their independent reading level). Of course, our long-term goal for students is not fluent oral reading, which for proficient readers is much slower than silent reading; oral reading fluency is a goal *en route* to fluent silent reading.

In a chapter titled "Kids Need to Learn to Read Fluently," Allington (2001) includes a "general range of adequate reading rates by grade levels" and some reminders about interpreting students' reading rate. I have listed these in Figure 12.2.

Please note that the rates in Figure 12.2 are for words per minute (WPM). In Chapter 11, when we were focusing on word accuracy, we discussed using words correct per minute during oral reading (Figure 11.8).

Students who read extended text too slowly are likely to have difficulty connecting the ideas and concepts to form a coherent message, learning the information provided in text, or following the intricacies of character development and plot in stories. While beginning readers seem to comprehend quite well with low levels of fluency when reading picture or simple picture informational texts, they are probably assisted with meaning-making by the corresponding illustrations. When the texts become lengthier (and the illustrations more sparse), fluency becomes more important to comprehension because the capacity of our short-term memory is limited. In general, as students advance from grade to grade, their reading rates must also advance, or they will be unable to handle the academic tasks and the information provided in their content area textbooks.

We have some students who are very accurate in reading words, but they are not fluent readers. Some read word-for-word without phrasing or emphasis; other students lack the skill to use phrasing, text signals such as punctuation, and emphasis and stress effectively, impeding their comprehension processes. To use a simple example, think about how many times you have heard beginning readers or older struggling readers read right though punctuation as if the author did not include it. Try reading this passage orally, word by word, without using punctuation as cues to phrasing and intonation. How does this affect meaning?

"Mom, have you seen my blue Nikes? I bet Anna hid them."

"I didn't!" said her sister.

Martina walked into the kitchen where her mom was working. There were her sneakers tucked under the counter, right where she'd left them last night.

Mother smiled.

We want to tend and monitor the development of students' oral reading fluency so they have it when they need it, and more importantly, to help them develop good pace, phrasing, rhythm and appropriate emphasis/stress when reading silently, because fluency supports comprehension. We also want our students to be able to easily vary their reading rate based on the nature of the text and their own purposes for reading.

Self-monitoring, also known as application of metacognitive knowledge, is another basic process that is integral to our understanding of connected text. Good readers monitor their comprehension of text as they read; they are metacognitive. This means they have knowledge about themselves as learners and their purposes for reading, knowledge about the nature of the task and how well they are engaging with it, and knowledge about the strategies they may employ in accomplishing their tasks and reaching their goals (Garner, 1987).

Good readers, including good beginning readers, are aware of when they understand the text and when they are having difficulties with some aspect of it. When they have a problem, they know how to fix it. They may begin by rereading; they may review the surrounding information; they may seek additional information; or they may decide to diagram or outline the connections made thus far.

However, applying metacognitive and self-regulatory processes to reading comprehension takes far more than simply being aware of when one understands what is being read and how to "fix" problems when they occur. The application of metacognitive knowledge by proficient readers is ongoing and flexible; it includes an awareness of the comprehension processes and strategies (Figure 12.1) that are in one's personal toolkit and which strategies are best bets for use with particular text. Proficient readers have metacognitive control—conscious executive control—of their reading comprehension processes; this is why they have such mental agility in their use of a variety of processes. The good news is that these metacognitive and self-monitoring processes can be taught (Bransford, Brown, & Cocking, 1999; Garner, 1987).

It takes time and much practice within the domain of cognitive activity—in our case, much practice in reading—to develop metacognitive knowledge. But from the very beginning of formal reading instruction, we want students to try to make sense of what they read and to employ the strategies they have to support their efforts. For example, if the text in a Touchy-Feely book states, "The teddy bear has a brown *furry* tummy" on a page that includes a picture with a teddy bear that has a furry tummy for the reader to touch, and the student reads, "The teddy bear has a brown *f-f-funny* tummy," we want our beginning reader to pause, study the text and picture, reflect, and use whatever she knows about teddy bears, book illustrations, and phonics to read the sentence accurately.

I realize I may be offending some readers by pushing accuracy. But I am trying to make the point that we need to encourage even young students to use multiple clues and multiple cognitive processes as they interact with text. We want them to develop word consciousness, meaning consciousness, and confidence in their ability to read accurately and skillfully. A major difference between good and poor readers lies in their understanding of their own comprehension processes: poor readers are less likely to understand lapses in comprehension, and when they do detect them, they are less able to repair them

(Palinscar, Winn, David, Snyder, & Stevens, 1993).

Think about what Clay and Imlach's study (1971, cited in Allington, 2001, as "the classic study on the development of reading fluency," p. 71) tells us about reading for meaning and the use of multiple clues by beginning readers. These authors examined the reading behaviors of 100 beginning readers. Those who were making the most progress read more accurately, more quickly, and with better phrasing (five- to seven-word phrases in comparison to one- and two-word phrases) and expression than lower-progress readers. The high-progress readers also "spontaneously self-corrected four or five times as many of their word pronunciation errors as did the lower-progress readers" (Allington, 2001, p. 71).

Adeptness in monitoring for understanding and expertise in directing cognitive processes support comprehension of connected text. Self-monitoring works much like having an expert director in our minds—one who evaluates our understanding continuously, reflects on our purposes, and selects optimal processes to facilitate reading with understanding.

Assessing Student Progress

As I always say, "Begin by assessing a few things well." You may want to start by looking carefully at the comprehension of exposition or of narration. Or you may decide to assess a few key expository or narrative *results* and a few key reading comprehension *processes*.

By *reading comprehension results,* I simply mean the results of traditional content knowledge we usually assess when we measure students' comprehension of text. For example, in assessing students' understanding and use of the content of expository text, we often determine whether students get the main idea, can locate information, can synthesize information from multiple sources, and can see actual or potential uses for the information. In understanding and relating to narrative, we often assess whether they follow the story sequence, recognize critical events, and relate to the characters or to their experiences. And for both genres, we sometimes assess the quality of students' summaries, their evaluations of text presentations, and their hypotheses about the author's purpose.

By *reading comprehension processes,* I mean those cognitive processes and strategies that proficient readers employ, such as activating prior knowledge and monitoring for meaning. (See the processes listed in Figure 12.1.) To put it more simply, *comprehension results* describe *what* students understand or take away from their reading; *comprehension processes* describe *how* they do this.

Figure 12.3 outlines possibilities for curriculum content and assessment. I have divided it into sections that address comprehension results (understanding of content) and comprehension processes (how readers engage with text). These sections provide eight big questions we can use to assess students' reading comprehension development.

Comprehension Results:

1. How well do students understand and use exposition?
2. How well do students understand and relate to narrative?

Comprehension Processes or Strategies:

3. How do students use prior knowledge?
4. How do students connect ideas, build concepts and relationships, or follow the message or story?
5. How do students engage actively with the text?
6. What recall and remembering strategies do students use?
7. How fluent are students?
8. How well do students self-monitor and self-regulate their reading processes?

Students are often assessed on reading comprehension results—what they understand or can do after reading. They are assessed on the processes or strategies they use in seeking to understand the text or apply information from it far less frequently. However, if a faculty is trying to help students improve in reading comprehension, they will need to inquire into these processes—into *how* students make meaning.

Think about how you can use Figure 12.3 in assessing reading curriculum emphases in your classroom or school. Look at the five points listed under Question 4, "How do students connect ideas, build concepts or relationships, or follow

——————————— FIGURE **12.3** ———————————

A Range of Reading Comprehension Results and Processes for Assessment Consideration

Comprehension Results—Indicators of Content Knowledge and Response to Text

1. Expository Results (Understanding and Use of Content):
   Do students follow the message, get the main ideas, recognize vital information, locate the information they need, summarize accurately, synthesize accurately from single and multiple sources of information, evaluate the quality of text presentations, make well-grounded hypotheses about the author's purpose, and see actual or potential uses of the information?

2. Narrative Results (Understanding and Relating to Content):
   Do students follow the story, recognize critical events or pivotal information in the shaping of the characters or design of the plot, relate to the characters or to their experiences, summarize what they have read, evaluate the quality of text presentations, make well-grounded hypotheses about the author's purpose, and see connections to their lives or to the larger society within which they live?

Comprehension Processes and Strategies

3. How do students use prior knowledge (word, world, linguistic, and discourse)?
   - How is that knowledge activated?
   - Do students show awareness of when prior knowledge interferes with understanding or learning?

4. How do students connect ideas, build concepts or relationships, or follow the message or story?
   - Can they determine the importance of and make connections between ideas?
   - How do they use text structures and story grammar?
   - How do they use graphics provided in the text?
   - How do they use visual representations (including mental imagery)?
   - Can they develop mental or written summaries?

5. Do students engage actively with the text?
   - Can they establish purpose?
   - Can they make predictions and be aware of differences between expectations and text?
   - Do they make inferences?
   - Can they relate the text to their current knowledge and personal experiences (type of prior knowledge)?
   - Can they integrate new information with what is currently known?
   - Do they generate and respond to their own questions?
   - Do they monitor for meaning?

6. What recall and remembering strategies do students use?
   - Do they preview, read, and review?
   - Do they reread?
   - Do they rehearse and paraphrase?
   - Do they summarize periodically (outlines, diagrams, or mental or written summaries)?

Basic Processes That Support Comprehension of Connected Text

7. What are students' levels of fluency (rate, accuracy, phrasing, and expression)?

8. How do students use self-monitoring and metacognitive knowledge?

the message or story?" Where are these processes, and the strategies or plans that enable them, explicitly taught in your curriculum? How are they assessed in your setting? What data inform you about students' level of skill in applying these processes? How are these data organized to support instructional planning? If a visitor were to ask your students what they do to "get the message" or "follow the story," how many of these processes would be described?

While your curriculum may include far more connection-making processes than the ones listed in Question 4, you certainly want the following strategies present and taught for meaning-making:

- How to identify, track, and synthesize important ideas.
- How to use text structure and story grammar.
- How to use the graphics provided in text.
- How to use visual representations (including mental imagery and representing connections using tools such as Venn diagrams and semantic webs).
- How to use summaries during and after reading.

As you review Figure 12.3, you'll notice overlap between some results and processes. Think about how this works and its implications for assessment and instruction. Accurate summaries are listed under *Comprehension Results* because written or oral summaries are one way we can determine if students understood the content they read. Developing summaries is also included in

Comprehension Processes under Question 4 because some readers use mental or written summaries to help them track ideas and follow the message or story. And it is also under Question 6 because some readers use summarizing as a process for moving information into their long-term memory.

Instruments and Procedures for Assessing Multiple Components

Let's imagine we're helping a faculty who have a pretty good assessment system accompanying their basal reading series. The school district uses the *Stanford Achievement Test (SAT-9)* annually at grades 3, 4, 6, and 8. But staff members, concerned about the number of students who are not reading on grade level and about low scores on the *SAT-9,* want to know more about individual student performance in reading comprehension, the progress groups of students are making, and how to support the reading comprehension development of their students.

The faculty needs to think about instruments and techniques that can be used for assessing student performance while reading connected text; provide useful performance and progress data on individuals, class groups, and grade level groups; and used in multiple classes and grade levels. Of course, they don't have forever to implement changes. They must balance quality assessment with the utility of the results for planning instruction and guiding curriculum changes. What kind of instruments and procedures will be most useful to them in their quest? Let's review three assessment techniques for studying student progress in reading comprehension: the use of informal reading inventories, real books, and retelling checklists.

Informal Reading Inventories. It's hard to beat informal reading inventories (IRIs), IRI processes with graded passages or books, or instruments like the *Gray Oral Reading Tests-4* (Wiederholt & Bryant, 2001) for assessing the reading of connected text and using the information within and across classrooms. As described in Chapter 11, these instruments can be used to assess students' word recognition and analysis skills, text reading level and fluency, and reading comprehension. The faculty is especially interested in students' comprehension of exposition, so they want something that will make it easy to assess student performance and progress in this component and others. To this end, here are two different examples of commercially published informal reading inventories they could use: the *Qualitative Reading Inventory-3* (Leslie & Caldwell, 2001) and the *Basic Reading Inventory* (Johns, 1997).

The authors describe the *Qualitative Reading Inventory-3 (QRI-3)* as being "designed to provide diagnostic information about (1) conditions under which students can identify words and comprehend text successfully, and (2) conditions that appear to result in unsuccessful word identification, decoding, and/or comprehension" (p. 1). The instrument contains 10 graded word lists for preprimer through high school. For the sets of graded passages, there are five passages at the preprimer level, four narrative and one expository; five passages for each level from primer through 2nd

grade, three narrative and two expository; and six passages for each level from grade 3 through 6, three narrative and three expository. For junior high and high school, there are three passages each for literature, social studies, and science.

Using these materials and the administration, analysis, and scoring guidelines provided, a student's level of knowledge and skill can be assessed in comprehension of connected text (narrative and expository), in text-reading processes that support comprehension (reading rate for fluency, self-monitoring), and in vocabulary and word analysis skills (sight words in and out of context, contextual analysis, and self-monitoring).

The comprehension assessment components of the *QRI-3* are special strengths. Each passage is accompanied by two tasks for assessing prior knowledge: one is a series of three or four questions to ask the student about his knowledge of ideas in the text; the second is a standard stem in which the examiner includes the title of the passage and the concepts from the questions and asks the student to predict what the passage will be about. To analyze students' understanding of what has been read, retelling scoring guides are included for each passage. And the traditional lists of questions that accompany each passage include both explicit and implicit comprehension questions.

Another choice the faculty could make is the *Basic Reading Inventory: Pre-Primer Through Grade Twelve & Early Literacy Assessments* (Johns, 1997). The author describes the overall purpose of the *Basic Reading Inventory (BRI)* as a tool for helping teachers "provide responsive instruction to individual students" (p. 4). This informal reading inventory contains three word lists for preprimer through grade 12, three sets of graded passages for preprimer through grade 8, and two sets of longer passages (250 words), one narrative and one expository, for grades 3 through 12.

The authors of both instruments provide rationales for what is assessed and why it is assessed or scored as it is. They stress the flexibility available to the teacher or examiner in selecting various components as needed for different students, and the role of the teacher or examiner as reflective decision maker. They are extremely careful to remind readers and users that any "score" is only an estimate of student knowledge or performance and that other sources of data are needed to have an accurate profile of student development in reading.

Both instruments provide guidelines for the analysis of oral reading miscues, and the coding system identifies substitutions, insertions, omissions, reversals, repetitions, and self-corrections. Worksheets are provided for teachers and examiners to further analyze substitutions and mispronunciations in terms of graphic similarity and semantic acceptability. However, to use either measure for assessing reading performance and progress in grades 1 through 3, I would add standard procedures for gathering more specific information on decoding skills and on structural/morphological analysis. This would not be difficult to do; it could be done by simply analyzing

the words that students cannot read with automaticity. If I wanted more information on phrasing and expressiveness for fluency, I would simply expand the coding used when recording the data from oral reading of the passages.

If reading comprehension is your focus area, and you are trying to assess both reading comprehension results and processes or strategies, the *QRI-3* is probably your better choice. For measuring progress across the year and grades, it has more passages, both narrative and expository. With this said, the results from both inventories yield information on student reading level (in grade level terms), reading rate for fluency, sight words or level of automatic word recognition in and out of context, and comprehension of narrative and expository text. Results from both instruments can be used by the classroom teacher to design individual and group instruction and create appropriate learning experiences. And, while the authors might be appalled at this suggestion, student results can be aggregated and used by leadership teams and faculties for studying the performance of groups of students and for evaluating the effects of the reading program. However, for this to happen, school administrators have to ensure that teachers have time to study the instruments, use them, discuss student responses and their own questions, and decide which sections they will use as a collective body.

Sometimes, as faculty members begin to use IRIs as a group, questions about student responses lead them to create additional administration guidelines. If the IRI is used for more than a couple of years, they also have to "add in" comparable passages to avoid too much student familiarity with those included in the IRI. And they have to make decisions about when the inventories will be administered, how often they will be used, and how the data will be shared. Most faculties who have made the effort to use the results from IRIs across several grade levels or schoolwide have found that working with a common instrument helped them in their discussions of literacy, in planning lessons and units together, and in considering actions to take as a school community.

Using Real Books for Reading Comprehension Assessment. If you're interested in using books instead of passages for assessing student progress in reading—and you do not already have a sturdy system in place—I recommend using a good up-close, standard measure first, then transitioning to a system that allows you to use real books. If you're already using the benchmark books for Guided Reading (Fountas & Pinnell, 1998, 2001), grade level teams will need to select the books they'll set aside for assessment and develop a standard set of questions and a retelling checklist for each book. Another useful source for kindergarten through grade 2 teachers is *Best Books for Beginning Readers* (Gunning, 1997). In this book, the author provides a list of 1,000 children's books arranged in eight levels by order of difficulty, beginning with picture books in which the illustrations carry the message and leading up to books with short chapters that contain 500 to 1,000 words.

Gunning also includes a sort of mini-informal reading inventory, "Graduated Word Lists and Primary Reading Passages Inventory," that faculties can use along with the book selections at first.

Using Retelling for Comprehension Assessment. Because a retelling asks students to render their version of the story or exposition, this assessment procedure allows the teacher to learn more about what students think is important and how they interpret the storyline or message. When retelling is used, the student is asked to tell as much about the passage or book as she can remember, while the examiner records information about the responses using an outline of the story or a general scoring rubric. The retelling occurs after the student has read the passage orally or silently and before she responds to any comprehension questions that may be asked.

From kindergarten to 6th grade, a good informal reading inventory or graded passages or leveled books—along with standard procedures for recording behaviors, written responses to text, and a few key questions to stimulate student think-alouds about the comprehension processes and strategies they use—can form an integrated system for assessing reading comprehension as well as emergent literacy skills and vocabulary and word analysis skills.

Organizing Reading Comprehension Results

Most instruments, including those cited here, provide forms for organizing individual student results. In Chapter 10, we discussed how we could take the individual student results from an instrument for assessing phonological and phonemic awareness and generate classroom summaries so that a teacher could have a profile of results for his classroom and study student progress three times during the year. Then we looked at how to use class summaries to develop grade level summaries of student performance (see Figure 10.1).

In Chapter 11, we followed a similar pattern using the results from the *GORT-4* on word accuracy and fluency (to represent sight word acquisition and estimate vocabulary growth). While assessing word accuracy and reading rate, we also looked at comprehension to double-check that students understood the meanings of words and were not just decoding them. Again, we reviewed the use of individual student results collected three times during the year along with forms for compiling class summaries and grade level summaries. (See the tables in Figures 11.6 and 11.7, and the analysis of Figure 11.4.)

I won't bore you by taking you through the same process again. Once you have an instrument or set of instruments that provides the information you need about student progress in understanding and using expository text, understanding and relating to narrative, primarily fiction text, and using comprehension processes and strategies, you simply develop the forms that facilitate your use of the results. I have included many table shells in this book to facilitate the organization and use of results and to serve as models. Also, the application of the "Tips for Collective Use of

Up-Close Measures" in Chapter 7 can improve the accuracy of results and serve as planning reminders.

I am going to share one form for organizing results (Figure 12.4) and one figure that displays the results of reading comprehension from both up-close and norm-referenced measures (Figure 12.5).

The table in Figure 12.4 can be used to develop a classroom summary using the results from individual student profiles, whether you use instruments like the *GORT-4*, the *QRI-3*, or the *BRI*, or your own leveled passages or books. Space has been provided for recording comprehension, word accuracy, and fluency (in reading rate) scores because it's useful to study them together until students are reading around 150 words per minute orally and 200 words per minute silently (a good 5th grade reading rate).

Figure 12.5 displays reading comprehension results from a 2nd grade teacher's classroom. The first three columns after each student's name have fluency (reading rate) scores using grade level passages from September, January, and May. The next three columns have students' independent level reading comprehension scores from the *Basic Reading Inventory* for the same three time periods. And the final two columns list students' norm-referenced scores for the fall (October) of 2nd grade and student results from the fall of 3rd grade. This teacher has a pretty good picture of the students' progress in reading comprehension. She used these assessment results throughout the year to group students, plan literacy activities, and guide instructional moves.

FIGURE 12.4

Table for Class Summary of Reading Vocabulary, Comprehension, and Rate

On CD-ROM
Table 26

School: _____	Teacher: _____	Grade: _____

No. of Students in Class: _____ School Year: _____ Instrument(s) Used: _____

Student Name	M or F	ESL/ Special Ed.	Highest Independent Level		
			Accuracy	Comprehension	Rate

It's a good idea to compare how students perform on different measures as you build a picture of their reading progress. We want students seeking meaning from the beginning of their interactions with print and employing a range of comprehension processes and strategies. Thus, we want to make sure our classrooms and schools are supporting the development of proficiency and monitoring student progress in both nonfiction and fiction. We also want to do more than teach and assess comprehension results, finding out if students understood the text. We want comprehension processes and strategies as part of our K–8 reading curriculum goals and assessment content.

Questions to Explore for Reading Comprehension

Note: The "Questions to Explore" in Chapters 10 and 11 also include many relevant items.

The list of questions in Figure 12.6 about the reading program is provided to help you think about how reading comprehension is supported in kindergarten, 1st grade, and special needs classrooms in your school. The questions address inquiries and actions in Cell 4 of the Action Research Matrix, "Information About Your School's Learning Environment." This is not intended to be an exhaustive list; instead, it addresses areas that often need to be strengthened and

FIGURE 12.5

Reading Comprehension Results from Multiple Measures: Class Summary

School: Rochelle Elementary   Teacher: Teal   Grade: 2   School Year: 2001–2002

No. of Students in Class: 22   Instrument(s) Used: Basic Reading Inventory, Iowa Tests of Basic Skills

Student Name	M or F	Reading Rate			Reading Comprehension (BRI)				Reading Comprehension (ITBS) National Grade Equivalents	
		9/01	1/02	5/02	9/01	1/02	5/02		10/01 (Grade 2)	10/02 (Grade 3)
	M	57	105	152	3	4	4		2.8	6.2
	M	71	119	146	4	5	6		2.8	5.1
	F	38	72	104	P	2	3		2.4	3.5
	F	151	180	198	2	3	6		3.3	4.8
	M	9	14	35	PP	PP	1		1.3	1.6
	M	4	20	41	<PP	P	1		1.4	1.7
	F	23	52	80	P	2	3		2.1	3.1
	M	30	52	83	1	2	3		2.1	2.7
	F	82	134	136	5	6	5		3.8	5.4
	F	31	74	118	2	4	6		2.1	6.2
	F	2	38	72	<PP	PP	3		1.6	3.1
	F	22	59	86	1	3	3		1.8	moved
	F	16	44	65	1	2	3		2.1	moved
	M	62	100	135	3	3	4		3.1	3.7
	M	3	moved							moved
	F	34	66	109	2	4	5		3.2	5.4
	M	40	97	115	3	3	6		2.2	moved
	F	48	82	105	4	2	4		2.4	3.3
	M	25	54	88	1	2	3		2.1	3.2
	F	97	138	166	4	6	7		3.2	6.2
	M	18	40	moved	P	1	moved		1.6	moved
	M	20	56	66	PP	P	2		1.8	2.1

some of the common omissions in literacy programs at these levels.

A Short List of Recommended Resources

➤ Routman, R. (2003). *Reading essentials: The specifics you need to teach reading well*. Portsmouth, NH: Heinemann.

The voice of the author (also a teacher)—caring, competent, and joyous about learning—permeates the book. See especially the chapters on teaching comprehension (Chapter 8), sharing your reading life (Chapter 3), and building a classroom library (Chapter 5).

➤ Duke, N. K., & Pearson, P. D. (2002). Effective practices for developing reading comprehension. In A. E. Farstrup & S. J. Samuels (Eds.), *What research has to say about reading instruction* (3rd ed.), pp. 205–242. Newark, DE: International Reading Association.

An easy-to-read summary of the current state of knowledge about teaching reading comprehension. The authors include a brief section on building a comprehension curriculum and provide short but explicit descriptions of comprehension strategies.

➤ Keene, E. O., & Zimmerman, S. (1997). *Mosaic of thought: Teaching comprehension in a reader's workshop*. Portsmouth, NH: Heinemann.

This is a good resource for study groups who want to learn more about teaching comprehension strategies.

➤ Caldwell, J. S. (2002). Comprehension of narrative and expository text. In *Reading assessment: A primer for teachers and tutors*. New York: Guilford Press; and Blachowicz, C., & Ogle, D. (2001). Finding a starting point: Ways to assess comprehension. In *Reading comprehension: Strategies for independent learners*. New York: Guilford Press.

These two books provide good advice and examples of comprehension assessments. Both include sections on using retellings and think-alouds for assessment. Caldwell's book is especially useful in learning how to modify IRIs and using IRI processes instead of complete inventories. Blachowicz and Olge's book is especially useful for upper elementary school teachers.

➤ Block, C. L., & Pressley, M. (Eds.). (2002). *Comprehension instruction: Research-based best practices*. New York: Guilford Press; and Sweet, A. P. & Snow, C. E. (eds.) (2003). *Rethinking reading comprehension*. New York: Guilford Press.

These two texts serve much like handbooks of research on reading comprehension. If you teach children to read or work with their teachers, read Vellutino's chapter "Individual differences as sources of variability in reading comprehension in elementary school children" in *Rethinking Reading Comprehension* (pp. 51–81).

➤ If you decide to strengthen the use of nonfiction in your school, the following four articles provide a set of good choices for collective study. They include rationale and explicit suggestions for getting started:

– Moss, B. (1995). Using children's nonfiction tradebooks as read-alouds. *Language Arts, 72*(2), 122–126.

– Moss, B., Leone, S., & Dipillo, M. L. (1997). Exploring the literature of fact: Linking reading and writing through information trade books. *Language Arts, 74*(6), 418–429.

– Duthie, C. (1994). Nonfiction: A genre study for the primary classroom. *Language Arts, 71,* 97–104.

– Guillaume, A. M. (1998). Learning with text in the primary grades. *The Reading Teacher, 51,* 476–486.

FIGURE **12.6**

Questions to Explore for Reading Comprehension

Curriculum Materials

1. Students need books, books, books. Do they have easy access to them in classrooms, in the school library, and in the community?

2. How many magazines are in each classroom collection? Most school libraries have subscriptions to a range of magazines written for young children and adolescents. But every classroom needs a rich supply that students can read during self-selected reading periods. Along with the most common ones like *Ranger Rick* and *National Geographic Geo*, here are a few other choices that might be popular with your students:

Children Ages 6 to 10	*Children Ages 8 to 14*
• *Barbie*	• *Calliope*
• *Black Belt for Kids*	• *Earthsavers*
• *Chickadee*	• *Koala Club*
• *Owl*	• *Soccer, Jr.*
• *Stone Soup*	• *Sports Illustrated for Kids*
• *Zoobooks*	

Instruction

3. How are comprehension processes and strategies taught throughout your school? It's not easy to analyze invisible cognitive processes so they can make it into our reading curriculum. And it's even more complex to teach them! It's no wonder that Durkin (1978/1979) found in her study of reading comprehension instruction that teachers primarily assessed reading comprehension results but were not teaching students *how to* get these results. Out of some 11,587 minutes of classroom observation during reading periods, she noted, only 45 minutes were devoted to comprehension instruction. The results, or products, of reading were being assessed regularly, with teachers asking questions such as "What is the main idea?" "Who is the main character?" and "What was the sequence of events?" but there was almost no instruction on how to get those products.

   While I believe progress has been made in increasing the amount of comprehension instruction through the use of explicit instruction in comprehension, think-alouds, reciprocal teaching, and the use of the reading-writing connection, we are not where we need to be 25 years after we were so clearly confronted with the problem. And while there is still much to be learned about how comprehension works and develops, reading field scholars and cognitive psychologists did respond and provide us with instructional strategies that could help us teach comprehension more effectively (Duffy et al., 1987; Palinscar & Brown, 1984; Pearson & Dole, 1987; Pressley et al., 1992, 1995; Taylor, 1982). Once again, we have an implementation problem. But the good news is that knowledge of the problem is the first step in solving it, because we do know how to support the implementation of instructional strategies (Joyce & Showers, 2002).

4. What is the read-aloud balance for sharing informational texts and narrative fiction texts with students?

—————————— FIGURE **12.6** CONTINUED ——————————

5. How and where is the reading-writing connection explicitly demonstrated to help students understand and use the relationship between text structures as readers and organizational patterns as writers?

6. Are students taught how to skim materials for specific information? Are they learning how to find a range of resources about a topic they are exploring?

Assessment

7. How are you teaching students to self-assess their reading comprehension processes and strategies? Do they have a plan of action to enable comprehension before reading, during reading, and after reading?

At an early age, students can monitor their comprehension. Bransford, Brown, and Cocking (1999) remind us: "Between 5 and 10 years of age, children's understanding of the need to use strategic effort in order to learn becomes increasingly sophisticated, and their ability to talk about and reflect on learning continues to grow throughout the school years" (p. 86).

Organizing for Learning—Schedules and Time

8. Especially in grades 4 and above, when you look at a typical school day, how much time do students have to discuss the selections they are reading? Time to talk about and share our reading is important at all grade levels, but as students age, become better readers, and read lengthier selections, they often need more time for discussions, just as we do.

13

Reading Habits

How do we help students develop healthy reading habits? Think about how much your students read; are they reading enough to become fluent? To become knowledgeable about the world beyond their immediate setting? What do they choose to read?

A major goal of any reading program is the development of lifetime reading habits that include reading from many different genres for learning and for leisure. We want our students to read, and we want them to read a lot! We want our students to believe they can learn *to* read and learn *from* reading. We want them to read for entertainment and engagement with the ideas and emotions of others. We feel passionate about the habit of reading because it has meant so much to us. We don't want any child to miss what we have.

The rationale for developing a habit of reading for learning was discussed in Chapter 11. Extensive reading is highly correlated with the development of a large sight word vocabulary and with better academic achievement. Aside from the types of development it supports, it is a goal in its own right. Extensive reading brings knowledge and pleasure.

Of all the components of reading development we have discussed, this is the easiest one to implement and maintain. So much of what we need to do to get most students reading more is in our control. We don't need to learn more about the structure of the discipline of language arts or new instructional strategies to generate wide reading. Actions for immediate, widespread improvement and schoolwide implementation are in our repertoire already:

- Modeling and sharing our own learning from and engagement with text is one way we encourage students to read. Anyone who has taught elementary school knows that many students immediately want to read what the teacher has just read to them. In fact, some of you probably keep a short stack of books on your desk each day that you read or read excerpts from because you know what a powerful invitation your sharing is and how it affects your students.

- Making sure students have access to a wide range of books of different genres and reading levels, including many books at their independent reading level, is a basic and important way to support student reading. Classroom library collections that include science and social studies trade books such as *Into the Sea* (Guiberson, 1996), *Frogs* (Badger, 1995), and *The Boys' War* (Murphy, 1990) help us teach our curriculum standards and help students learn and expand concepts. The research on the importance of access to books and how critical easy access is to supporting literacy development continues to accumulate (Neuman & Celano, 2001).

- Providing time during every school day—several times in fact—for students to read is another way to help build a reading habit. Whatever content we're teaching, whether we're using direct instruction or concept formation models of teaching, student learning is facilitated if students read, write, and discuss the ideas. Time to read books and excerpts from science and social studies trade books needs to be part of every school day.

In addition, if students use some of their time beyond the school day to read, they'll have even more opportunity to build a healthy reading habit.

The Just Read Process

Teachers and faculty can systematically study the amount of reading by students using an approach called the Just Read process (Joyce & Wolf, 1996; Wolf, 1998). This technique was designed to

- Assist students in becoming independent readers;
- Involve all students in the school;
- Improve school and home connections;
- Encourage parents and families to recognize the importance of wide reading outside the school setting and involve them more formally in supporting their children's literacy development; and
- Provide school faculties with a tool for expanding students' reading beyond the school day and for studying amount and type of reading.

In the first studies of Just Read (Joyce & Showers, 2002; Joyce & Wolf, 1996), the students in the highest-reading schools gained twice as much in quality of writing as did the students in the lowest-reading schools—an indication of the effects of reading on writing. There is increasing evidence that children who read more outside of school also perform better academically in school. And, as adults, most of us know that the benefits of a healthy reading habit nourish spirit and mind for years to come.

Assessing Amounts of Reading

The Just Read process is very simple and direct. First, at a set time each week, each

---
FIGURE 13.1

Table for Just Read:
Student Weekly Reading Log

On CD-ROM
Table 27

| Student's Name: _____ | | Gender: M F | Grade: _____ |
| Teacher: _____ | | School Year: _____ | |

Date		Title of Book Read	Pages	Book Finished?
	1.			
	2.			
	3.			
	4.			
	5.			
	6.			
	7.			
	8.			
	9.			
	10.			
	11.			
	12.			
	13.			
	14.			
	15.			
	16.			
	17.			
	18.			
	19.			
	20.			
			Number of books completed this week	
			Number of books completed to date	

student fills out a reading log like that shown in Figure 13.1. (Students who cannot write yet have their forms filled out by parents or other adults.) Weekly collection is important because longer time periods, such as monthly collection, do not work as well, since parts of the reading are too distant and therefore difficult to remember and celebrate.

Next, the student records are consolidated into class records on forms like that shown in Figure 13.2. Generally, both male and female totals are developed because of the traditional large gender differences in reading competence and habits. Thus, we want to keep an eye on the gender variable and be prepared

to increase the strength of our invitations and support, if needed.

In the primary grades, the amounts of reading are celebrated weekly. Classes set goals and watch themselves meet and exceed them. The teacher and students celebrate as a class, for Just Read not only celebrates the students who read the most, but also everyone who is reading and the accomplishments of the community of students.

Looking over the class record, teachers note any student who has not finished a book that week and talks to the student. They want to help students find books that will engage their interests and that the students can easily read and

─── FIGURE 13.2 ───

Table for Just Read: Class Log—Males

On CD-ROM
Table 28

School: _____   Teacher: _____   Grade: _____

No. of Male Students in Class: _____   School Year: _____

Names of Students (Alphabetically)	Number of Books Completed This Week	Check if Zero
1.		
2.		
3.		
4.		
5.		
6.		
7.		
8.		
9.		
10.		
11.		
12.		
13.		
14.		
15.		
16.		
17.		
18.		
19.		
20.		
Total		

understand. Parents and caregivers who have not been reading to their kindergarteners may be called and tactfully asked to help their child by having someone read to him. In some neighborhoods, the parent or older sibling who speaks the best English reads to several children.

Data analysis now moves to the school level, using forms like that shown in Figure 13.3. Celebrations will be held at the school as various goals are reached, and end-of year celebrations set up the summer reading campaign. A few years ago, I had the privilege of attending the end-of-year celebration at

Kaiser Elementary School in Newport/ Costa Mesa Unified School District in California as the 400 students, with their parents and teachers, cheered their collective reading of 80,000 titles that school year. That's a lot of reading.

Establishing Benchmarks— How Much Is Enough?

Once again, let's turn to the external knowledge base in reading and see what it has to offer. In *Reading and Writing Grade by Grade: Primary Literacy Standards for Kindergarten Through Third Grade*, the New Standards Primary

—————————— FIGURE 13.3 ——————————

Table for Just Read: Elementary School Summary

On CD-ROM

Table 29

School: _____   Grade: _____   School Year: _____

No. of Classes/Teachers: _____   Total No. of Students: _____   Dates: _____

Year-to-Date Summary	Females		Males		Total	
	No. of books	No. of students	No. of books	No. of students	No. of books	No. of students
Number of books completed this week by kindergarten						
Number of books completed this week by grade 1						
Number of books completed this week by grade 2						
Number of books completed this week by grade 3						
Number of books completed this week by grade 4						
Number of books completed this week by grade 5						
Number of books completed this week by grade 6						
Number of books completed this week by all grades						
Number of books completed by all grades to date						
Total average number of books completed per student to date						

Summary for Week of: _____	Females		Males		Total	
	No. of books	No. of students	No. of books	No. of students	No. of books	No. of students
Number of students completing zero (0) books this week						
Number of students completing one (1) book this week						
Number of students completing two (2) books this week						
Number of students completing three (3) books this week						
Number of students completing four (4) books this week						
Number of students completing five (5) books this week						
Number of students completing six to ten (6–10) books this week						
Number of students completing more than ten (10) books this week						

Literacy Committee (1999) classifies "vocabulary building as a reading habit because the key to robust vocabulary is reading a lot" (p. 27). In this excellent resource, the authors define what they mean by "a lot":

Kindergarten Students: Read or reread—independently or with another student or adult—two to four familiar books each day. Listen to one or two books read aloud each day at school and at home.

First Grade Students: Read—independently or with assistance—four or more books a day. Hear two to four books or other texts read aloud every day.

Second Grade Students: Read one or two short books or long chapters every day. Listen to and discuss every day one text that is longer and more difficult than what can be read independently.

Third Grade Students: Read 30 chapter books a year. Listen to and discuss at least one chapter read aloud every day. (New Standards Primary Literacy Committee, 1999, p. 22)

If we followed this pattern (unless our benchmarks are higher), our 4th through 6th grade reading habits benchmarks might look something like this:

- *4th Grade Students:* Read 40 chapter books a year. Listen to at least one text excerpt read aloud and discuss at least one nonfiction or fiction piece every day.
- *5th Grade Students:* Read 45 books a year, at least one-half of them chapter books. Listen to at least one text excerpt read aloud and discuss at least one nonfiction or fiction piece every day.
- *6th Grade Students:* Read 50 books a year, at least one-half of them chapter books. Listen to at least one text excerpt read aloud and discuss at least one nonfiction or fiction piece every day.

Collecting and analyzing these simple data, working together to increase students' reading, and celebrating successes can help faculties make great progress toward building a culture of readers. The collective efforts of the faculty are important in developing the school as a center for literacy. And the more fully we can engage parents and caregivers in sharing literacy experiences with their children, the more likely it is that these children will become proficient readers.

PART FOUR

Pulling It All Together for Sustained Collective Inquiry

Schools teach in three ways—by what they teach, by how they teach, and by the kind of place they are (Downey, 1967). Many schools and districts have a long way to go before they have high-quality, coherent reading programs provided to all students. Along with all of the student learning goals and curriculum benchmarks we have for our students, we also have a grand opportunity to model individual and cooperative learning and create a healthier, more productive learning environment for everyone.

This last section is about organizing collective work on assessing student performance and progress in reading, analyzing the components of the reading program, and supporting the implementation of changes you elect to pursue. Basically, it's a brief how-to manual for using schoolwide or districtwide action research to improve student achievement. Use this as a resource as you review your own reading program and make plans for change.

14

Organizing Schoolwide Action Research and Professional Development

This final chapter is about planning collective inquiry and action as a school leadership team or faculty. Initial tasks include deciding where to begin, identifying what work needs to be done and by whom, and designing a route that's likely to get you where you want to go.

I've provided many forms for collecting data about student performance in Chapters 4 through 13. In this chapter, we'll consider tools for collecting information about what and how we are teaching. I'll also discuss how to identify promising changes, support ourselves in expanding knowledge and practice, and study the implementation of desirable changes.

Most of the examples presented assume that there is a school leadership team or facilitation team, that the tasks involve exchanges between the team and the faculty, and that some tasks are being conducted by the team and others are being performed by the entire faculty. This is what you saw when you visited Elwood Elementary in Chapter 1. The faculty had established shared governance of curriculum and instruction and developed routines for identifying priorities and supporting their learning.

Selecting a Focus for Collective Study

I recommend that faculties or school teams begin by selecting one dimension or component from Figure 2.1 for focused study. While you need data on student performance to help you assess student progress and design optimal instruction, you don't need mounds of data to help you decide where to begin. Select any reading component or dimension in which students need to be more skilled and which would advance literacy development for a majority of your students, and use that as an entry point for your inquiry into student performance and reading program quality.

You may remember that based on the student performance data they had in reading, Elwood's faculty could have selected either reading comprehension or vocabulary as a collective priority. They decided that working on expanding reading vocabulary and word analysis skills would help more students immediately. And some teachers and parents were concerned about how phonics were taught, so this focus gave faculty members an opportunity to engage in disciplined inquiry into their phonics curriculum and instruction and into current knowledge about what works.

Along with the study of student data, leadership teams and study groups can review reading program components in documents such as *Every Child a Reader* (Hiebert, Pearson, Taylor, Richardson, & Paris, 1998), Chapters 2 and 10–13 in this book, and *Reading and Writing Grade by Grade* (New Standards Primary Literacy Committee, 1999); reflect on the evidence presented; and make immediate changes in materials and time use. However, making changes in thinking about how reading develops and implementing new instructional strategies will, and should, take more time.

For example, if you decide that the argument presented here for a better fiction/nonfiction balance in the reading program is credible and needs to be addressed in your school, it's relatively easy to increase the size of classroom collections and make some different choices in what is read to students. However, if you want all faculty members to select well-written trade books that match the curriculum concepts they are teaching in science and social

studies, and you want students to use the text structures to comprehend and remember the ideas presented in these books, more time will be needed. More time is required not only for staff development in analyzing the quality and content of trade books and for training in new instructional strategies, but also for reading and discussing articles, assessing the current learning environment, and integrating new knowledge into a conceptual framework for teaching reading. Therefore, even after identifying actions that can be taken immediately, a faculty generally needs to focus on a single dimension or component of reading development for in-depth work.

As a faculty thinks about the dimensions and their components (see Figure 2.1) and identifies a collective priority, they'll need to consider the depth of study needed to effect changes in knowledge and practice and the breadth of impact on the reading program. Some dimensions are simply too big as a unit—there's too much information to be studied, too much new learning required, and too many changes needed in curriculum, instruction, and assessments. Think about the dimension "Comprehension of Connected Text." In most settings, focusing on either "Understanding and Learning from Expository Nonfiction Text" or "Understanding and Relating to Narrative Text (Primarily Fiction)" will be a multiyear endeavor before student performance and reading program quality are where the faculty would like them to be. However, the components in "Building Reading Vocabulary" ("Sight Words," "Phonics and Decoding Skills," "Structural/Morphological Analysis," and "Contextual Analysis") are so intertwined in purpose and utility that I would advise working on them as a group. Also, the amount of learning required by faculty members and the complexity of the content is far less dense in "Building Reading Vocabulary" than it is in "Comprehension of Connected Text."

Some components—such as "Understanding and Learning from Expository Nonfiction Text"—involve the entire K–6 staff and can be productively pursued for two or three years. Other components— such as "Phonological and Phonemic Awareness"—involve primarily kindergarten and 1st grade teachers, and in-depth study and program modifications may take only one or two semesters.

Be disciplined. Avoid making too many dimensions of reading development a collective priority. In 30 years of work in schools, I've never seen a school or district faculty that could do everything skillfully in the beginning. Having too many priorities either results in a big mess with a great deal of uncertainty about what has been accomplished or in a shallow, activities-checked-off process. Such experiences create cynicism and comments like, "Initiatives come and go, but schools stay the same." Establishing a few parameters about what will be studied initially, how it will be studied, and which grade levels will be addressed are major decisions for the leadership team and staff. Only you know your context and student performance data well enough to decide which component or dimension to study first as you inquire into reading program quality and build

an information base to support student progress.

Think about Elwood. The faculty wanted to provide a high-quality, multi-dimensional reading program in every classroom, but its collective disciplined inquiry at first focused on only one dimension: expanding reading vocabulary and word analysis skills. This focus guided the faculty's use of resources, its professional development time, and its selection of persons to provide technical assistance. It encouraged them to inquire into how they were teaching students to build reading vocabulary and use word analysis skills. And it helped them realize they had little common data and no up-close standard measures (across classrooms) to inform them about student progress in acquiring sight word vocabulary or in using phonics, structural analysis, or context.

You'll want to transform the component or dimension the faculty selects as a priority into a student learning goal, just as Elwood's faculty did when they changed the dimension "Building Reading Vocabulary" into the goal "To expand reading vocabulary and word analysis skills." For example, the component "Understanding and Learning from Expository Nonfiction Text" can become "To improve students' comprehension of expository nonfiction text," or the component "Phonological and Phonemic Awareness" could be modified to read "To increase students' phonological and phonemic awareness skills." The statement of the collective priority as a student-learning goal is both practical and symbolic. The goal sets the parameters for the up-close student learning data that will be collected and studied across classrooms; for the information about current curriculum, instruction, and assessment procedures that needs to be analyzed and assembled; and for the extensiveness of the study of the external knowledge base. Symbolically, it's our belief in the value of education and in student learning that binds educators in common cause, despite all the differences in teaching styles and approaches, prior knowledge and experiences, and political affiliations. Student learning goals can unify faculties and generate purposeful energy.

Using the Action Research Matrix

The cells of the Action Research Matrix form a structured process for making informed decisions and taking collective action. If you look at the Action Research Matrix in Figure 14.1, you can see the actions that the Elwood faculty are engaging in as they work on their priority goal. You can see some of the external information they have studied (Cells 2 and 5) and some of the information they are gathering about their learning environment (Cell 4). And you can see the benchmarks they have established (Cell 3), using the results of their current measures of reading performance (Cell 1) and promising changes they have decided to make in the learning environment (Cell 6).

The matrix design provides a strategy that faculties can use to keep the study of student performance and development tightly connected to the study of the learning environment. Using it as a guide for collective work provides a coherent approach to studying the effects of our actions on student learning. It also serves as a reminder to maintain our focus until we have the results we want for students and for ourselves.

Studying the External Knowledge Base (Matrix Cells 2 and 5)

No one withholds her competence. We are all—teachers, coordinators, directors, consultants, and administrators—doing the best we can. If this yields high student achievement for all students in all the academic and social goals your school has, then information from the external knowledge base may not be the critical resource for you that it is for the rest of us.

If you wish to improve student proficiency in reading, your problem with using external information is not a lack of it but how to sift, sort, and select high-quality resources for collective study and how to then derive useful ideas and actions to pursue in the school and classroom. I'm going to describe two techniques for screening information prior to facultywide dissemination, and then introduce a simple cooperative learning activity that helps faculties distill information from external resources.

The first screening technique can be implemented once your faculty has selected a student learning focus. The leadership team can identify three persons who are knowledgeable about reading and literacy and for whom they have great respect, and contact them. After telling them what you're working on,

————— FIGURE 14.1 —————

Elwood's Action Research Matrix

Schoolwide Focus: To expand reading vocabulary and word analysis skills

	Learner (Students)		Learning Environment (School)	
On-Site Information (Information at the school level)	**1. Current student information** N = 622 students 60% free/reduced-price lunch Race/ethnicity: 43% White 38% Black 16% Hispanic 3% Other • NRT Reading Total • 3rd Grade: 29% at or above 50th percentile; 71% at or below 49th percentile • 5th Grade: 33% at or above 50th percentile; 67% at or below 49th; 10% of 5th grade did not take test • CBM Vocabulary, grades 2–5: 35–40% Proficient & Advanced; 60–65% below Proficiency	**3. Student performance and responses we would like to see** • NRT Reading Total 3rd & 5th Grade: 40% at 50th percentile or above • CBM Vocabulary, grades 2–5: 55% Proficient or Advanced • Students will begin to assess their own vocabulary growth and use of word analysis skills • Students will increase the amount of independent reading they do in and out of school	**4. Information about the current learning environment in our school** • Mostly games, puzzles, worksheets, and dictionary activities are used to teach word meaning—few conceptual activities for sight word acquisition or meaning • In word analysis skills, K–2 were teaching phonics systematically • Teachers were sharing fiction with their students regularly, but not nonfiction • Most classrooms had four times more fiction books available than nonfiction	**6. Learning environment we would like to see** • Increase teacher read-alouds of nonfiction, prekindergarten–grade 5 • Provide more time for students to read books at their independent level and time to discuss them • Teach students at least two strategies for building vocabulary, K–5 • Teach students to assess their vocabulary building and word analysis strategies, K–5 • Use the picture word inductive model for teaching vocabulary K–5 and word analysis skills K–2 • Establish some common vocabulary measures, 1–5
External Information (Study of literature, standards, & best practices)	**2. External information about learners/students** Some faculty members began to realize that their expectations of students were too low. Some of the information they studied included the following: • Student data from five schools with similar demographics where students were excelling in reading and vocabulary year after year • K–3 student expectations from *Preventing Reading Difficulties* (Snow et al., 1998, pp. 80–83) • *Reading and Writing Grade by Grade* (New Standards Primary Literacy Committee, 1999) • "Phases of Acquisition in Learning to Read Words and Instructional Implications" (Ehri, 1999)		**5. External information about the learning environment** • The goal of phonics instruction is to help students build an extensive sight vocabulary (Ehri, 1999) • Having students use dictionaries or write definitions is not an effective approach to building vocabulary or word meaning (Nagy & Scott, 2000; Stahl, 1999) • Instruction needs to include reading aloud to students (Stahl, 1999), student-friendly explanations (Beck et al., 2002), how to use analogies (Cunningham & Cunningham, 1992; Gaskins et al., 1996/97); teaching students word analysis strategies (Graves & Watts-Taffe, 2002), explicit instruction and inductive lessons (Calhoun, 1999), and time for students to read books at their independent level and discuss them (New Standards, 1999) • Most textbooks do not include enough information about key concept words for students to understand the concepts or add the words to their sight vocabulary (Stahl, 1999) • The best way to expand vocabulary is wide reading; amount of reading is the main determinant of vocabulary growth (Anderson & Nagy, 1992)	

ask them to recommend three to five research studies and one or two conceptual pieces related to the learning focus. These documents will provide a good starting place. If there is one document that all three recommended, start with that one. Look for agreement from your live resources and within the documents; you're looking for converging evidence.

Another technique is to read through research syntheses or compilations and identify sections to study. From those sources, the leadership team can identify additional documents that seem promising. Again, look for common citations and get those first.

Whichever technique you use for initial screening, you'll probably end up with more documents than a faculty can inquire into with depth. The leadership team will need to study the base set and select three or four documents for facultywide study.

Generally, leadership teams and faculties find that *a mixture of resources* works best. This is what the Elwood team had. For whole-faculty study, one or two research pieces (maybe one synthesis of research in your focus area and one study) and one or two easy-to-read and easy-to-transfer-into-practice pieces may be enough for the year. For example, if your district or school is worried about students' poor performance in reading at the end of 1st grade, and you find when studying the learning environment that many kindergarten teachers are using a letter-a-week program, part of your staff development time might include a cooperative reading and analysis of "Emergent Literacy Skills, Early Instruction, and

Individual Differences as Determinants of Difficulties in Learning to Read: The Case for Early Intervention" (Vellutino & Scanlon, 2001) from the *Handbook of Early Literacy Research,* as well as a reading and analysis of "Letting Go of 'Letter of the Week' " (Bell & Jarvis, 2001) in *Primary Voices K–6.* The Vellutino and Scanlon piece would be for K–3 or K–6 faculty members, not just prekindergarten and kindergarten teachers.

Whatever technique you use for gathering information, before all faculty members are asked to read a document, the leadership team needs to analyze it and decide whether it's a treasure or not. Team members need to agree that the authors present a good theoretical basis for their ideas, and if the document describes instructional practices, that it provides a clear description of teacher and student moves. For research studies, consider the above *plus* determine whether the authors describe in detail the attributes of the intervention and how to implement it, whether it be a complex instructional strategy or some simple organizational variable, such as increasing the amount of discussion time available to students following independent reading. Also, describe the population and setting, present their results clearly, and describe how the results were determined. Journal editors often try to reduce the length of articles, so if you find pieces that seem especially useful but you still have questions, contact the author or institution and ask more questions.

You may be thinking, "Well, Emily, how do I *know* if it's 'good research'?"

Some would say, "If it's been published in a peer-reviewed research journal, it's been vouched for" (International Reading Association, 2002; Stanovich & Stanovich, 2003; U.S. Department of Education, 2002). I will tell you, however, that I have been leading staff development sessions in schools and districts for 25 years, and these sessions have often included the reading and analysis of research. This research has spanned from Durkin's (1978–1979) study of reading comprehension instruction, which I felt every elementary teacher should read and discuss, to Englert and colleagues' (1991) modeling of writing strategies and metacognitive processes, to Kamberelis's (1999) study of genre development and learning in K–2 classrooms. In that time, I have seen many, many "research articles" from peer-reviewed research journals that I would never ask a teacher to read. While I agree with the argument that evidence about educational interventions needs to be presented carefully and accurately and needs to be available to the larger community, I do not agree that the only trustworthy evidence of success can be found in refereed (indicating that the articles are approved for publication by a panel of independent reviewers) research journals.

Others might tell you, "Look in the *What Works Clearinghouse* (http://w-w-c.org)," a new federally sponsored initiative to help states, districts, and schools "sort through the claims" about what works. I think we'll just have to wait and see whether this Web site is a useful source of information or not. (If you wish to become a more knowledge-able consumer of educational research, see the resources listed at the end of the chapter.)

I worry that we are being led to disregard almost all of the reading and educational research and scholars many of us have relied on for years. Since the Reading Excellence Act of 1998, some of us have moved from being pleased at the increased emphasis on informed decision making and use of evidence to being afraid of where we're going. However, there is hope. While much of the narrowing of what represents good research is being done under the auspices of the U.S. Department of Education (USDOE), the No Child Left Behind (NCLB) Act defines scientifically based reading research as " . . . research that applies rigorous, systematic, and objective procedures to obtain reliable and valid knowledge relevant to reading development, reading instruction, and reading difficulties" (see http://www.ed.gov/policy/elsec/leg/esea02/pg4.html#sec 1208). NCLB does not legislate that we attend only to the results of experimental studies as we improve our reading curriculum and select instructional practices. (See Appendix A for the USDOE's definition of "scientifically based reading research" and a brief description of the implications of this definition.)

When you think about the components of reading development in Figure 2.1 in terms of No Child Left Behind's *Reading First* and the USDOE's criteria for scientifically based reading research, "Phonics and Decoding" and "Phonological and Phonemic Awareness" have the most extensive federally acceptable research base, and "Structural/Morphological Analysis," "Extensive Reading," and "Positive Attitude Toward Reading" the least.

Cooperative Processing of Worthy Resources. How can you turn good resources into information that can be used to make informed, collective decisions in your setting? Using structured response sheets can help faculties develop common knowledge and engage in focused discussions about information from the external knowledge base. Such forms are designed to help readers juxtapose the ideas of others with their own classroom and school practices. Figure 14.2 is an example.

Faculty members complete these forms individually as they analyze what the author has stated or implied about curriculum, instruction, assessment, or the organization of the learning environment. They discuss individual responses in their peer coaching groups and develop a group response. If someone is in doubt about whether a colleague's statement is accurate, he simply asks the person to identify the portions of the text that support that statement. Then a whole-faculty structured response sheet is prepared.

Cooperative processing of just three or four worthy pieces a year can go a long way toward helping a faculty determine which actions should be tested as hypotheses in their school action plans. Use of something like the structured response sheets needs to become a routine part of staff development, for such activities help us build our knowledge of the structure of the discipline and best

practices within it. And the summary documents that represent the faculty's synthesis of information also make good documentation of the evidence that supports the curriculum modifications and instructional practices you've selected for implementation.

The leadership team will need to develop an in-school information retrieval system. It could be something as simple as a filing cabinet placed in the media center or the teachers' workroom, preferably somewhere inviting. Inside would be copies of all the documents collected (three copies of each in each file), not just those that were used in cooperative processing activities. A staff member would simply sign the file folder when she checks out an item and crosses her name out when it's returned. Copies of books and journals purchased for screening information and to support professional development also need to be easily accessible to all faculty members. You'll only need one or two copies of some books; of others, you'll need a copy for every faculty member.

Gathering Information About the Learning Environment in Your School (Matrix Cell 4)

Many times, I've seen district or school staff move from analyzing current student data to setting benchmarks or performance targets, to identifying changes they would like to make in their schools or classrooms. In terms of the Action Research Matrix, they have "hopped" from Cell 1 to Cell 3 to Cell 6. Not only have they ignored a disciplined analysis of information from the

--- FIGURE 14.2 ---

Structured Response Sheet

Title of Document or Videotape _____

Author(s) or Presenter(s) _____

1. What does this author say to us about content? About what we teach? What knowledge, skill, and processes in the focus area need to be a part of daily/yearly curriculum? What about materials for use in classrooms and the larger learning environment?

2. What does this author say about instruction? About how we teach? What recommendations are made or can be directly inferred about the design of instruction or presentation of content?

3. What does this author say about assessing student learning? Are there suggestions about measuring students' knowledge, skill, or transfer of knowledge/skill? About the use of results by staff or students?

4. What does this author say to us about organizing students and staff?

external knowledge base as described in the preceding section, they have not taken time to study the current learning environment.

Remember how the leadership team and faculty at Elwood Elementary worked together to collect information about how vocabulary and word analysis skills were being taught, how they were being assessed, and which curriculum resources had been especially effective? They were also studying the extent and nature of read-alouds by teachers in prekindergarten through grade 5. Their student performance data (Cells 1 and 3), their study of the external knowledge base (Cells 2 and 5), and their investigation into the current learning environment (Cell 4) all combined to help them select actions for study or implementation (Cell 6—what they included in their school action plan).

As faculty members consider the student performances they would like to bring about, and as they read and analyze information from the external knowledge base, they often identify many aspects of current practices that need to be investigated. Keeping focused primarily on the collective goal, here are some of the common lines of investigation:

1. *Curriculum* (what we are teaching): What current lesson and unit objectives, concepts, and materials are intended to support student attainment of the goal? How is this content treated in textbooks, local curriculum or standards documents, and other resource materials being used (e.g., quality of presentation,

depth of coverage, support for transfer, accessibility)? Are any key curriculum materials needed to support student learning either missing or scarce?

2. *Instruction* (how we are teaching): What instructional strategies and practices are currently being used to support goal attainment in the focus area? How much time is provided for instruction specifically aimed at developing student knowledge and skill?

3. *Assessment (*what and how we are assessing): What student knowledge and performances are being assessed in the focus area and at which grade levels? How are we assessing them? How often? Do we have good, standard, up-close measures in use across classrooms and grades? How are the results used in planning lessons, units, and whole-school/curriculum modifications?

4. *Organization of the learning environment* (how students and staff are organized in our learning community): What kinds of grouping patterns are used during instructional time? How are staff deployed, including paraeducators? How are special programs and regular education integrated? Is adequate, uninterrupted time for reading and literacy instruction protected?

A faculty may wisely opt to inquire into only two or three aspects of current practice at a time. For example, imagine your school has just selected improving reading comprehension of either exposition or narrative fiction as a priority. Considering what you know about your context, and after reading and analyzing several resources, you may decide to inquire only into how reading comprehension is assessed and into the size of classroom book collections to start your investigation.

Gathering Information About Assessment Practices. Your school leadership team might work together and answer the following questions about reading comprehension assessment:

1. Are there any up-close, standard reading comprehension measures used by all team members? If there are, please describe them.
2. Are there any measures used predominantly in kindergarten classrooms? If there are, please describe them. (Have a separate item for each grade level.)
3. Are there any measures used predominantly in special classes? If there are, please describe them.
4. Are there any summative, norm-referenced measures of reading comprehension administered? If so, at what grade levels?

Once team members have put together their summary, it should go to the whole faculty for discussion and clarification. Then faculty members should address this question: *"Does our system for assessing student progress in comprehension provide a profile of student development K–6?"* If not, what's missing that will most help classroom teachers plan instruction *and* help the faculty analyze

student progress across the grades? (Of course, I'm going to bet that standard, up-close measures are missing, just as they were at Elwood Elementary.)

Gathering Information About Curriculum Materials. A simple form like Figure 14.3 can be used to assess classroom book collections. Then one or two members of the leadership team can organize a schoolwide profile so faculty members can see what quantity looks like in every classroom. Next, you should compare your findings to what you believe is needed and to recommendations from the external knowledge base, and decide if action needs to be taken.

Gathering Information About Instructional Practices. After reading "Effective Practices for Developing Reading Comprehension" (Duke & Pearson, 2002) or "Questioning the Author: A Year-Long Classroom Implementation to Engage Students with Text" (Beck, McKeown, Worthy, Sandora, & Kucan, 1996), you may decide to collect information about how reading comprehension is being taught. To gather this information, ask teachers to keep a log for five days. Ask them to jot down what they do when they're teaching "reading comprehension." I know some of us are doing that almost all day, but for this purpose, I am talking about something the teacher does that directly addresses the development of the comprehension results and processes in Figure 11.2.

The data from the logs will most likely be lists of actions and materials and brief descriptions of instructional practices. It will be a bit messy, but see what you discover. You're trying to

---
FIGURE **14.3**

Assessing the Quantity of Books in Classroom Collections

Teacher: _____   **Grade:** _____   **Date:** _____

Purpose and Procedures: This activity will help determine how many books your students have access to and help you assess the balance of fiction and nonfiction books in your classroom. Simply count the number of books available for students to read at this time.

- Do not count books that are in the cupboards or closets (even though you may rotate them out at some time during the year).

- Do not count magazines and textbooks.

- These books may be owned by the school, media center, or teachers.

Number of Available Books

Total Number of Books	Number of Fiction Books	Number of Nonfiction Books

---

develop a picture of what students are experiencing under the guise of reading comprehension instruction. You know the rest of the story—summarize, discuss, compare, and decide whether action is needed. (Depending on your context, grade level teams may do the first analysis and summary.)

Generally, the more engaged faculty members are in thoughtful study and discussion of the external knowledge base, the more questions they have about their own practices. (Of course, this doesn't apply to everyone. We do have a few closed minds in some settings. But the good news is there aren't many.) The Questions to Explore sections in Chapters 10 through 12 list some common inquiries in instruction, curriculum materials, assessment, and organization of the reading dimensions addressed in this book.

Supporting and Studying the Implementation of Desirable Changes (Matrix Cell 6)

Once you've selected one or more instructional strategies that need to be in widespread use throughout your school, you're ready to organize practice-oriented staff development and study of implementation. I'll share two tools you can use as you plan staff development: one is a set of critical attributes for designing staff development, and the other is a sample implementation log.

There are many forms of professional development with various content and purposes (Killion, 2003; National Staff Development Council, 2001). Some have been mentioned in this book (for example, reading and discussing articles, studying student data, analyzing student work, and planning staff development sessions for colleagues). Some forms target individuals, and others target study groups, leadership and facilitation teams, and/or faculties. But the kind of professional development I'm going to address is often called the *staff development training model,* and its components are similar to the explicit instruction model in reading. I believe it's our best bet when we want to expand knowledge and skills rapidly and when we do not have time to proceed one-by-one as individuals perceive a need.

Designing Effective Practice-Oriented Staff Development. The staff development training model, as developed and tested by Joyce and Showers (1982, 1995, 2002), is designed to support making changes in knowledge and skill and to transfer these changes into classroom practice. While the purpose of such staff development is to improve student learning, the desired outcomes include helping participants gain executive control of new or expanded instructional practices.

If your intent is to have widespread and expert use of the instructional strategies mentioned in this book—such as explicit instruction, inductive models of teaching, questioning the author, reciprocal teaching, and think-alouds—you'll want a series of workshops that include these attributes: presentation of the theoretical base supporting the strategy, multiple demonstrations of the strategy, opportunities to rehearse and practice the strategy, and expert coaching.

You'll also want to build the following workplace activities and time for them into your school calendar and action plan: peer coaching sessions in which teachers and administrators plan and rehearse lessons and talk about student responses; routines for the regular collection and analysis of implementation data; and time for expert coaches and team leaders to observe, study implementation data, and design future workshops. A knowledgeable staff development provider (either someone in your own school or someone from the outside community) and the support of colleagues and the organization make successful implementation more likely.

Studying the Implementation of Instructional Strategies. Implementation means to accomplish what we set out to do. Successful implementation of an instructional strategy depends on one's assimilation of the rationale, strategic moves, and curriculum content into consistent and appropriate use in the classroom. After a faculty selects an instructional strategy, the leadership team can begin to plan staff development and the study of implementation.

For example, let's look at the simplest of the five actions Elwood selected to help expand reading vocabulary and word analysis skills: "Increase read-alouds to students in prekindergarten through grade 5."

After collecting data on their current use of read-alouds of fiction and nonfiction and discussing the findings in their study groups, Elwood's leadership team suggested to the faculty that they work first on increasing nonfiction read-alouds. They suggested this because most teachers, except for a few at the upper grades, were regularly reading fiction to their students, but not nonfiction. In addition, when teachers assessed the size and nature of their classroom book collections and kept their first log of fiction and nonfiction read-alouds, many more questions surfaced about how to use nonfiction. Also, during their discussions and while they were summarizing the data on classroom collections and use of read-alouds, team members realized that more of *them* were comfortable with the fiction books they were using and that they were less certain about the attributes of quality nonfiction.

When they had their first workshop, the staff development provider used Figure 14.4, "Nonfiction Read-Aloud Implementation Log," as she explained the purposes of and demonstrated brief read-alouds for use in science and social

studies. She had participants use the same form during the workshop when they planned lessons and rehearsed read-alouds with their peer coaching partners. Elwood used this form to collect implementation data.

Good implementation logs can be used in planning lessons, observing peer coaching partners, and observing live or videotaped demonstrations. We're not very experienced at studying implementation, even though it is basically studying our own learning and progress at the individual and organizational levels. To do so effectively, first we must simply find out who's trying the new curriculum or strategies and how often. After a while, we can begin to study how well they are being used, documenting novice, intermediate, and expert use. Each time we collect data, we can look at them and figure out how to support ourselves in moving forward.

Designing School Action Plans

Of course, having a good plan doesn't mean that student achievement will automatically increase or that the quality of your reading program will necessarily improve, but these consequences will be far more likely. The school action plan pulls together what the faculty has learned and how it will be pursued. Remember that at Elwood, the action plan came to symbolize a public commitment to selected actions and continuing inquiry. It includes the actions of the Action Research Matrix (Cells 1–6) and professional development activities. At the most basic level, it is a "living plan"

——————— FIGURE 14.4 ———————

Nonfiction Read-Aloud Implementation Log

Name/Grade Level or Role: _____   **Date:** _____

School/Organization: _____

Review: A read-aloud is simply reading aloud to your students. Read-alouds of expository prose can be brief, sharing as little as a sentence and illustration or a single paragraph. When you're looking for good models to share and discuss with students, look for (1) passages that address concepts that fit into curriculum content across disciplines; and (2) passages that are well-written, especially in terms of how the author(s) announce and support major points. One of the major instructional purposes of nonfiction read-alouds is to provide an opportunity for students to learn science, social studies, mathematics, and other curriculum concepts and vocabulary. Our long-term goal, however, is for students to use similar text as learners and independent readers.

Title, author, and page number(s) of nonfiction book used:

1. Concepts addressed from social studies, science, mathematics, other:

2. Language arts concepts and processes represented in the text selection:

3a. Organization of the lesson and reflections on the attributes of the read-aloud:

3b. Reflections on student responses:

4. Questions about using read-alouds:

In the last five days, have you worked with your peer coaching partner to select and rehearse read-alouds? _____ Yes _____ No If "Yes," how many times? _____

In the last five days, have you demonstrated a read-aloud (with students) for your peer coaching partner? _____ Yes _____ No If "Yes," how many times? _____

for concerted action, identifying what will be done, who will do it, when it will be done, which resources will be used, and how progress will be assessed. Both effects on student learning and the implementation of selected actions are measured. And faculty members look at data from both sources as they determine progress and make decisions for further action.

Following is a list of questions to use in designing or assessing action plans. The questions address many of the building blocks of successful school improvement (Joyce, Calhoun, & Hopkins, 1999).

1. Does the plan *allocate time for the whole staff to pursue a major student-learning goal*? How many times will the whole staff be working together? Weekly is optimum; every other week will keep things going well as long as peer coaches are working together weekly.

2. Does the plan include *formative assessment measures to keep the staff regularly informed about student progress*? For up-close measures, do you have two or three administration times, times allocated for organizing the data, and times allocated for sharing the data as a staff and for planning their use?

3. How does the plan support the *continuous study of the knowledge base* in the focus area?

4. How many *research-based actions and strategies are being pursued* by the staff as a whole? Is there enough time allocated to pursue the selected strategies?

5. Have provisions been made for *practice-oriented staff development at the school level*? Have provisions been made for *technical assistance throughout the year*? Are dates scheduled for staff development and for the leadership team to work with the technical assistant or staff development provider?

6. What provisions have been made for *the study of implementation of strategies*? What provisions have been made for the analysis of implementation data?

7. What groups and structures are in place to support an informed professional citizenry (a facilitation/leadership team, peer coaching teams, a system for making decisions)? Does the plan indicate *times for the leadership team to meet and plan and times or provisions for peer coaching partners to meet*?

8. Are there any *policies* at the school, district, or state levels that impede the pursuit of the actions described in the plan and *that need to be addressed*?

Most of the building blocks of successful school improvement are under the control of school faculties and school and district administrators. We have long denied ourselves and our students just celebrations of learning by using year-to-year scheduled adoptions; by reacting frantically to initiatives from the district, state, or federal government; or by failing, for whatever reasons, to implement a good curriculum widely and to assess the effects of our actions carefully.

How do schools successfully improve student proficiency in reading? By the choices we make and the actions we take. Plan a good course of study for yourselves, just like you would for students.

Thinking About Sources of Reading Research

In Chapters 10 through 13, you saw citations for the major published compilations and syntheses of reading research from the last 15 years, for research studies in peer-reviewed journals, and for easy-to-read, less technical articles and books. Research syntheses and articles from peer-reviewed journals are good sources of information. However, good information can also be found in articles and documents written by scholars or practitioners and published in educational journals, available from sources such as *The Reading Teacher* (for example, Hoffman, Roser, & Battle, 1993, "Reading Aloud in Classrooms: From the Modal to a 'Model' "); *Language Arts* (for example, Invernizzi, Abouzeid, & Bloodgood, 1997, "Integrated Word Study: Spelling, Grammar, and Meaning in the Language Arts Classroom"); and *Educational Leadership* (for example, Juel, Biancarosa, Coker, & Deffes, 2003, "Walking with Rosie: A Cautionary Tale of Early Reading Instruction"), as well as books such as *Making Facts Come Alive: Choosing Quality Nonfiction Literature K–8* (Bamford & Kristo, 1998) or *Explaining Reading: A Resource for Teaching Concepts, Skills, and Strategies* (Duffy, 2003).

Below are brief descriptions of three common types of research resources:

1. *Research handbooks* are generally compiled by two or more scholars who invite colleagues to address a particular topic. They include chapters on topics of current or longstanding interest, such as "Chapter 26: Beginning Reading Instruction: Research on Early Interventions" (Hiebert & Taylor, 2000). Some examples include the following:

   - *Handbook of Reading Research: Vol. II* (Barr, Kamil, Mosenthal, & Pearson, 1991)
   - *Handbook of Reading Research: Vol. III* (Kamil, Mosenthal, Pearson, & Barr, 2000)
   - *Handbook of Early Literacy Research* (Neuman & Dickinson, 2001)

2. *Large-scale, federally funded research reviews* are generally compiled by a panel of scholars appointed by a funding agency and charged with collecting, interpreting, and synthesizing research in a given domain. Examples include the following:

   - *Preventing Reading Difficulties in Young Children* (Snow, Burns, & Griffin, 1998)
   - *Report of the National Reading Panel: Teaching Children to Read: An Evidence-Based Assessment of the Scientific Research Literature on Reading and Its Implications for Reading Instruction—Reports of the Subgroups* (National Reading Panel, 2000)

3. The articles in *peer-reviewed research journals* include research studies or

syntheses that have been reviewed for quality and accuracy by other professionals within a field. Examples of these include *Reading Research Quarterly, American Educational Research Journal, Review of Educational Research, Journal of Educational Psychology, Elementary School Journal, Journal of Literacy Research,* and *Research in the Teaching of English.*

A Short List of Recommended Resources

Becoming a More Knowledgeable Consumer of Educational Research

➤ Huck, S. W. (2000). *Reading statistics and research* (3rd ed.). New York: Longman.

This is a resource I've found useful ever since its first edition came out in 1974 (Huck, Cormier, & Bounds). It helped me early on as a teacher struggling to comprehend some of the research articles I read and later to evaluate the quality of the research methodology and the appropriateness of the statistics used. Now in its third edition (Huck, 2000) and almost twice its original size, it's still a handy reference for

helping individuals or teams learn to analyze and screen educational research.

➤ Bogdan, R. C., & Biklen, S. K. (1992). *Qualitative research for education: An introduction to theory and methods* (2nd ed.). Boston: Allyn & Bacon.

For questions about qualitative studies, it's nice to have Bogdan and Biklen (1992) in your head or on your reference shelf.

➤ Miles, M. B., & Huberman, A. M. (1994). *Qualitative data analysis* (2nd ed.). Thousand Oaks, CA: Sage.

This is a good how-to guide for collecting and analyzing qualitative data. However, as a research consumer, I've always appreciated the authors' sets of "relevant queries" that can be applied to qualitative work and used to judge the quality of conclusions presented. Many of the questions they provide for readers apply to both quantitative and qualitative studies. Here is an example of one such question:

> Has the researcher been explicit and as self-aware as possible about personal assumptions, values and biases, affective states—and how they may have come into play during the study? (p. 278)

In the Name of Science—The Rapidly Disappearing Evidence Base

Beginning in 1998, districts that were allocated federal funds to improve reading achievement and instruction K–3 through the Reading Excellence Act (REA) were required to use these monies to support instructional practices that come from "scientifically based reading research." While that doesn't sound like a bad idea, let's follow this trail deeper into the forest. The REA guidelines were as follows:

The term "scientifically based reading research"—

(A) Means the application of rigorous, systematic, and objective procedures to obtain valid knowledge relevant to reading development, reading instruction, and reading difficulties.

(B) Shall include research that—

    i. Employs systematic, empirical methods that draw on observation or experiment;

    ii. Involves rigorous data analyses that are adequate to test the stated hypotheses and justify the general conclusions drawn;

    iii. Relies on measurements or observational methods that provide valid data across evaluators and *observers,* and across multiple measurements and observations; and

    iv. Has been accepted by a peer-reviewed journal or approved by a panel of independent experts through a comparatively rigorous, objective, and scientific review. (Section 2252 (5) [Reading Excellence Program Overview])

This definition was still available as of May 2004 at www.ed.gov/policy/elsec/leg/esea02/pg4.html#sec1208 and is the one used in Reading First. If you're not familiar with Reading First, it is a formula grant program to states included in the No Child Left Behind Act. (It replaces the REA grants.) Funds are allocated to states based on the number of children between the ages of 5 and 17 who come from families below the poverty line. The intent of Reading First is to support states, districts, and schools in using scientifically based reading research to improve reading programs K–3. Its goal is worthy: to have all students between kindergarten and 3rd grade read at grade level or above.

The reading content of Reading First matches the "findings" of the National Reading Panel Report (2000).

Teaching Children to Read, the report of the National Reading Panel (2000), appeared to use the above definition and requirements, but extended their "rigor" by largely limiting its examination to experimental and quasi-experimental studies of reading. Here is a statement from the NRP report:

> Unfortunately, only a small fraction of the total reading research literature met the Panel's standards for use in the topic analyses. (p. 27, in the Methodology section of the Introduction)

Many of us who work in and with school districts and school leadership teams have become more and more concerned as we watch how the definition of "scientifically based reading research" in Reading First and the NRP report are being used to restrict the literacy curriculum and reading experiences of our children. Long-established scholars in our field have been direct in reminding us to be cautious when interpreting or applying the findings of the report:

> What are we to make of a report that so boldly lays claim to what science, rigor, and objectivity are in reading research, and first denigrates, then ignores, the preponderance of research literature in our field? (Cunningham, 2000, p. 51)

> I find it puzzling that scientists as good as the ones on the [National Reading] Panel could have convinced themselves to take these conceptually and methodologically narrow approaches. (Pressley, 2001a; Pressley, 2001b)

Now, let's go to conferences provided to help states and districts develop their Reading First grants and interventions (for example, Student Achievement and School Accountability Conference, October 2002) and materials provided by the United States Department of Education, such as Assistant Secretary Whitehurst's presentation on "Evidence-Based Education (EBE)." If you read Whitehurst's slides, you'll find that true experimental studies that have random assignment to conditions are "the gold standard" educators should use when identifying studies of effective instructional practices (http://www.ed.gov.offices/admins/tchrqual/evidence/whitehurst.html?exp=0).

While Stanovich and Stanovich (2003) assign more value to peer-reviewed research journals than I would, and assign more value to correlational methods and qualitative studies than the U.S. Department of Education currently does, their monograph is a nice place to begin if you're struggling with justifying effective practices. Their opening remarks include the following excerpt:

> Standards- and assessment-based educational reforms seek to obligate schools and teachers to supply evidence that their instructional methods are effective. . . . Evidence of instructional effectiveness can come from any of the following sources:
>
> - Demonstrated student achievement in **formal testing** situations implemented by the teacher, school district, or state;
> - **Published findings of research-based evidence** that the instructional methods being used by teachers lead to student achievement; or

- **Proof of reason-based practice** that converges with a research-based consensus in the scientific literature. This type of justification of educational practice becomes important when direct evidence may be lacking (a direct test of the instructional efficacy of a particular method is absent), but there is a theoretical link to research-based evidence that can be traced. (p. 1, boldface in primary source)

For an easy-to-read analysis of the current definitions of scientifically based research and their implications for our work, see "Into the Mix: Policy, Practice, and Research" (Laitsch, 2003).

B

A Guide to the CD-ROM

The CD-ROM accompanying this book provides downloadable versions of the table shells presented throughout the book. You are welcome to use them as templates or distribute and use them in your school. The forms have been created in Microsoft Excel, the leading spreadsheet software. Each form is presented in a separate document and has been designed for data entry. Each document also contains directions and a sample, filled-in version of the form, which reflects the print version of the examples presented in this appendix.

Disk Contents

Name of the Electronic File	Name of Table on CD-Rom	Text Example	Page
Table 1	Enrollment	Figure 4.1	37
Table 2	Student Characteristics: Race and Ethnicity	Figure 4.1	37
Table 3	Student Characteristics: Gender	Figure 4.1	37
Table 4	Student Characteristics: Socioeconomic Status	Figure 4.1	38
Table 5	Student Characteristics: Native Languages	Figure 4.1	38
Table 6	Student Characteristics: English Language Proficiency	Figure 4.1	38
Table 7	Student Attendance and Suspension: Presence and Absence for Instruction	Figure 4.3	42
Table 8	Student Participation in Special Categorical Programs: By Grade Level and Gender	Figure 4.4	45

Name of the Electronic File	Name of Table on CD-Rom	Text Example	Page
Table 9	Student Participation in Special Categorical Programs: By Student Need	Figure 4.4	45
Table 10	Analysis of Efforts of Special Programs to Raise Student Achievement	Figure 4.5	46
Table 11	K–5 Student Achievement in Reading: Grades or Progress Indicators by Gender	Figure 5.1	51
Table 12	Retention: Number and Ethnicity by Grade Level for School Year	Figure 5.3	53
Table 13	Standardized Tests: Participation Rate	Figure 6.8	70
Table 14	Standardized Test Scores, by Gender: Reading Comprehension	Figure 6.9	70
Table 15	Standardized Test Scores: Growth Analysis	Figure 6.10	71
Table 16	Concepts About Print: Individual Student	Figure 7.1	78
Table 17	Concepts About Print: Class Summary	Figure 7.1	79
Table 18	Concepts About Print: Grade Level Summary	Figure 7.1	79
Table 19	Phonological and Phonemic Awareness: Individual Student	Figure 10.1	107
Table 20	Phonological and Phonemic Awareness: Class Summary	Figure 10.1	107
Table 21	Phonological and Phonemic Awareness: Grade Level Summary	Figure 10.1	108
Table 22	Phonemic Awareness: Grade Level Summary	Figure 10.1	108
Table 23	Sight Word and Word Analysis Skills: Class Summary	Figure 11.6	140
Table 24	Building Reading Vocabulary—Fluency (Words Correct Per Minute): Grade Level Summary	Figure 11.7	142
Table 25	Sight Word Recognition: Class Summary	Figure 11.10	147
Table 26	Reading Vocabulary, Comprehension, and Rate: Class Summary	Figure 12.4	174
Table 27	Just Read: Student Weekly Reading Log	Figure 13.1	182
Table 28	Just Read: Class Log—Males	Figure 13.2	183
Table 29	Just Read: Elementary School Summary	Figure 13.3	184

Minimum System Requirements

- *Program:* Excel 97 or Version 7.0
- *Operating System:* Windows 98 or NT 4.0, or Macintosh OS 9
- *RAM:* 16 MB
- *Drive:* 2X CD-ROM drive

Getting Started

Insert the CD-ROM into your computer's CD drive and click on the appropriate drive icon to launch it. You will see a directory of the MS Excel documents.

To Download Documents

The documents on the CD-ROM are *read-only*. To download a document, open it by double-clicking on the document name. Under the File pull-down menu, choose *Save As*. Save the document to your hard drive, using a new file name. It is important to use a different name; otherwise, the document may remain a read-only file.

To Use the Forms

Once you have saved the documents to your hard drive, follow the embedded instructions in each form to customize it for your school's use (e.g., adding your school's name). Please note that calculations in the forms are entry-protected. To change programming or calculation options, or to add or subtract cells and text, you will need to turn off the sheet protection. Consult MS Excel programming guidelines for specific instructions. Finally, it is important that those responsible for reviewing and "signing off" on electronic financial forms that contain automated calculations remember to always give these forms the same degree of scrutiny that they would give to old-fashioned paper forms.

References

Adams, M. J. (1990). *Beginning to read: Thinking and learning about print.* Cambridge, MA: MIT Press.

Adams, M. J., Foorman, B. R., Lundberg, I., & Beeler, T. (1998). *Phonemic awareness in young children: A classroom curriculum.* Baltimore: Paul Brookes Publishing.

Adams, M. J., & Huggins, A. W. F. (1985). The growth of children's sight vocabulary: A quick test with educational and theoretical implications. *Reading Research Quarterly, 20*(3), 262–281.

Allington, R. L. (1983). The reading instruction provided readers of differing abilities. *Elementary School Journal, 83,* 548–559.

Allington, R. L. (1991). The legacy of "Slow it down and make it more concrete." In J. Zutell & S. McCormick (Eds.), *Learner factors/ teacher factors: Issues in literacy research and instruction* (40th Yearbook of the National Reading Conference, pp. 19–30). Chicago: National Reading Conference.

Allington, R. L. (2001). *What really matters for struggling readers: Designing research-based programs.* New York: Longman.

Allington, R. L. (2003). The six Ts of effective elementary literacy instruction. Accessed March 5, 2003: http://www.readingrockets. org/article.php?ID=413

Anderson, L. W., & Bourke, S. F. (2000). *Assessing affective characteristics in the schools* (2nd ed.). Mahwah, NJ: Lawrence Erlbaum.

Anderson, R. C. (1996). Research foundations to support wide reading. In V. Greaney (Ed.), *Promoting reading in developing countries* (pp. 55–77). Newark, DE: International Reading Association.

Anderson, R. C., & Freebody, P. (1981). Vocabulary knowledge. In J. Guthrie (Ed.), *Comprehension and teaching: Research reviews* (pp. 77–117). Newark, DE: International Reading Association.

Anderson, R. C., & Nagy, W. E. (1992, Winter). The vocabulary conundrum. *American Educator, 16*(4), 14–18, 44–47. (ERIC Document Reproduction Service No. ED 354 489)

Applebee, A. N., Langer, J. A., Mullis, I. V. S. (1988). *Who reads best? Factors related to reading achievement in grades 3, 7, and 11* (Report No: 17-R-01). Princeton, NJ: Educational Testing Service.

Applebee, A. N., Langer, J. A., Mullis, I. V. S., Latham, A. S., & Gentile, C. A. (1994). *NAEP 1992 writing report card* (Report No. 23-W01). Washington, DC: U.S. Government Printing Office.

Armbruster, B. B., Lehr, F., & Osborn, J. (2001). *Put reading first: The research building blocks for teaching children to read.* Jessup, MD: National Institute for Literacy.

Bamford, R. A., & Kristo, J. V. (1998). *Making facts come alive: Choosing quality nonfiction literature K–8.* Norwood, MA: Christopher-Gordon.

Barr, R., Kamil, M. L., Mosenthal, P., & Pearson, P. D. (Eds.). (1991). *Handbook of reading research: Vol. II.* Mahwah, NJ: Lawrence Erlbaum.

Baumann, J. F., Edwards, E. C., Font, G., Tereshinski, C. A., Kameenui, E.

213

J., & Olejnik, S. (2002). Teaching morphemic and contextual analysis to fifth-grade students. *Reading Research Quarterly, 37*(2), 150–176.

Bear, D. R., Invernizzi, M., Templeton, S., & Johnston, F. (2000). *Words their way: Word study for phonics, vocabulary, and spelling instruction* (2nd ed.). Upper Saddle River, NJ: Merrill/Prentice-Hill.

Beck, I., & McKeown, M. (1991). Conditions of vocabulary acquisition. In R. Barr, M. L. Kamil, P. Mosenthal, & P. D. Pearson (Eds.), *Handbook of reading research: Vol. II* (pp. 789–814). Mahwah, NJ: Lawrence Erlbaum.

Beck, I. L., McKeown, M. G., Hamilton, R. L., & Kucan, L. (1997). *Questioning the author: An approach for enhancing student engagement with text.* Newark, DE: International Reading Association.

Beck, I. L., McKeown, M. G., & Kucan, L. (2002). *Bringing words to life: Robust vocabulary instruction.* New York: Guilford Press.

Beck, I. L., McKeown, M. G., & McCaslin, E. S. (1983). Vocabulary development: All contexts are not created equal. *The Elementary School Journal, 83*(3), 177–181.

Beck, I. L., McKeown, M. G., Worthy, J., Sandora, C. A., & Kucan, L. (1996). Questioning the author: A year-long classroom implementation to engage students with text. *The Elementary School Journal, 96*(4), 385–414.

Beck, I. L., Perfetti, C. A., & McKeown, M. G. (1982). The effects of long-term vocabulary instruction on lexical access and reading comprehension. *Journal of Educational Psychology, 74*(4), 506–521.

Bell, D., & Jarvis, D. (2001). Letting go of "Letter of the Week." *Primary Voices K–6, 11*(2), 11–24.

Berkowitz, S. J., & Taylor, B. M. (1981). The effects of text type and familiarity on the nature of information recalled by readers. In M. Kamil (Ed.), *Directions in reading: Research and instruction.* Washington, DC: National Reading Conference.

Biemiller, A. (1999, April). *Estimating vocabulary growth for ESL children with and without listening comprehension instruction.* Paper presented at the annual meeting of the American Educational Research Association. Montreal, Canada.

Blachowicz, C., & Ogle, D. (2001). *Reading comprehension: Strategies for independent learners.* New York: Guilford Press.

Block, C. L., & Pressley, M. (Eds.). (2002). *Comprehension instruction: Research-based best practices.* New York: Guilford Press.

Bogdan, R. C., & Biklen, S. K. (1992). *Qualitative research for education: An introduction to theory and methods* (2nd ed.). Boston: Allyn & Bacon.

Bond, G. L., & Dykstra, R. (1967). The Cooperative Research Program in first-grade reading instruction. *Reading Research Quarterly, 2*(4), 5–142. (Reprinted in 1997, *Reading Research Quarterly, 32*(4), 348–427.)

Bransford, J. D., Brown, A. L., & Cocking, R. R. (Eds.). (1999). *How people learn: Brain, mind, experience, and school.* Washington, DC: National Academy Press.

Brown, A. L., Bransford, J. D., & Campione, J. C. (1983). Learning, remembering, and understanding. In J. H. Flavel & E. M. Markman (Eds.), *Handbook of child psychology: Vol. 3 cognitive development* (4th ed.) (pp. 78–166). New York: Wiley.

Bryk, A. S., Sebring, P. B., Kerbow, D., Rollow, S., & Easton, J. (1998). *Charting Chicago school reform.* Boulder, CO: Westview Press.

Caldwell, J. S. (2002). *Reading assessment: A primer for teachers and tutors.* New York: Guilford Press.

Calhoun, E. F. (1994). *How to use action research in the self-renewing school.* Alexandria, VA: Association for Supervision and Curriculum Development.

Calhoun, E. F. (1999). *Teaching beginning reading and writing with the Picture Word Inductive Model.* Alexandria, VA: Association for Supervision and Curriculum Development.

Calhoun, E. F. (2002). Action research for school improvement. *Educational Leadership, 59*(6), 18–24.

Calkins, L., Montgomery, K., Santman, D., & Falk, B. (1998). *A teacher's guide to standardized reading tests.* Portsmouth, NH: Heinemann.

Camilli, G., Vargas, S., & Yurecko, M. (2003, May 8). Teaching children to read: The fragile link between science and federal education policy. *Education Policy Analysis Archives, 11*(15). Accessed August 10, 2003: http://epaa.asu.edu/epaa/v11n15/

Carroll, J. B., Davies, P., & Richman, B. (1971). *The American heritage word frequency book.* New York: American Heritage Publishing.

Chall, J. S. (1967). *Learning to read: The great debate.* New York: McGraw-Hill.

Chall, J. S. (1983). *Learning to read: The great debate* (2nd ed.). New York: McGraw-Hill.

Chall, J. S., Jacobs, V., & Baldwin, L. (1990). *The reading crisis: Why poor children fall behind.* Cambridge, MA: Harvard University Press.

Cipielewski, J., & Stanovich, K. (1992). Predicting growth in reading ability from children's exposure to print. *Journal of Experimental Child Psychology, 54,* 74–89.

Clay, M. M. (1987). Learning to be learning disabled. *New Zealand Journal of Educational Studies, 22,* 155–173.

Clay, M. M. (1989). Concepts about print: In English and other languages. *The Reading Teacher, 42*(4), 268–277.

Clay, M. M. (1993). *An observation survey of early literacy achievement.* Portsmouth, NH: Heinemann.

Clymer, T. (1963/1996). The utility of phonic generalizations in the primary grades. *The Reading Teacher, 50*(3), 182–187.

Cooley, W. (1993). The difficulty of the educational task: Implications for comparing student achievement in states, school districts, and schools. *ERS Spectrum, 11,* 27–31.

Cunningham, J. W. (2002). The National Reading Panel report [A review]. In R. L. Allington (Ed.), *Big brother and the national reading curriculum: How ideology trumped evidence* (pp. 49–74). Portsmouth, NH: Heinemann.

Cunningham, P. M. (1990). The Names Test: A quick assessment of decoding ability. *The Reading Teacher, 44,* 124–129.

Cunningham, P. M. (2000). *Phonics they use: Words for reading and writing* (3rd ed.). New York: Longman.

Cunningham, P. M., & Cunningham, J. W. (1992). Making words: Enhancing the invented spelling-decoding connection. *The Reading Teacher, 46*(2), 106–115.

Dale, E., & O'Rourke, J. (1976). *The living word vocabulary: The words we know.* Elgin, IL: Dome.

Darling-Hammond, L., & Ball, D. L. (1998). *Teaching for high standards: What policymakers need to know and be able to do.*

Philadelphia: University of Pennsylvania Graduate School of Education, Consortium for Policy Research in Education.

Dolch, E. W. (1936). A basic sight vocabulary. *Elementary School Journal, 36,* 456–460.

Dole, J. A., Duffy, G. G., Roehler, L. R., & Pearson, P. D. (1991). Moving from the old to the new: Research on reading comprehension instruction. *Review of Educational Research, 61*(2), 239–264.

Donahue, P. L., Finnegan, R. J., Lutkus, A. D., Allen, N. L., & Campbell, J. R. (2001). *The nation's report card: Fourth-grade reading 2000* (NCES 2001-499). Washington, DC: National Center for Education Statistics. (Available at http://nces.ed.gov)

Downey, L. (1967). *The secondary phase of education.* Boston: Ginn & Co.

Duffelmeyer, F. A., Kruse, A. E., Merkley, D. J., & Fyfe, S. A. (1994). Further validation and enhancement of The Names Test. *The Reading Teacher, 48*(2), 118–128.

Duffy, G. G. (2003). *Explaining reading: A resource for teaching concepts, skills, and strategies.* New York: Guilford.

Duffy, G. G., Roehler, L. R., Sivan, E., Rackliffe, G., Book, C., Meloth, M., Vavrus, L., Wesselman, R., Putnam, J., & Bassiri, D. (1987). Effects of explaining the reasoning associated with using reading strategies. *Reading Research Quarterly, 22*(3), 347–368.

Duke, N. K. (2000). For the rich it's richer: Print experiences and environments offered to children in very low- and very high-socioeconomic status first-grade classrooms. *American Educational Research Journal, 37*(2), 441–478.

Duke, N. K. (2001). Effective comprehension instruction in the primary grades. Paper presented at the CIERA Summer Institute, Michigan State University. East Lansing, MI.

Duke, N. K. (2002). *Comprehension.* PowerPoint presentation for the Iowa Department of Education, Des Moines. Ann Arbor, MI: Center for the Improvement of Early Reading Achievement.

Duke, N. K., & Pearson, P. D. (2002). Effective practices for developing reading comprehension. In A. E. Farstrup & S. J. Samuels (Eds.), *What research has to say about reading instruction* (3rd ed.) (pp.

205–242). Newark, DE: International Reading Association.

Durkin, D. (1978–79). What classroom observations reveal about reading comprehension instruction. *Reading Research Quarterly, 14*(4), 481–533.

Duthie, C. (1994). Nonfiction: A genre study for the primary classroom. *Language Arts, 71,* 97–104.

Eakin, E. (2002, July 14). 'Sexual selections': Show me your plumage. *The New York Times Book Review,* p. 26.

Ehri, L. C. (1991). Development of the ability to read words. In R. Barr, M. L. Kamil, P. Mosenthal, & P. D. Pearson (Eds.), *Handbook of reading research: Vol. II* (pp. 383–417). Mahwah, NJ: Erlbaum.

Ehri, L. C. (1994). Development of the ability to read words: An update. In R. B. Ruddell, M. P. Ruddell, & H. Singer (Eds.), *Theoretical models and processes of reading* (4th ed.) (pp. 323–358). Newark, DE: International Reading Association.

Ehri, L. C. (1995). Phases of development in learning to read words by sight. *Journal of Research in Reading, 18*(2), 116–125.

Ehri, L. C. (1998a). Essential processes in learning to read words. In P. D. Pearson (Ed.), *New York State Reading Symposium: Final Report* (pp. 39–58). Albany, NY: New York State Education Department.

Ehri, L. C. (1998b). Word reading by sight and by analogy in beginning readers. In C. Hulme & R. M. Joshi (Eds.), *Reading and spelling: Development and disorders* (pp. 87–111). Mahwah, NJ: L. Erlbaum Associates.

Ehri, L. C. (1999, April). *Phases of acquisition in learning to read words and instructional implications.* Paper presented at the annual meeting of the American Educational Research Association. Montreal, Canada.

Ehri, L. C., Nunes, S., Stahl, S., & Willows, D. M. (2001). Systematic phonics instruction helps students learn to read: Evidence from the National Reading Panel's meta-analysis. *Review of Educational Research, 71*(3), pp. 393–447.

Elmore, R. F. (2000). *Building a new structure for school leadership.* Washington, DC: The Albert Shanker Institute.

Englert, C. S., Raphael, T. E., Anderson, L. M., Anthony, H. M., & Stevens, D. D. (1991). Making strategies and self-talk visible: Writing instruction in regular and special education classrooms. *American Educational Research Journal, 28*(2), 337–372.

Fielding, L. G., & Pearson, P. D. (1994). Reading comprehension: What works. *Educational Leadership 51*(5), 62–68.

Fountas, I. C., & Pinnell, G. S. (2001). *Guiding readers and writers, Grades 3–6: Teaching comprehension, genre, and content literacy.* Portsmouth, NH: Heinemann.

Fry, E. B. (1980). The new instant word list. *The Reading Teacher, 34,* 284–289.

Fry, E. B. (1999). *1000 instant words.* Westminster, CA: Teacher Created Materials.

Fullan, M. G. (2001). *The new meaning of educational change* (3rd ed.). New York: Teachers College Press.

Fullan, M. G., & Stiegelbauer, S. (1991). *The new meaning of educational change* (2nd ed.). New York: Teachers College Press.

Garner, R. (1987). *Metacognition and reading comprehension.* Norwood, NJ: Ablex.

Gaskins, I. W., Downer, M., Anderson, R. C., Cunningham, P. M., Gaskins, R. W., Schommer, M., & the Teachers at Benchmark School. (1988). A metacognitive approach to phonics: Using what you know to decode what you don't know. *Remedial and Special Education, 9,* 36–41.

Gaskins, I. W., Ehri, L. C., Cress, C., O'Hara, C., & Donnelly, K. (1996/1997). Procedures for word learning: Making discoveries about words. *The Reading Teacher, 50*(4), 312–327.

Gaskins, R. W., Gaskins, J. C., & Gaskins, I. W. (1991). A decoding program for poor readers—and the rest of the class, too! *Language Arts, 68,* 213–225.

Graesser, A., Golding, J. M., & Long, D. L. (1991). Narrative representation and comprehension. In R. Barr, M. L. Kamil, P. Mosenthal, & P. D. Pearson (Eds.), *Handbook of reading research: Vol. II* (pp. 171–205). Mahwah, NJ: Erlbaum.

Graves, M. F. (1992). The elementary vocabulary curriculum: What should it be? In M. J. Dreher & W. H. Slater (Eds.), *Elementary school literacy: Critical issues* (pp. 101–131). Norwood, MA: Christopher-Gordon.

Graves, M. F., & Watts-Taffe, S. M. (2002). The place of word consciousness in a research-based vocabulary program. In A. E. Farstrup & S. J. Samuels (Eds.), *What research has to say about reading instruction* (3rd ed.). Newark, DE: International Reading Association.

Gray, W. S. (1960). *On their own in reading.* Glenview, IL: Scott Foresman.

Guillaume, A. M. (1998). Learning with text in the primary grades. *The Reading Teacher, 51,* 476–486.

Gunning, T. G. (1996). *Creating reading instruction for all children* (2nd ed.). Boston: Allyn and Bacon.

Gunning, T. G. (1997). *Best books for beginning readers.* Boston: Allyn and Bacon.

Harp, B. (1996). *The handbook of literacy assessment and evaluation.* Norwood, MA: Christopher-Gordon.

Hasbrouck, J. E., & Tindal, G. (1992). Curriculum-based oral reading fluency norms for students in grades 2 through 5. *Teaching Exceptional Children, 24,* 41–44.

Haycock, K. (2002). *Achievement in America–2001.* [PowerPoint presentation] Available at www2.edtrust.org

Heimlich, J. E., & Pittelman, S. D. (1986). *Semantic mapping: Classroom applications.* Newark, DE: International Reading Association.

Hiebert, E. H. (1991). Research directions. *Language Arts, 68,* 482.

Hiebert, E. H., Pearson, P. D., Taylor, B. M., Richardson, V., & Paris, S. G. (1998). Early concepts: Concepts of print, letter naming, and phonemic awareness. In *Every child a reader: Applying reading research in the classroom* (Topic 2 in the series). Ann Arbor, MI: University of Michigan School of Education, Center for the Improvement of Early Reading Achievement.

Hiebert, E. H., Pearson, P. D., Taylor, B. M., Richardson, V., & Paris, S. G. (1998). Phonics and word recognition accuracy. In *Every child a reader: Applying reading research in the classroom* (Topic 3 in the series). Ann Arbor, MI: University of Michigan School of Education, Center for the Improvement of Early Reading Achievement.

Hiebert, E. H., & Raphael, T. E. (1998). *Early literacy instruction.* Ft. Worth, TX: Harcourt Brace.

Hiebert, E. H., & Taylor, B. M. (2000). Beginning reading instruction: Research on early interventions. In M. L. Kamil, P. B. Mosenthal, P. D. Pearson, & R. Barr (Eds.), *Handbook of reading research: Volume III* (pp. 455–482). Mahwah, NJ: Lawrence Erlbaum.

Hoffman, J. V., Roser, N. L., & Battle, J. (1993). Reading aloud in classrooms: From the modal to a "model." *Reading Teacher, 46*(6), 496–503.

Huck, S. W. (2000). *Reading statistics and research* (3rd ed.). New York: Longman.

Huck, S. W., Cormier, W. H., & Bounds, W. G. (1974). *Reading statistics and research.* New York: Harper & Row.

International Reading Association. (2002). *What is evidence-based reading instruction? A position statement of the International Reading Association.* Newark, DE: Author.

Invernizzi, M. A., Abouzeid, M. P., & Bloodgood, J. W. (1997). Integrated word study: Spelling, grammar, and meaning in the language arts classroom. *Language Arts, 74,* 185–192.

Jenkins, J. R., Stein, M. L., & Wysocki, K. (1984). Learning vocabulary through reading. *American Educational Research Journal, 21*(4), 767–787.

Johns, J. L. (1997). *Basic Reading Inventory: Pre-primer through grade twelve & early literacy assessments* (7th ed.). Dubuque, IA: Kendall/Hunt.

Johnson, R. S. (1996). *Setting our sights: Measuring equity in school change.* Los Angeles: The Achievement Council.

Johnston, F. R. (1999). The timing and teaching of word families. *The Reading Teacher, 53*(1), 64–75.

Johnston, P., & Allington, R. (1991). Remediation. In R. Barr, M. L. Kamil, P. Mosenthal, & P. D. Pearson, (Eds.), *Handbook of reading research: Volume II* (pp. 984–1012). White Plains, NY: Longman.

Joyce, B., & Calhoun, E. (1996). *Learning experiences in school renewal: An exploration of five successful programs.* Eugene, OR: ERIC Clearinghouse on Educational Management.

Joyce, B., & Calhoun, E. (1998). *Learning to teach inductively.* Boston: Allyn and Bacon.

Joyce, B., Calhoun, E., Carran, N., Simser, J., Rust, D., & Halliburton, C. (1996). In B. Joyce & E. Calhoun (Eds.), *Learning experiences in school renewal: An exploration of the five successful programs* (pp. 52–93). Eugene, OR: ERIC Clearinghouse on Educational Management.

Joyce, B., Calhoun, E., & Hopkins, D. (1999). *The new structure of school improvement: Inquiring schools and achiev-*

ing students. Buckingham, England: Open University Press.

Joyce, B., Hrycauk, M., Calhoun, E., & Northern Lights Kindergarten Teachers. (2003). Learning to read in kindergarten: Has curriculum development bypassed the controversies? *Phi Delta Kappan, 85*(2), 126–132

Joyce, B., & Showers, B. (1982). The coaching of teaching. *Educational Leadership, 40*(1), 4–16.

Joyce, B., & Showers, B. (1995). *Student achievement through staff development* (2nd ed.). White Plains, NY: Longman.

Joyce, B., & Showers, B. (2002). *Student achievement through staff development* (3rd ed.). Alexandria, VA: Association for Supervision and Curriculum Development.

Joyce, B., & Wolf, J. M. (1996). Readersville: Building a culture of readers and writers. In B. Joyce & E. Calhoun (Eds.), *Learning experiences in school renewal: An exploration of five successful programs* (pp. 95–115). Eugene, OR: ERIC Clearinghouse on Educational Management.

Juel, C. (1988). Learning to read and write: A longitudinal study of fifty-four children from first through fourth grades. *Journal of Educational Psychology, 80*(4), 437–447.

Juel, C. (1992). Longitudinal research on learning to read and write with at-risk students. In M. J. Dreher & W. H. Slater (Eds.), *Elementary school literacy: Critical issues* (pp. 73–99). Norwood, MA: Christopher-Gordon.

Juel, C. (1996). *Phonemic awareness: What is it?* Needham, MA: Silver Burdett Ginn.

Juel, C., Biancarosa, G., Coker, D., & Deffes, R. (2003). Walking with Rosie: A cautionary tale of early reading instruction. *Educational Leadership, 60*(7), 13–18.

Kamberelis, G. (1999). Genre development and learning: Children writing stories, science reports, and poems. *Research in the Teaching of English, 33,* 403–460.

Kameenui, E. J. (2002). *Analysis of reading assessment instruments for K–3.* Eugene, OR: University of Oregon, Institute for the Development of Educational Achievement. Available: http://idea.uoregon.edu/assessment/index.html

Kameenui, E. J., & Simmons, D. (2000). *Consumer's guide to evaluating a core reading program: A critical elements analysis.* Eugene, OR: University of Oregon, Insti-tute for the Development of Educational Achievement. Available: http://reading.uoregon.edu/resources.php

Kameenui, E. J., Simmons, D., Cornachione, C., Thompson-Hoffman, S., Ginsburg, A., Marcy, E., et al. (2002). *A practical guide to reading assessments.* Newark, DE: International Reading Association.

Kamil, M. L., Mosenthal, P. B., Pearson, P. D., & Barr, R. (Eds.) (2000). *Handbook of reading research: Volume III.* Mahwah, NJ: Lawrence Erlbaum.

Karweit, N. (1999). *Grade retention: Prevalence, timing, and effects. Technical report #33.* Baltimore: John Hopkins University, Center for Research on the Education of Students Placed At Risk (CRESPAR).

Keene, E. O., & Zimmerman, S. (1997). *Mosaic of thought: Teaching comprehension in a reader's workshop.* Portsmouth, NH: Heinemann.

Killion, J. (2003). Use these 6 keys to open doors to literacy. *Journal of Staff Development, 24*(2), 10–16.

Krashen, S. (1993). *The power of reading: Insights from the research.* Englewood, CO: Libraries Unlimited.

Laitsch, D. (2003). Into the mix: Policy, practice, and research [Electronic version]. *ASCD Infobrief, 34,* 1–9.

Langer, J. A. (1986). *Children's reading and writing: Structures and strategies.* Norwood, NJ: Ablex.

Langer, J. A., Applebee, A. N., Mullis, I. V. S., & Foertsch, M. A. (1990). *Learning to read in our nation's schools: Instruction and achievement in 1988 at grades 4, 8, and 12.* Princeton, NJ: Educational Testing Service.

Langer, J. A., Bartolome, L., Vasquez, O., & Lucas, T. (1990). Meaning construction in school literacy tasks: A study of bilingual students. *American Educational Research Journal, 27*(3), 427–471.

Learning Research and Development Center at the University of Pittsburgh and the National Center on Education and the Economy. (1997). *Performance standards: Elementary school English language arts, mathematics, science, and applied learning.* Pittsburgh, PA: Author.

Leslie, L., & Caldwell, J. (2001). *Qualitative Reading Inventory–3.* New York: Longman.

Liberman, I. Y., Shankweiler, D., Fischer, F. W., & Carter, B. (1974). Explicit syllable and phoneme segmentation in the young child. *Journal of Experimental Child Psychology, 18,* 201–212.

Mariotti, A. S., & Homan, S. P. (2001). *Linking reading assessment to instruction: An application worktext for elementary classroom teachers* (3rd ed.). Mahwah, NJ: Lawrence Erlbaum.

McGill-Franzen, A., & Allington, R. (1991). The gridlock of low-achievement: Perspectives on policy and practice. *Remedial and Special Education, 12,* 20–30.

McGill-Franzen, A., & Goatley, V. (2001). Title I and special education: Support for children who struggle to learn to read. In S. B. Neuman & D. K. Dickinson (Eds.), *Handbook of early literacy research* (pp. 471–483). New York: Guilford.

McKenna, M. C., & Kear, D. J. (1999). Measuring attitude toward reading: A new tool for teachers. In S. J. Barrentine (Ed.), *Reading assessment: Principles and practices for elementary teachers* (pp. 199–214). Newark, DE: International Reading Association.

McKenna, M. C., Kear, D. J., & Ellsworth, R. A. (1995). Children's attitudes toward reading: A national survey. *Reading Research Quarterly, 30*(4), 934–956.

McKenna, M. C., & Stahl, S. (2003). *Assessment for reading instruction.* New York: Guilford Press.

McKeown, M. G. (1993). Creating effective definitions for young word learners. *Reading Research Quarterly, 28,* 16–31.

Merriam-Webster (1994). *Webster's tenth new collegiate dictionary.* Springfield, MA: Author.

Miles, M. B., & Huberman, A. M. (1994). *Qualitative data analysis* (2nd ed.). Thousand Oaks, CA: Sage.

Millard, E. (1997). *Differently literate: Boys, girls, and the schooling of literacy.* London: Falmer Press.

Miller, G. A., & Gildea, P. M. (1987). How children learn words. *Scientific American, 257*(3), 94–99.

Morris, R. (1997, September). *How new research on brain development will influence educational policy.* Paper presented at Policy Makers Institute, Georgia Center for Advanced Telecommunications Technology. Atlanta, GA.

Moss, B. (1995). Using children's nonfiction tradebooks as read-alouds. *Language Arts, 72* (2), 122–126.

Moss, B., Leone, S., & Dipillo, M. L. (1997). Exploring the literature of fact: Linking reading and writing through information trade books. *Language Arts, 74*(6), 418–429.

Nagy, W. E., & Anderson, R. C. (1984). How many words are there in printed school English? *Reading Research Quarterly, 19,* 304–330.

Nagy, W. E., Anderson, R. C., & Herman, P. A. (1987). Learning word meanings from context during normal reading. *American Educational Research Journal, 24*(2), 237–270.

Nagy, W. E., & Herman, P. A. (1987). Breadth and depth of vocabulary knowledge: Implications for acquisition and instruction. In M. G. McKeown & M. E. Curtis (Eds.), *The nature of vocabulary acquisition* (pp. 19–35). Hillsdale, NJ: Erlbaum.

Nagy, W. E., Herman, P. A., & Anderson, R. C. (1985). Learning words from context. *Reading Research Quarterly, 20*(2), 233–253.

Nagy, W. E., & Scott, J. A. (2000). Vocabulary processes. In M. L. Kamil, P. B. Mosenthal, P. D. Pearson, & R. Barr (Eds.), *Handbook of reading research: Vol. III* (pp. 269–284). Mahwah, NJ: Erlbaum.

Nagy, W. E., Winsor, P., Osborn, J., & O'Flahavan, J. (1994). Structural analysis: Some guidelines for instruction. In F. Lehr & J. Osborn (Eds.), *Reading, language, and literacy: Instruction for the twenty-first century* (pp. 45–58). Hillsdale, NJ: Lawrence Erlbaum.

National Center for Educational Statistics (1995). *NAEPFact: Listening to children read aloud: Oral fluency.* (Available at http://nces.ed.gov/pubs/95762.html)

National Center for Educational Statistics (2001). *The nation's report card: Reading 2000.* (Available at http://nces.ed.gov/nationsreportcard)

National Center for Educational Statistics (2003). *National assessment of educational progress (NAEP), 1992, 1994, 1998, 2000, and 2002 assessments.* Washington, DC: U.S. Department of Education, Institute of Education Sciences. (Available at http://nces.ed.gov/nationsreportcard/reading)

National Center for Educational Statistics (2003). *The nation's report card: Reading highlights 2002* (NCES 2003-534). Washington, DC: Author. (Available at http://nces.ed.gov/nationsreportcard)

National Reading Panel (2000). *Teaching children to read: An evidence-based assessment of the scientific research literature on reading and its implications for reading instruction—Reports of the subgroups.* Washington, DC: National Institute of Child Health and Human Development. (Available at http://www.national readingpanel.org)

National Staff Development Council. (2001). *Revised standards for staff development.* Reston, VA: Author.

Neuman, S. B. (1999). Books make a difference: A study of access to literacy. *Reading Research Quarterly, 34*(3), 286–311.

Neuman, S. B., & Celano, D. (2001). Access to print in low-income and middle-income communities. *Reading Research Quarterly, 36*(1), 8–26.

Neuman, S. B., & Dickinson, D. K. (Eds.). (2001). *Handbook of early literacy research.* New York: Guilford Press.

New Standards Primary Literacy Committee. (1999). *Reading and writing grade by grade: Primary literacy standards for kindergarten through third grade.* Learning Research and Development Center at the University of Pittsburgh and the National Center on Education and the Economy. (Ordering information available at http://www.ecee.org)

Newkirk, T. (1989). *More than stories: The range of children's writings.* Portsmouth, NH: Heinemann.

No Child Left Behind Act of 2001. (2002). Public Law 107-110, Title IX, General Provisions, Section 9102 (Definition 37). Available: http://www.ed.gov/legislation/ESEA02

Palinscar, A. S., & Brown, A. L. (1984). Reciprocal teaching of comprehension fostering and monitoring activities. *Cognition and Instruction, 1*(2), 117–175.

Palinscar, A. S., Winn, J., David, Y., Snyder, B., & Stevens, D. (1993). Approaches to strategic reading instruction reflecting different assumptions regarding teaching and learning. In L. J. Meltzer (Ed.), *Strategy assessment and instruction for students with learning disabilities: From theory to practice* (pp. 247–292). Austin, TX: Pro-Ed.

Pappas, C. C. (1991a). Fostering full access to literacy by including information books. *Language Arts, 68,* 449–462.

Pappas, C. C. (1991b). Young children's strategies in learning the "book language" of information books. *Discourse Processes, 14,* 203–225.

Pappas, C. C. (1993). Is narrative primary? Some insights from kindergarteners' pretend readings of stories and information books. *Journal of Reading Behavior, 25*(1), 97–129.

Pearson, P. D. (1992). Reading. In M. C. Alkin (Ed.), *Encyclopedia of educational research: Volume III* (pp. 1075–1085). New York: Macmillan.

Pearson, P. D., & Camperell, K. (1994). Comprehension of text structures. In R. B. Ruddell, M. R. Ruddell, & H. Singer (Eds.), *Theoretical models and processes of reading* (4th ed.) (pp. 448–468). Newark, DE: International Reading Association.

Pearson, P. D., & Dole, J. A. (1987). Explicit comprehension instruction: A review of research and a new conceptualization of instruction. *Elementary School Journal, 88*(2), 151–165.

Pikulski, J. J. (1997/2001). *Emergent Literacy Survey/K–2 with phonemic awareness screening.* Boston: Houghton Mifflin.

Pinnell, G. S., & Fountas, I. C. (1998). *Word matters: Teaching phonics and spelling in the reading/writing classroom.* Portsmouth, NH: Heinemann.

Pinnell, G. S., & Fountas, I. C. (1999). *Matching books to readers: Using leveled books in guided reading, K–3.* Portsmouth, NH: Heinemann.

Pinnell, G. S., & Fountas, I. C. (2001). *Using leveled books: Grades 3–6.* Portsmouth, NH: Heinemann.

Pittelman, S. D., Heimlich, J. E., Berglund, R. L., & French, M. P. (1991). *Semantic feature analysis: Classroom applications.* Newark, DE: International Reading Association.

Popham, W. J. (2001a). *Classroom assessment: What teachers need to know* (3rd ed.). Boston: Allyn and Bacon.

Popham, W. J. (2001b). *The truth about testing: An educator's call to action.* Alexandria, VA: Association for Supervision and Curriculum Development.

Pressley, M. (2000). What should comprehension instruction be the instruction of? In M. L. Kamil, P. B. Mosenthal, P. D.

Pearson, & R. Barr (Eds.), *Handbook of reading research: Vol. III* (pp. 545–561). Mahwah, NJ: Erlbaum.

Pressley, M. (2001a, December). *What I have learned up until now about research methods in reading education.* Oscar Causey Award address presented at the National Reading Conference, San Antonio, TX.

Pressley, M. (2001b). *Effective beginning reading instruction.* Executive summary and paper commissioned by the National Reading Conference. Chicago: National Reading Conference.

Pressley, M. (2002). Comprehension strategies instruction: A turn-of-the-century status report. In C. C. Block & M. Pressley (Eds.), *Comprehension instruction: Research-based best practices.* New York: Guilford.

Pressley, M., & Afflerbach, P. (1995). *Verbal protocols of reading: The nature of constructively responsive reading.* Hillsdale, NJ: Erlbaum.

Pressley, M., Brown, R., El-Dinary, P. B., & Afflerbach, P. (1995). The comprehension instruction that students need: Instruction fostering constructively responsive reading. *Learning Disabilities Research & Practice, 10*(4), 215–224.

Pressley, M., El-Dinary, P. B., Gaskins, I., Schuder, T., Bergman, J., Almasi, L., & Brown, R. (1992). Beyond direct explanation: Transactional instruction of reading comprehension strategies. *Elementary School Journal, 92,* 511–554.

Pressley, M., Wharton-McDonald, R., Mistretta-Hampston, J. M., & Echevarria, M. (1998). The nature of literacy instruction in ten grade 4/5 classrooms in upstate New York. *Scientific Studies of Reading, 2,* 159–194.

Puma, M., Karweit, N., Price, C., Ricciuti, A., Thompson, W., & Vaden-Kiernan, M. (1997). *Prospects: Final report on student outcomes.* Washington, DC: U.S. Department of Education, Office of Planning & Evaluation Services.

Purcell-Gates, V. (1998). Growing successful readers: Homes, communities, and schools. In J. Osborn & F. Lehr (Eds.), *Literacy for all: Issues in teaching and learning.* New York: Guilford Press.

Purcell-Gates, V., & Dahl, K. (1991). Low-SES children's success and failure at early literacy learning in skills-based classrooms. *Journal of Reading Behavior, 23,* 1–34.

Quammen, D. (1996). *The song of the dodo: Island biogeography in an age of extinctions.* New York: Simon & Schuster.

RAND Reading Study Group. (2001). *Reading for understanding: Toward an R&D program in reading comprehension.* Prepared for the Office of Educational Research and Improvement, U.S. Department of Education. Santa Monica, CA: RAND.

Read, C. (1971). Preschool children's knowledge of English phonology. *Harvard Educational Review, 41,* 1–34.

Roller, C. M. (1998). *So . . . what's a tutor to do?* Newark, DE: International Reading Association.

Routman, R. (2003). *Reading essentials: The specifics you need to teach reading well.* Portsmouth, NH: Heinemann.

Rupley, W. H., Logan, J. W., & Nichols, W. D. (1998/1999). Vocabulary instruction in a balanced reading program. *The Reading Teacher, 52*(4), 336–346.

Schmoker, M. (2001). The "crayola curriculum." *Education Week, 21*(8), 42, 44.

Shanahan, T. (2001). Response to Elaine Garan. *Language Arts, 79*(1), 70–71.

Slavin, R. E., Karweit, N. L., & Wasik, B. A. (1994). *Preventing early school failure.* Boston: Allyn & Bacon.

Snow, C. E., Burns, M. S., & Griffin, P. (Eds.). (1998). *Preventing reading difficulties in young children.* Washington, DC: National Academy Press.

Spiro, R. J., & Taylor, B. M. (1987). On investigating children's transition from narrative to expository discourse: The multidimensional nature of psychological text classification. In R. J. Tierney, P. L. Anders, & J. N. Mitchell (Eds.), *Understanding readers' understanding.* Hillsdale, NJ: Erlbaum.

Stahl, S. A. (1983). Differential word knowledge and reading comprehension. *Journal of Reading Behavior, 15,* 33–50.

Stahl, S. A. (1999). *Vocabulary development.* Cambridge, MA: Brookline Books.

Stahl, S. A., Duffy-Hester, A. M., & Stahl, K. A. D. (1998). Everything you wanted to know about phonics (but were afraid to ask). *Reading Research Quarterly, 33*(3), 338–355.

Stahl, S. A., & Murray, B. A. (1994). Defining phonological awareness and its relationship to early reading. *Journal of Educational Psychology, 86,* 221–234.

Stahl, S. A., & Murray, B. A. (1998). Issues involved in defining phonological awareness and its relation to early reading. In J. Metsala & L. C. Ehri (Eds.), *Word recognition in beginning literacy* (pp. 65–87). Mahwah, NJ: Erlbaum.

Stanovich, K. E. (1986). Matthew effects in reading: Some consequences of individual differences in the acquisition of literacy. *Reading Research Quarterly, 21*(4), 360–407.

Stanovich, K. E. (2000). *Progress in understanding reading: Scientific foundations and new frontiers.* New York: Guilford Press.

Stanovich, P. J., & Stanovich, K. E. (2003). *Using research and reason in education: How teachers can use scientifically based research to make curricular & instructional decisions.* Jessup, MD: National Institute for Literacy.

Stein, N. L., & Trabasso, T. (1982). What's in a story: An approach to comprehension and instruction. In R. Glaser (Ed.), *Advances in the psychology of instruction* (Vol. 2) (pp. 213–268). Hillsdale, NJ: Erlbaum.

Sternberg, R. J. (1987). Most vocabulary is learned from context. In M. G. McKeown & M. E. Curtis (Eds.), *The nature of vocabulary acquisition* (pp. 89–105). Hillsdale, NJ: Erlbaum.

Sternberg, R. J., & Powell, J. S. (1983). Comprehending verbal comprehension. *American Psychologist, 38*(8), 878–893.

Sulzby, E., & Teale, W. (1991). Emergent literacy. In R. Barr, M. L. Kamil, P. Mosenthal, & P. D. Pearson (Eds.), *Handbook of reading research: Vol. II* (pp. 727–757). Mahwah, NJ: Erlbaum.

Swanborn, M. S. L., & de Glopper, K. (1999). Incidental word learning while reading: A meta-analysis. *Review of Educational Research, 69*(3), 261–285.

Sweet, A. P., & Snow, C. E. (Eds.) (2003). *Rethinking reading comprehension.* New York: Guilford Press.

Taylor, B. M. (1982). Text structure and children's comprehension and memory for expository material. *Journal of Educational Psychology, 74,* 323–340.

Taylor, B. M., Pearson, P. D., Clark, K., & Walpole, S. (2000). Effective schools and accomplished teachers: Lessons about primary-grade reading instruction in low-income schools. *Elementary School Journal, 101*(2), 121–165.

Taylor, B. M., & Samuels, S. J. (1983). Children's use of text structure in the recall of expository material. *American Educational Research Journal, 20*(4), 517–528.

Taylor, S. E., Frackenpohl, H., White, C. E., Nieroda, B. W., Browning, C. L., & Birsner, P. (1979). *EDL core vocabularies in reading, mathematics, science, and social studies.* New York: EDL/McGraw-Hill.

Teale, W. H. (1989). The promise and challenge of informal assessment in early literacy. In L. M. Morrow & J. K. Smith (Eds.), *Assessment for instruction in early literacy* (pp. 45–61). Englewood Cliffs, NJ: Prentice-Hall.

Torgeson, J. K., & Mathes, P. G. (2000). *A basic guide to understanding, assessing, and teaching phonological awareness.* Austin, TX: Pro-Ed.

Treiman, R. (1993). *Beginning to spell.* New York: Oxford University Press.

Trelease, J. (2001). *The read-aloud handbook.* New York: Penguin.

U.S. Department of Education. (1999). *Promising results, continuing challenges: The final report of the national assessment of Title I.* (http://www.ed.gov/offices/OUS/eval/exsum. html)

U.S. Department of Education. (2002). Guidance for the Reading First program: Section B-2: What is scientifically based reading research. (Available at http://www.ed.gov/print/programs/reading first/grant.html)

Vellutino, F. R. (2003). Individual differences as sources of variability in reading comprehension in elementary children. In A. P. Sweet & C. E. Snow (Eds.), *Rethinking reading comprehension* (pp. 51–81). New York: Guilford Press.

Vellutino, F. R., & Scanlon, D. M. (2001). Emergent literacy skills, early instruction, and individual differences as determinants of difficulties in learning to read: The case for early intervention. In S. B. Neuman & D. K. Dickinson (Eds.), *Handbook of early literacy research* (pp. 295–321). New York: Guilford Press.

Vierra, A., & Pollock, J. (1992). *Reading educational research* (2nd ed.). Scottsdale, AZ: Gorsuch Scarisbrick.

White, T. G., Slater, W. H., & Graves, M. F. (1989). Yes/no method of vocabulary assessment: Valid for whom and useful for what? In S. McCormick & J. Zutell (Eds.) *Cognitive and social perspectives for literacy research and instruction* (pp. 391–398). Chicago: National Reading Conference.

White, T. G., Sowell, J., & Yanagihara, A. (1989). Teaching elementary students to use word-part clues. *Reading Teacher, 42*(4), 302–308.

Whitehurst, G. J. (2002). *Evidence-based education* [Slide Presentation]. Available: http://www.ed.gov/offices/OESE/SASA/eb/index/html1

Whitehurst, G. J., & Lonigan, C. J. (2001). Emergent literacy: Development from prereaders to readers. In S. B. Neuman & D. K. Dickinson (Eds.), *Handbook of early literacy research* (pp. 11–29). New York: Guilford Press.

Wiederholt, J. L., & Bryant, B. R. (2001). *Gray Oral Reading Tests* (4th ed.). Austin, TX: Pro-Ed.

Wiggins, G. (1998). *Educative assessment: Designing assessments to inform and improve student performance.* San Francisco: Jossey-Bass.

Wolf, J. M. (1998). Just read. *Educational Leadership, 55*(8), 61–63.

Wollman-Bonilla, J. E. (2000). Teaching science writing to first graders: Genre learning and recontextualization. *Research in the Teaching of English, 35*(1), 35–65.

Woodcock, R. W. (1987). *Woodcock Reading Mastery Tests—Revised.* Circle Pines, MN: American Guidance Service.

Worthy, J., & Broaddus, K. (2001–2002). Fluency beyond the primary grades: From group performance to silent, independent reading. *The Reading Teacher, 55*(4), 334–343.

Wylie, R. E., & Durrell, D. D. (1970). Teaching vowels through phonograms. *Elementary English, 47,* 787–791.

Yopp, H. K. (1995a). Read-aloud books for developing phonemic awareness: An annotated bibliography. *The Reading Teacher, 48,* 538–543.

Yopp, H. K. (1995b). Yopp-Singer Test of Phoneme Segmentation. *The Reading Teacher, 49,* 20–29.

Alphabet Books Cited

Bannatyne-Cugnet, J. (1992). *A prairie alphabet.* Montreal, Canada: Tundra Books.

Bond, M. (1996). *Paddington's ABC.* New York: Puffin.

Gág, W. (1961). *The ABC bunny.* New York: Coward-McCann.

Onyefulu, I. (1993). *A is for Africa.* New York: Cobblehill Books.

Pandell, K., & Wolfe, A. (1996). *Animal action ABC.* New York: Dutton Children's Books.

Pienkowski, J. (1995). *A to Z sticker book.* New York: Random House.

Seuss, Dr. (1963). *Dr. Seuss's ABC.* New York: Random House.

Nonfiction Children's Books Cited

Arnosky, J. (2000). *All about turtles.* New York: Scholastic.

Badger, D. (1995). *Frogs.* New York: Barnes & Noble.

Berger, M. (1994). *Growing pumpkins.* New York: Newbridge.

Byron, B. (1981). *Wheels.* New York: Thomas Y. Crowell.

Carson, R. (1962). *Silent spring.* Boston: Houghton Mifflin.

Dorros, A. (1997). *A tree is growing.* New York: Scholastic.

Dussling, J. (1998). *Bugs! Bugs! Bugs!* New York: Dorling Kindersley.

Guiberson, B. Z. (1996). *Into the sea.* New York: Henry Holt.

Heller, R. (1983). *The reason for a flower.* New York: Grosset & Dunlap.

Kitchen, B. (1994). *When hunger calls.* Cambridge, MA: Candlewick Press.

Lacey, E. A. (1993). *What's the difference? A guide to some familiar animal look-alikes.* New York: Clarion Books.

Latimer, J. P., & Nolting, K. S. (1999). *Backyard birds.* Boston: Houghton Mifflin.

Morris, A., & Heyman, K. (1992). *Tools.* New York: Mulberry.

Murphy, J. (1990). *The boys' war: Confederate and Union soldiers talk about the Civil War.* New York: Clarion Books.

O'Neil, A. (1998). *Cats.* New York: Kingfisher.

Overbeck, C. (1982). *How seeds travel.* Minneapolis, MN: Lerner Publications.

Peterson, C., & Upitis, A. (1994). *Extra cheese, please: Mozzarella's journey from cow to pizza*. Honesdale, PA: Boyds Mill.

Fiction Children's Books Cited

Campbell, R. (1982). *Dear zoo*. New York: Simon & Schuster.

Carle, E. (1976). *Do you want to be my friend?* New York: HarperCollins.

Cazet, D. (1990). *Never spit on your shoes*. New York: Orchard Books.

DiCamillo, K. (2000). *Because of Winn-Dixie*. Cambridge, MA: Candlewick.

Eastman, P. D. (1961). *Go, dog, go!* New York: Random House.

Galdone, P. (1975). *The gingerbread boy*. New York: Seabury.

Galdone, P. (1968). *Henny Penny*. New York: Scholastic.

George, J. C. (1983). *The talking earth*. New York: HarperCollins.

Kitamura, S. (1987). *Lily takes a walk*. New York: Dutton.

Lobel, A. (1986). *The Random House book of Mother Goose*. (1986). New York: Random House.

London, J. (1903/2000). *The call of the wild*. New York: Scholastic.

Martin, B. (1967). *Brown bear, brown bear, what do you see?* New York: Holt, Hinehart & Winston.

Ochs, C. (1991). *Moose on the loose*. Minneapolis, MN: Carolrhoda.

Seuss, Dr. (1957). *The cat in the hat*. New York: Random House.

Silverstein, S. (1974). *Where the sidewalk ends*. New York: Harper & Row.

Viorst, J. (1968/1993). *Sunday morning*. New York: Aladdin.

Yolen, J., & Regan, L. (1996). *Welcome to the sea of sand*. New York: Putnam.

Electronic Media Cited

The American heritage talking dictionary. (1996). Softkey Multimedia.

Broderbund.com (consumer Web site for Broderbund).

Index

Page numbers followed by an *f* indicates a figure.

225

About the Author

Emily Calhoun is Director of the Phoenix Alliance, which provides long-term support to school districts and state/regional agencies that are committed to improving student achievement through investing in staff learning. Her major work is helping school, district, and state staff study the effects of curriculum and instruction on student learning and strengthen the learning environment for all.

Emily has taught at the elementary, secondary, and university levels, and has served as an intermediate service agency consultant (K-12), district language arts coordinator, and coordinator of the Georgia League of Professional Schools. She has written several books to support schoolwide and individual inquiry into student achievement and the development of literacy, including *How to Use Action Research in the Self-Renewing School* (ASCD, 1994), *Teaching Beginning Reading and Writing with the Picture Word Inductive Model* (ASCD, 1999), and co-authored with Bruce Joyce and David Hopkins *The New Structure of School Improvement* (Open University Press, 1999).

Related ASCD Resources

Using Data to Assess Your Reading Program

At the time of publication, the following ASCD resources were available; for the most up-to-date information about ASCD resources, go to www.ascd.org. ASCD stock numbers are noted in parentheses.

Audio

Creating Strategic Readers: Helping Students Understand Text in the Content Areas by Sue Beers (3 audiotapes, #203081)

Doing It All! Getting Big Results While Nurturing Lifelong Readers by Marie Carbo (#203190 audiotape; #503283 CD)

Improving Reading Is Everyone's Business by Brenda Hunter (#203122 audiotape; #503215 CD)

Stopping Reading Failure for Struggling Readers in Grades 3-8 by J. David Cooper (#202152 audiotape)

Multimedia

Literacy Across the Curriculum Professional Development Planner and Resource Package (#703400)

The Multiple Intelligences of Reading and Writing: Making the Words Come Alive Books-in-Action Package (10 books and 1 video) Educational consultant: Thomas Armstrong (#703381)

Reading Strategies for the Content Areas: An ASCD Action Tool by Sue Beers and Lou Howell (#703109)

Strategies for Teaching Writing: An ASCD Action Tool by Roger Caswell and Brenda Mahler (#704015)

Networks

Visit the ASCD Web site (www.ascd.org) and search for "networks" for information about professional educators who have formed groups around topics like "Language, Literacy, and Literature: Whole Language Perspective and Practice." Look in the "Network Directory" for current facilitators' addresses and phone numbers.

Online Resources

Visit ASCD's Web site (www.ascd.org) for the following professional development opportunities:

Professional Development Online: *Successful Strategies for Literacy and Learning* among others (for a small fee; password protected)

Print Products

Capturing All of the Reader Through the Reading Assessment System: Practical Applications for Guiding Strategic Readers Volume 3, First Edition by Rachel Billmeyer (#303358)

Collaborative Analysis of Student Work: Improving Teaching and Learning by Georgea M. Langer, Amy B. Colton, and Loretta S. Goff (#102006)

Educational Leadership: What Research Says About Reading (entire issue, March 2004) Excerpted articles online free; entire issue online and accessible to ASCD members

Mapping the Big Picture: Integrating Curriculum and Assessment K-12 by Heidi Hayes Jacobs (#197135)

Reading Topic Pack (#198215)

Teaching Beginning Reading and Writing with the Picture Word Inductive Model by Emily Calhoun (#199025)

Teaching Reading in the Content Areas: If Not Me, Then Who? 2nd Edition by Rachel Billmeyer and Mary Lee Barton (#397258)

Teaching What Matters Most: Standards and Strategies for Raising Student Achievement by Richard W. Strong, Harvey F. Silver, and Matthew J. Perini (#100057)

The Threads of Reading: Strategies for Literacy Development by Karen Tankersley (#103316)

Videos

The Lesson Collection: Reading Strategies, Tapes 1-8 (#499257)

Reading in the Content Areas Video Series (3 videos) (#402029)

Reporting Student Progress (with facilitator's guide) (#495249)

Using Classroom Assessment to Guide Instruction (3 videos & facilitator's guide) (#402286)

For more information, visit us on the World Wide Web (http://www.ascd.org), send an e-mail message to member@ascd.org, call the ASCD Service Center (1-800-933-ASCD or 703-578-9600, then press 2), send a fax to 703-575-5400, or write to Information Services, ASCD, 1703 N. Beauregard St., Alexandria, VA 22311-1714 USA.